THE ILLUSTRATED GUIDE TO THE 20TH CENTURY

First published in 1999 by Mustard
Mustard is an imprint of Parragon

Parragon
Queen Street House
4 Queen Street
Bath
BA1 1HE, UK

ISBN 1 84164 356 4

Produced for Parragon by Foundry Design & Production
a part of The Foundry Creative Media Company Ltd
Crabtree Hall, Crabtree Lane
Fulham, London, SW6 6TY

A copy of the CIP data for this book is available from the
British Library.

printed in Spain

THE ILLUSTRATED GUIDE TO THE 20TH CENTURY

Contents

Introduction

AT THE TURN of the year 1900, the world was on the brink of a revolution in hundreds of different areas of human life, culture and society. The first signs of this revolution were already showing in some fields; in others, nobody could have guessed what the twentieth century would have in store. As we look back now, poised on the edge not just of a new century, but a new millennium, it hardly seems feasible that humankind could have achieved so much, and suffered so greatly, in just one hundred years.

At the beginning of the century man had scarcely been airborne, communication even with somebody from the next town could take a considerable amount of time and surgical procedures were difficult, often fatal. Today, aircraft can travel faster than the speed of sound, we can speak to directly to someone on the opposite side of the globe, and human organs can be transplanted successfully.

Individual nations, and indeed the world at large, were once divided into distinct classes, the rich and the poor, those who had everything and those who had nothing; many groups suffered persecution, prejudice and oppression. For many of these the battle has now been won and throughout a large part of the globe, freedom of thought and expression are an accepted – and expected – part of everyday life. Many peoples and nations once lived in isolation or under the control of alien empirical governments, but now trade and travel have opened up the world and the idea of an empire is an old-fashioned concept.

The twentieth century has been one of constant change and flux, but as the decades passed a pattern emerged, and it was generally one of advance, progression and enlightenment. This is not to suggest that improvement has been the overall characteristic in all aspects of twentieth-century life. As the human mind advances, so to does the human desire to expand, to control, to be the best – and while international competition has given rise to some of the greatest achievements in the history of the world, it has also been the cause of some of the worst examples ever recorded of man's inhumanity towards man.

There can be no doubt that this has been a century of warfare unlike any other witnessed before. A build-up of events from the turn of the century eventually led to one of the greatest and all-encompassing disasters of modern times. The First World War, which began as a dispute between the empire of Austria-Hungary and Serbia, eventually escalated into a conflict that drew in most of the world. Necessity became the mother of invention and new weapons – such as gas – were created and new methods, for example tank warfare, came into being. Out of disaster, though, was also born progress, most notably in terms of medical and surgical procedures. The scale and nature of illness and injuries caused by the first war meant that new treatments and cures had to be found, resulting in huge leaps forward for medical science. Such disaster and such advance continued through the century, not just in the Second World War, but as a result of continued conflict both between nations and internally. Perhaps the ultimate symbol of this is the development and use of nuclear weapons since 1945: weapons that have the potential to destroy whole countries and shake the foundations of life as we know it.

In the course of the century, empires have risen and fallen, countries have been formed, boundaries shifted, and national identities dissolved and subsumed. Britain's return of Hong Kong to China in 1997 marked the last bastion of an empire that once covered one-third of the globe. Shifts in power have always occurred, but the speed and effects of such changes have never been more profoundly felt than in the twentieth century.

Within different societies, the struggles for freedom, acceptance and equal rights have been long, marred with setbacks and strong opposition. In the United States, for example, two great leaders of the Civil Rights Movement, Martin Luther King Jr and Malcolm X, were assassinated before the Civil Rights Act finally put an official end to years of inequality. Unofficially, of course, racial prejudice is still practised in a more covert way in many countries, but we are moving in the right direction. Other groups or minorities have also achieved recognition and acceptance this century. Although women had been campaigning for the vote and other social equalities since the 1880s, it wasn't until the First World War that they really had the opportunity to prove themselves. At the end of the conflict women in the US were finally granted the right to vote and other countries soon followed America's example; it was the first step along a road that would alter the very fabric of society as it had previously been known.

These are just a few examples of the many thousands of events that have helped to shape the world as it is today. *The Illustrated Guide to the 20th Century* takes a chronological look, decade by decade, at all the most significant events of the past one hundred years, from a truly global point of view. In addition, the book offers a series of themes allowing the reader to trace the developments of the century from different perspectives, including politics, industry, science, art and exploration. It is fascinating to see how events unfold and interrelate, and as we delve back into this retrospective of humankind's incredible development over the past years – at one of the greatest turning points in history – we can only wonder, in awe at what the human mind can conceive and execute, what the twenty-first century will bring.

Key to themes

- Art and Design
- Culture, Sport and the Arts
- Exploration and Discovery
- Human Rights and Society
- Medicine and Health
- Natural World
- Power and Politics
- Religion and Belief
- Science and Technology
- Trade and Industry
- War and Peace

Chapter 1
1900–1909

1900
THE BOER WAR

The Boer War began in 1899 between British colonists in South Africa and the neighbouring natives of Dutch descent, the Boers. On 10 January 1900, General Lord Roberts was sent to replace Sir Redvers Buller as commander-in-chief of British forces in the area, in an attempt to bring a swift conclusion to the conflict. Early in February, Roberts ordered an army north to relieve the city of Kimberley, an object achieved four days later. Simultaneously, Roberts marched from Cape Colony into the Orange Free State. Attacked by the Afrikaaner general Piet Cronje on 27 February, Roberts forced the surrender of Cronje and his 4,000 troops. On 13 March, Roberts entered Bloemfontein, capital of the Orange Free State. Two months later, the besieged town of Mafeking, defended by troops under the command of Robert Baden-Powell, was relieved. Roberts captured Johannesburg on 31 May and Pretoria, the capital of the South African Republic, on 5 June.

1900
THE BOXER REBELLION

Throughout the late nineteenth century, Chinese resentment towards Japan and western countries had grown because of both their economic and political exploitation, and their humiliating military defeats of China. In 1899, in retaliation for this, a secret society of Chinese called the Boxers began terrorizing Christian missionaries. These attacks culminated in 1900, in the violent Boxer uprising in Beijing, which claimed the lives of many Chinese and foreigners. A large relief expedition consisting of British, French, Japanese, Russian, German and American troops relieved the besieged quarter and occupied Beijing on 14 August 1900. The relief forces retained possession of the city, seeking out and punishing anti-foreign actions, until a peace treaty was eventually signed on 7 September 1901.

Battle scene during the Boxer Rebellion in China in 1900.

Sigmund Freud, the founder of psychoanalysis, and pioneer in investigating the power of unconscious thought.

1900
FREUD PUBLISHES *THE INTERPRETATION OF DREAMS*

The founder of psychoanalysis, Sigmund Freud mined deep into the unconscious mind, in an attempt to find the causes of neurosis and anxiety. His study *The Interpretation of Dreams,* published in 1900, dealt with the puzzling problems of dreams and became the key text to his theories. Freud studied all the previous literature on the subject and then presented his views on the function of dreams and their sources. He stated that dreams could reveal things that had been hidden or repressed from the conscious mind. Freud believed that the stimulus for a dream was always an unconscious wish that had its origin in childhood. He threw a light on the inner nature of a child's mind that startled and repelled his contemporaries. He maintained that the hidden layers in a child's mind were full of sexual and hostile attitudes to its parents, the Oedipus complex being an example.

1 JULY 1900
First Zeppelin Launched

The first airship, created by Count Ferdinand von Zeppelin, takes flight near Lake Constance in front of a small group of intrigued spectators. The Zeppelin is made of aluminium and covered in cotton cloth; it is powered by hydrogen.

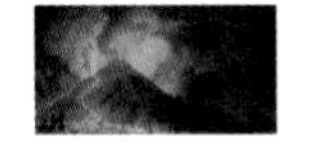

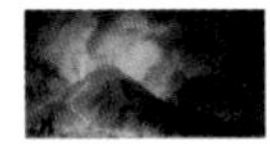

The Australian flag showing the British Union Jack and the Commonwealth star.

1901
BIRTH OF THE COMMONWEALTH OF AUSTRALIA

Royal Assent was given to the act that created the Commonwealth of Australia in July 1900. The first prime minister, Edmund Barton, formally took his place in history in January 1901. The governor-general, Lord Hopetoun, presided over the ceremony in front of 50,000 people from the four corners of the continent. A three-km (one-mile) long procession of British, Australian and Empire troops paraded through Sydney in celebration of the new Commonwealth. By May, the first Australian Federal Parliament had met in Melbourne, the state capital, but Australia would still continue to support the UK through the difficult times in the future.

1901
QUEEN VICTORIA DIES

Victoria, the only child of Edward, Duke of Kent, the fourth son of George III, was born on 24 May 1819 at Kensington Palace. She succeeded her uncle, William IV, becoming queen of Great Britain in 1837. In 1840 she married Prince Albert of Saxe-Coburg and Gotha. She soon demonstrated a good grasp of constitutional principles, a surprising maturity, a firm will and a conservative nature. When Melbourne's government fell in 1839 she exercised her perogative and refused to dismiss the ladies of the bedchamber. Peel then resigned, enabling the queen to prolong the preferred Melbourne administration until 1841. She had four sons and five daughters: Victoria, the Princess Royal; Albert Edward, later Edward VII; Alice; Alfred, Duke of Edinburgh and of Saxe-Coburg-Gotha; Helena; Louise; Arthur; Leopold and Beatrice. Always strongly influenced by her husband, she went into seclusion after his death from typhoid in 1861, which brought her temporary unpopularity. With Disraeli's administration she rose again in the public's favour, becoming Empress of India in 1876. From 1848 she regularly visited the Scottish Highlands, where she had a house at Balmoral built to Albert's designs. She died at Osborne House on the Isle of Wight on 22 January 1901, marking the end of a long and distinguished era in British history.

Queen Victoria, who died at Osborne House on the Isle of Wight in January 1901.

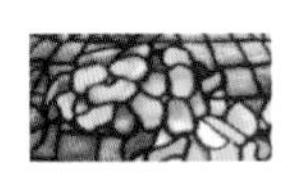

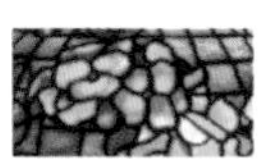

Lord Kitchener, British commander-in-chief during the Boer War, who led the relief of the siege of Mafeking.

1901
KITCHENER DEFEATS THE BOERS

No sooner had the British begun to reduce the number of troops in South Africa than Boer leaders – among them such soldiers and future statesmen as Louis Botha and Jan Christian Smuts – launched extensive and well-planned guerrilla warfare against the occupying British troops. The fighting continued for the next year and was only finally quelled through the severe tactics of the new British commander-in-chief, Lord Kitchener. He exhausted the Boers by devastating the Afrikaaner farms that sustained and sheltered the guerrillas, placing black African and Afrikaaner women and children in concentration camps and building a strategic chain of formidable iron blockhouses for his troops. British losses totalled about 28,000. Afrikaaner losses were about 4,000 soldiers, plus more than 20,000 civilians, who died from disease in concentration camps.

10 JANUARY 1901

Oil Struck in Texas

Oil is discovered in the Spindletop region of south-east Texas, USA. This discovery hails the dawn of a new era for the state, which has formerly been dominated by the cattle industry.

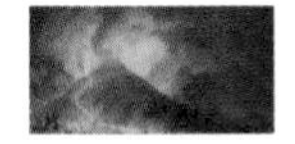

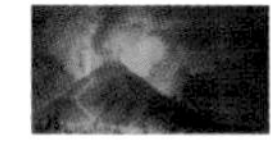

1901
US GOES ON GOLD STANDARD

The Gold Standard was first adopted by Great Britain in 1821. It was a policy by which gold could be exchanged for equal weights of gold coinage, coins could be melted down and bullion could be exported or imported freely. The Gold Standard, in effect, operated from about 1870 to the outbreak of the First World War. The US adoption of the Gold Standard in 1901 added extra weight to its importance. Although by this time gold coins were no longer in general circulation, extensive use could be made of the gold-exchange standard, which finally collapsed during the Depression of the 1930s. By 1937 not a single country remained on the full Gold Standard.

Guglielmo Marconi, the first man to succeed in transmitting radio waves across the Channel, pictured with one of the earliest wirelesses.

1901
FIRST TRANSATLANTIC RADIO TRANSMISSION

In radio transmissions, a microphone converts sound waves into electromagnetic waves, which are picked up by a receiving aerial and fed to a loudspeaker; this then converts them back into sound waves. The theory of electromagnetic waves had been developed by James Maxwell in 1864 and was confirmed by Heinrich Hertz in 1888. After experimenting with devices to convert electromagnetic waves into electrical signals, Italian Guglielmo Marconi succeeded in transmitting radio waves over 1.6 km (one mile) in 1895. In 1898 he transmitted signals across the English Channel and in 1901 established the first transatlantic communication; this worked between St John's in Newfoundland, USA, and Poldhu in Cornwall. Marconi shared the Nobel Prize for Physics in 1909 with Karl Braun.

1901
PRESIDENT MCKINLEY SHOT BY ANARCHIST

William McKinley was the 25th president of the United States, a Republican elected in 1896. He went to Congress in 1876 and was repeatedly re-elected. In 1892 he was made governor of Ohio, his name being identified with the high protective tariff carried in the McKinley Bill of 1890. His term as president was marked by the US's adoption of an imperialist policy, as shown by the Spanish-American War in 1898 and the annexation of Cuba and the Philippines. In November 1900, as in 1896, he secured a large majority and was re-elected. He was shot by anarchist Leon Czolgosz in 1901 in Buffalo, New York, and died eight days later.

1901
WORLD EXHIBITION OPENS IN PARIS

The 1901 World Exhibition was more whimsical and retrospective in tone than the 1889 Exhibition, which had unveiled the Eiffel Tower, described at the time as a 'ridiculous tower dominating Paris like a gigantic, black chimney'. At the front gate stood a statue of La Parisienne wearing a tight skirt and a charming hat of the latest style, symbolizing Paris as the fashion capital. Also featured were 'palaces'

The Eiffel Tower, the highlight of the 1889 Paris Exhibition; the 1901 Exhibition was more retrospective.

from every major country, which were dotted along the Rue des Nations and the Quai d'Orsay. The Electrical Illuminations and the Hall of Illusions were the most popular attractions of the year. The French hoped to restore the international image of their Empire through the Exhibition.

1902
US COMMISSION CHOOSES PANAMA AS SITE OF CANAL

In 1902, after a long battle in Congress between two rival groups of senators, the Americans finally decided to build a canal linking the Pacific and Atlantic Oceans across Panama. A French company, led by the engineer Ferdinand de Lesseps, had been trying to build such a canal since the late 1870s. After skilful negotiations by the New York lawyer William Nelson Cromwell, the French company agreed to be bought out for $40 million. An alternative route through Nicaragua had been finally put aside when eruptions from Mount Pelée on Martinique cost 30,000 lives: the pro-Panama group sent Nicaraguan stamps to each senator showing an erupting volcano. The canal project would shorten the route between the two US coasts by 13,000 km (8,000 miles).

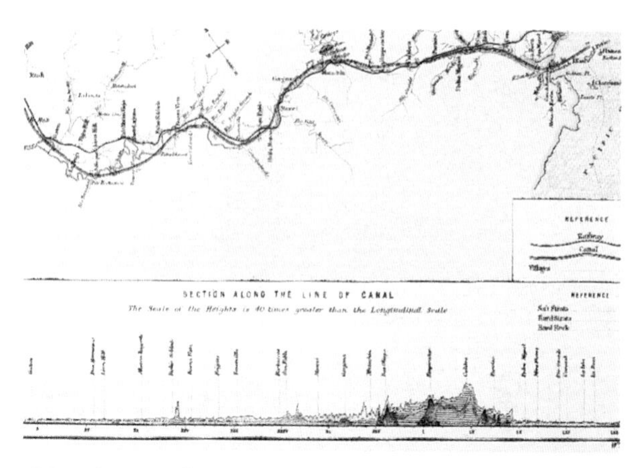

Map showing the Panama Canal during its construction.

10 DECEMBER 1902

Aswan Dam Completed

The massive project to build a dam on the Nile at Aswan to control the river's annual flood, allowing an even distribution of water throughout the year, is finally completed. The dam has been four years in construction.

Lamp designed by Louis Comfort Tiffany, demonstrating his trademark coloured glass.

1902
TIFFANY DESIGNS THE LOTUS LAMP

Art Nouveau was the western world's major decorative style of the early twentieth century. The emphasis was on curved patterns, based on natural forms, but its practitioners were unconcerned with creating the illusion of reality. In the United States Louis Comfort Tiffany combined metal with opalescent colours of glass to make beautiful jewellery, windows, bowls and, in particular, the Lotus Lamp of 1902. Tiffany was born in New York, the son of a jeweller, but, instead of entering the family business, he established a glassmaking plant. He invented a type of glowing, iridescent glass which became his hallmark. He called it Favrile, but it is known best by his name, Tiffany.

A cholera epidemic swept through Egypt in 1902, killing 9,000 people.

1902
9,000 DIE OF CHOLERA IN EGYPT

Cholera is an acute infection of the small intestines, caused by the bacterium *Vibrio cholerae* and characterized by violent diarrhoea and vomiting with rapid and severe depletion of body fluids and salts. As dehydration increases the person becomes comatose and may die of shock. In the period from 1898 to 1907, cholera caused at least 370,000 deaths in Africa. The most severe outbreak occurred in Egypt in 1902, causing the deaths of 9,000 people. The formerly high death rate was later significantly reduced by the invention of antibiotics, treatments to prevent dehydration and an effective vaccine.

1902
KARL LANDSTEINER DISCOVERS BLOOD GROUPS

In 1902, Austrian immunologist Karl Landsteiner first discovered that blood could be classified by the activity of its anti-

A priest blesses the dead surrounded, by the devastation caused by the Martinique volcano disaster.

gens. He realized that there are two main antigens (A and B) which give rise to four different blood groups; those having A only (A), having B only (B), having both (AB) and having neither (O). Landsteiner went on to help in the discovery of the Rhesus blood factors (1940) and his work earned him a Nobel Prize in 1930. His research and discoveries made successful blood transfusions possible and aided forensic medicine. In 1936 he wrote *The Specificity of Serological Reactions*, which helped establish the science of immunology. He also developed a test for syphilis.

1902
MARTINIQUE VOLCANO DISASTER

On 8 May 1902, the island of Martinique, a French island in the West Indies, was devastated when the volcano Mount Pelée exploded, unusually through its sides rather than through its peak. Smoke had been seen issuing from Pelée since early April and by 27 April birds and animals had been asphyxiated by poisonous gases from the ash. The explosion wiped out the entire city and population of St Pierre, a primary port. In all 36,000 people were killed instantly, either incinerated, suffocated by the gas or blasted to death. Every home was affected: either obliterated completely or partially destroyed and the city took four days to cool down enough for rescuers to enter.

13 DECEMBER 1902
Blockades in Venezuela

Great Britain and Germany begin blockading the coasts of Venezuela and attacking forts across the region, after the country declined to respond to an ultimatum put to them demanding recompense for damages inflicted during the government takeover three years ago.

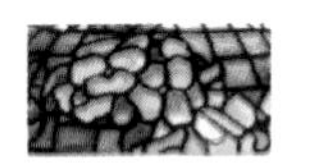

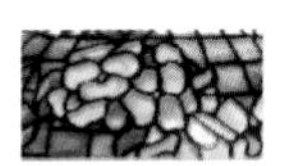

1902
PRINCE PETER KROPOTKIN'S MUTUAL AID

Prince Peter Kropotkin was born into a noble Russian family. Following exile from Russia for his anarchist views, he settled in London. His *Fields, Factories and Workshops* (1899) was a study of how small villages and decentralized communities could produce all their own food and material needs without relying upon landowners, big business, factory owners or the state. His major work, *Mutual Aid*, published in 1902, was a refutation of the views of the Social Darwinists, who justified capitalism because it encouraged the survival of the fittest. As a biologist and anthropologist, he was able to show that evolution often resulted in mutually beneficial co-operation between animals and between peoples in primitive societies. He rejected the communist alternative to capitalism because he felt his research proved that co-operation could arise naturally without being imposed by the state.

Prince Peter Kropotkin rejected the views of the Social Darwinists, followers of Darwin's (above) theories, with a belief in the justification of capitalism.

Emmeline Pankhurst (right), leader of the suffragette movement in England, with her daughter Christabel.

1903
SUFFRAGISM

Women had been campaigning to be allowed to vote since around 1880, but this campaign was generally conducted by peaceful means. In 1903, however, a leading British suffragette, Emmeline Pankhurst (1858–1928), founded the Women's Social and Political Union. This marked a change in the movement's methods and suffragism became more militant. Suffragettes employed more violent means to draw attention to their cause: they chained themselves to railings, smashed windows and set fire to pillar-boxes. Violence was matched by violence, notably the forcible feeding of suffragettes on hunger strike, which so damaged Mrs Pankhurst that it contributed to her death. Her efforts, however, made such a prominent issue of votes for women that after they had taken on men's jobs during the First World

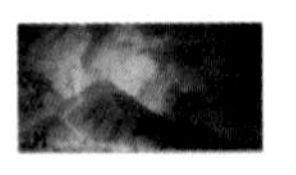

War, some were enfranchised in 1918. All adult women in Britain were allowed to vote after 1928.

1903
DU BOIS WRITES
THE SOULS OF BLACK FOLK

William Edward Burghardt Du Bois (1868–1963) was a lifelong advocate of world peace and a leading champion of the liberation of Africans – in particular, African-Americans. Du Bois was the first black to be awarded a PhD from Harvard. In more than 20 books and 100 scholarly articles, Du Bois championed the African-American culture through historical and sociological studies. *The Souls of Black Folk*, published in 1903, was a pioneering effort, arguing that an educated black elite should lead blacks to liberation. In 1905 Du Bois founded the Niagara Movement, a forerunner of the National Association for the Advancement of Colored People (NAACP), which he helped organize in 1909.

1903
POPE PIUS X CROWNED

Giuseppe Melchiorre Sarto became a parish priest in Venetia and a cardinal of Venice in 1893. He was elected pope in 1903 and crowned before an enormous crowd of 70,000 people. Unlike the previous pope, Leo XIII, he was uninterested in social reforms, instead concentrating on apostolic problems and making the defence of Roman Catholicism his cause. In particular, he condemned Modernism, a contemporary intellectual movement that sought to reinterpret traditional Catholic teaching in the light of nineteenth-century philosophical, historical and psychological theories. In 1907 he issued a decree rejecting Modernist teachings and suggesting remedies to eradicate it, urging immediate compliance with his censorship programme. He was canonized in 1954.

20 JULY 1903

Pope Leo XIII Dies

Pope Leo XIII dies after serving 25 years in office. His central concerns throughout this period had been bridging the gap between Christian sects and resolving the problems of class warfare. He was 93 years old.

Pope Pius X, who was crowned before a crowd of 70,000 people in 1903.

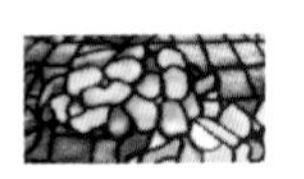

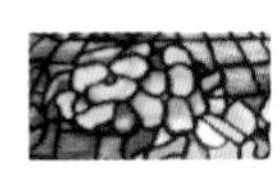

Antarctic explorer Captain Robert Scott.

1903
SCOTT REACHES ANTARCTICA'S SOUTHERNMOST POINT

Robert Falcon Scott said, 'I may as well confess that I have no predilection for polar exploration', and then set off on a journey to Antarctica. In 1901 the expedition ship *Discovery*, especially built to deal with pack ice, set sail. By January 1902, Scott had made winter camp on Ross Island and was making forays to explore the adjacent ice shelf and the mainland. His first venture towards the South Pole was hampered by the poor performances of the sledges and an outbreak of scurvy. In the summer of 1903, Scott tried again. He sledged up the Ferrar Glacier to the Polar Plateau, in a smooth 59 days. It was the furthest south any person had ever been.

1903
ARMY OFFICERS KILL KING AND QUEEN IN SERBIA

Since 1459 Serbia had been under the domination of the Turks. Uprisings in 1804–16, led by Kara George and Milosh Obrenovich, forced the Turks to recognize Serbia as an autonomous principality under Obrenovich. However, the assassination of George on Obrenovich's orders gave rise to a long feud between the two houses. Following a war with Turkey (1876–78), Serbia became an independent kingdom. In 1903, army officers assassinated the last king, Obrenovich, and his wife, after which the Karageorgevich dynasty was able to seize the throne. The restoration of this dynasty gave rise to a new pro-Russian orientation for Serbia, which brought it into conflict with Austria-Hungary; this in turn contributed to the First World War.

1903
POWERED FLIGHT

For many years, attempts had been made to get an aircraft that was heavier than air off the ground, but it took the considerable genius of American aviation pioneers Orville and Wilbur Wright, to achieve that dream. They invented the first successful self-propelled aeroplane after conducting tests with kites and then gliders. Before attempting powered flight they solved the essential problems of controlling a plane's motion in rising, descending and turning. The Wright brothers designed and built a 12–16 horsepower engine and propeller for their plane – originally named *Flyer 1* and commonly called *Kitty Hawk*. On 17 December 1903, on an isolated beach near Kitty Hawk, North Carolina, Orville achieved the first successful flight ever made in a self-propelled, heavier-than-air craft.

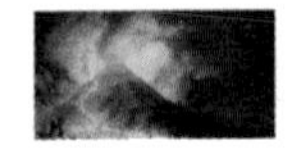

The Wright brothers' first successful flight at Kitty Hawk, North Carolina.

1904
NORWEGIAN CITY OF ALESUND BURNS DOWN

Located on the north-western coast of Norway, the town of Alesund was devastated by fire in the early hours of the morning of 23 January 1904. The furious winter storm spread a blaze akin to an explosion, covering the whole town centre in ashes and leaving between 10,000 and 12,000 people homeless. Following exceptional restoration work, including shipments of building materials sent by Emperor Wilhelm II of Germany, the town was completely rebuilt in the Art Nouveau style. Alesund remains one of the only towns like this in the world and looks very much like an illustration from a fairy tale. It now has a population of 36,000 and is the commercial and industrial capital of its region.

21 JULY 1904
Opening of the Trans-Siberian Railway

Siberia is finally opened up to Russia with the completion of the Trans-Siberian railroad after almost 13 years of building work. The railroad stretches for 7,360 km (4,600 miles) and has more than 1,000 stations along its route.

A train fitted with a snow plough pictured on the Trans-Siberian railway, which finally provided a direct route between Moscow and Vladivostok.

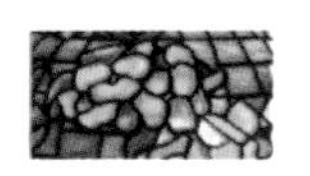

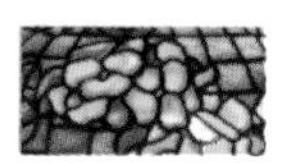

7 SEPTEMBER 1904

Britain to Trade in Tibet

The political and religious leader of Tibet, the Dalai Lama signs a treaty allowing Britain to establish trading posts in three cities in Tibet. The same treaty agrees that the country will not cede territories to foreign rule.

Puccini drew his inspiration for ***Madam Butterfly*** *from the play by David Belasco.*

1904
PREMIÈRE OF PUCCINI'S OPERA *MADAM BUTTERFLY*

Italian composer Giacomo Puccini was gifted with a vivid sense of the stage and a talent for beautiful harmonies and fine orchestration. It made him popular in the theatre, where his music seemed as brightly coloured and flowing as the drama taking place before the audience's eyes. In the summer of 1900, Puccini saw David Belasco's one-act play, *Madam Butterfly*. He was immediately drawn to the character of the little geisha and her tale of love and abandonment. He built an opera around it, using his melodic gifts to heighten the passion, tenderness and despair. *Madam Butterfly* premièred at La Scala in February 1904, and was revised in May with astounding success.

1904
THE RUSSO-JAPANESE WAR

War broke out between Japan and Russia, over Korea, in February 1904. The Russians had advanced into Korea and refused to withdraw. The war ended as a complete victory for the Japanese. Port Arthur was besieged and the Russian army was defeated at Mukden. The Russian Baltic Fleet was sent on a 35,400-km (22,000-mile) journey around the world to break the siege of Port Arthur, but was destroyed in just 45 minutes at the battle of Tsu Tshima. This was the first time that a major European power had been defeated by an Asian country and the war revealed the extent to which Japan had developed since the opening up of Japan by Commodore Matthew Perry and the coming to power of the Meiji, the 'illuminated reign' of the emperor Mutsuhito in 1868.

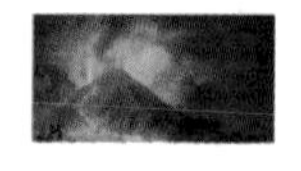

1904
VALVES AND TRANSISTORS

A major breakthrough in the development of complex machines run by electricity came in the shape of the valve tube. This was a sealed glass tube containing a vacuum; inside the vacuum were a cathode and anode which were able to create a one-way electrical current. This current could be turned on or off with the use of control electrodes. The two-diode thermionic valve appeared in 1904 and the three-diode amplification valve in 1906. Valves were commonly used until the advent of the transistor. The transistor is a semiconductor device with three or more terminals attached to electrode regions. The current between two of the electrodes is controlled by the others. This had the advantages of being smaller and being able to work on much lower voltage.

1904
HELEN KELLER GRADUATES

Helen Adams Keller (1880–1968) was an author, speaker and philanthropist whose dedicated work had an extraordinary and wide-ranging influence on the lives of the disabled. Keller had become blind and deaf at the age of 19 months as a result of brain fever and was unable to communicate or understand the world. She was patiently encouraged and taught by Anne Mansfield Sullivan, and she learned to read Braille and to write by using a special typewriter. In 1904, Keller graduated with honours from Radcliffe College and began a life of writing, lecturing and raising money for the disabled. The relationship between teacher and child was the subject of *The Miracle Worker*, a 1960 Pulitzer Prize-winning play and 1962 film by William Gibson.

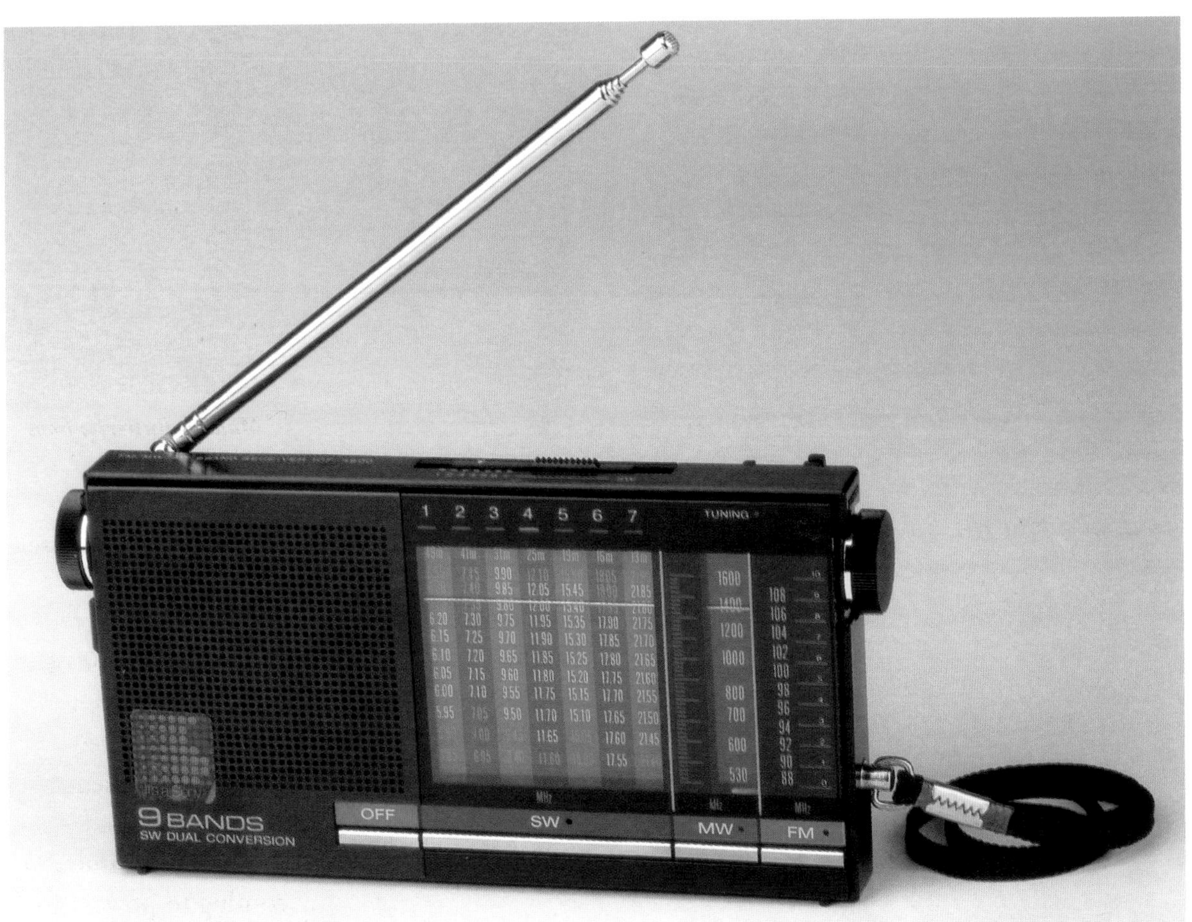

The transistor, used in later wirelesses and radios, superseded the use of the vacuum valve.

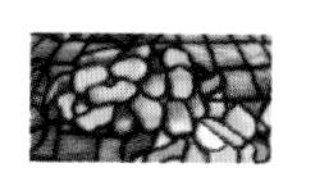

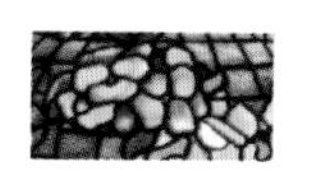

1904
THE ENTENTE CORDIALE

Throughout the second half of the nineteenth century, Britain had successfully avoided any long-term European commitments. British politicians took part in conferences and agreements, but undertook no treaty obligations. In 1902, however, Britain signed a treaty with Japan and in 1904 signed the much more significant Entente Cordiale with France. These treaties brought to an end the period of 'Splendid Isolation' that had characterized British foreign policy for so long. Three years later, Britain signed an entente with Russia, so creating the Triple Entente. This effectively meant that Europe was now divided into two armed camps, each made up of three powers and each with a series of built-in clauses, which involved automatic and immediate military action; it was an arrangement that would come into its own within a decade.

1904
PREMIÈRE OF *PETER PAN*

Peter Pan was a boy who never grew up; he was the leader of the Lost Boys who lived in Never Never Land, somewhere in the starry skies. He landed on the London stage in 1904. J. M. Barrie based his play on an earlier, less successful one, *The Little White Bird*, but the preparations for *Peter Pan* were shrouded in secrecy. The actress playing Wendy was alarmed to receive a notice reading 'Flying, 10.30 a.m.', along with a request for her to insure her life. The performance would involve the actors sweeping upwards on specially designed wires as they followed Peter beyond the clouds. The play was an outstanding success at its première, and even today remains one of the most popular children's entertainments of all time.

1904
DREADNOUGHT

The development of steel manufacturing allowed enormous steps to be made in the production of ships from 1870 onwards. By 1900, however, the thin steel battleships, with a displacement of 15,000 tons and a speed of 18 knots were fast becoming the norm. Britain had intensified the fleet build-up in 1899, concerned that the joint fleets of France and Russia rivalled its own. The first Dreadnought was laid down in 1904; this was a significant improvement on anything produced elsewhere in the world. This British vessel, with a speed of between 18–25 knots, boasted ten 12-in guns and would become the model for capital ships until the Second World War. Britain and Germany now dominated the seas around Europe.

The Dreadnought, the first steel battleship, unveiled in 1904.

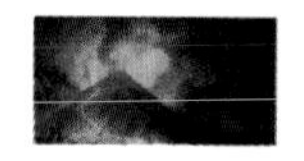

1905
NORWAY ATTAINS INDEPENDENCE

In June 1905, the Norwegian Parliament refused to recognize the Swedish monarchy and declared its independence from Sweden. A split in the union had been expected for some time. A referendum of the Norwegian people in August showed 80 per cent support for the dissolution of the union with Sweden. The terms of Norwegian independence were announced in Stockholm the following month, forcing the Swedish king, Oscar II, to abdicate formally from the Norwegian throne in October. A second referendum in Norway followed in November revealing 78 per cent support for the second son of the Danish King Frederick VII. Prince Carl formally accepted the throne of Norway on 18 November and was duly crowned as Haakon VII.

Robert Koch, the German bacteriologist who won the Nobel Prize for Medicine in 1905.

1905
ROBERT KOCH WINS NOBEL PRIZE FOR MEDICINE

German bacteriologist, Robert Koch, and his assistants devised techniques that enabled them to culture bacteria outside the body. Together they formulated the rule system, which determines if a bacterium is the cause of a particular disease or not. They won the Nobel Prize for Medicine in 1905. Koch's work on wounds, septicaemia and splenic fever won him a seat on the Imperial Board of Health. His researches in microscopy and bacteriology allowed him to identify the bacteria responsible for diseases such as anthrax, cholera and tuberculosis. His attempts at a lymph inoculation for tuberculosis were a failure, but his pioneering work meant that cures for these diseases were subsequently discovered.

22 JANUARY 1905

Bloody Sunday in Russia

In excess of 500 loyalist strikers are shot and killed during a march through St Petersburg in protest against poor working conditions and pay. The march is led by Father George Gapon, who survives the shots fired by troops attempting to disperse the protest.

1905
THE SCHLIEFFEN PLAN

Count Alfred von Schlieffen was the chief of the German general staff and in 1905 he drew a military strategy to counter a possible attack on two fronts by France and Russia. He believed that the immediate threat would come from France, but the more serious threat would come from Russia. The Schlieffen Plan involved a sudden attack through Belgium, a neutral country, which would outflank the French army and surround Paris. This would force the French to surrender; German forces could then be moved east by train to face the Russian armies. Schlieffen believed that the Russians would take six weeks to mobilize. The plan was to become fundamental to German strategy during the First World War.

1905
THE PROTESTANT ETHIC

The Protestant Ethic and the Spirit of Capitalism, published in 1905 by sociologist Max Weber (1864–1920), had significant influence on understanding capitalist attitudes and values. Weber traced the views that maximizing profit was the purpose of life and that leisure was evil, notions that were common amongst early industrialists, to the teachings of the sixteenth-century Protestant reformer John Calvin. Calvin taught that profit was God's reward to the obedient and hard-working, and that poverty was a result of sinful laziness. Biblical quotes supporting this view were often written on the walls of workshops. This marked a turning point in generally held work ethics and demonstrated a major shift from the medieval belief that proclaimed 'blessed are the poor'.

1906
MOUNT VESUVIUS ERUPTS

Mount Vesuvius in Italy has long been one of the most active volcanoes. In the twentieth century nearly 2,000 people have been killed by its eruptions, first in 1906 and then in 1944. The 1906 eruption began on 4 April when a fissure opened on the cone. Lava began to flow with increasing intensity over the next two days and 105 parishioners were killed in San Giuseppe when a 'lava bomb' devastated the local cathedral. The culmination of the eruption came with a great 'gas blow-off' on 8 April. So much ash was left by the explosion that 'hot avalanches' occurred for days and, when heavy rains fell, mudslides caused extensive damage in Ottaiano.

The eruption of Mount Vesuvius.

Magazine cover making light of the earthquake and fire which ravaged San Francisco in April 1906.

1906

SAN FRANCISCO EARTHQUAKE AND FIRE

The San Francisco quake and fire of 18 April 1906 caused the deaths of an estimated 700 people, obliterated 500 city blocks and caused $500 million of damage. On that day and for two days afterwards San Francisco was virtually burnt to the ground. The quake was created by shifting along the San Andreas Fault and measured 8.3 on the Richter Scale. Its epicentre was a few centimetres from the Golden Gate Bridge. The quake came in two shocks, one of 40 seconds the other of 75. The fire, caused not by the quake but by the disastrous efforts of troops trying to stop it with dynamite, lasted three days.

30 OCTOBER 1905

The October Manifesto

Tsar Nicholas II of Russia announces the October Manifesto, which puts the powers of the tsar under the control of a Duma (parliament), creating a constitutional monarchy; the attempt does little to relieve the tide of revolt sweeping through Russia.

Pablo Picasso, pioneer of the Cubist style, with examples of his work.

1907
THE BIRTH OF CUBISM

Cubism literally changed the perspective of art. Until 1907, artists had experimented with colour, depth and brush technique, but had represented objects and nature in a fairly straightforward way. Picasso and Braque created a new way of seeing the world. Strange angles, distorted surfaces and bizzare geometrical planes replaced portraiture and still lifes. Objects were no longer in scale and shapes were crammed on to the canvases seemingly haphazardly. The major work in the discovery of the Cubist principles was Picasso's savage painting *Les Demoiselles d'Avignon.* Braque made jagged shapes of everyday things, like guitars and houses. He shaded them with herringbone lines and used many sources of light. It was his attempt to 'materialize the new space', and it was disorientating and explosive. Cubism abandoned all the old ideas about art. The pictures of tables and chairs, newspapers, bottles and people were selected for their ordinariness, but were made extraordinary by the creative vision focused upon them.

1907
VICTORIA AND ALBERT MUSEUM OPENS IN LONDON

The Victoria and Albert Museum houses a rich collection of decorative and applied arts, spanning nearly every period and nation. It was founded in 1852 as the Museum of Manufacture with the mission of 'raising standards and improving public taste in contemporary industrial design'. On display were objects from the Great Exhibition of 1851. It moved to South Kensington, to become part of the Science Museum, and then became the Victoria and Albert Museum in 1899, when Queen Victoria laid the cornerstone of the new building, designed by Sir Aston Webb. It took some years to complete and was finally opened by King Edward VII in 1907.

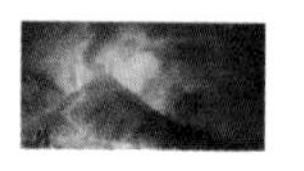

15 APRIL 1907
Japanese Leave Manchuria

The Japanese military withdraws its last troops from Manchuria, officially returning the area to Chinese control after its invasion and possession during the Russo-Japanese War.

1907
ROBERT BADEN-POWELL FOUNDS THE BOY SCOUTS

Sir Robert Stephenson Smyth Baden-Powell, 1st Baron Baden-Powell of Gilwell (1857–1941), was a British general who founded the Boy Scout and Girl Guide (Girl Scout) movement in the UK. Baden-Powell had written a book on military reconnaissance and scouting that became so popular with younger readers that he wrote *Scouting for Boys* in 1908. The American organization, Boy Scouts of America, begun in 1910, was founded on Baden-Powell's model. Boys attain rising rank within the organization through various accomplishments, each of which earns a rank or merit badge. Locally Cub Scouts are organized into dens and packs and Boy Scouts into patrols and troops.

Sir Robert Baden-Powell, founder of the Boy Scout movement and general in the British army.

Florence Nightingale, whose work in the Crimea revolutionized nursing practice.

1907
FLORENCE NIGHTINGALE AWARDED ORDER OF MERIT

Florence Nightingale trained as a nurse in Kaiserswerth and Paris and in 1853 became the superintendent of a hospital for invalid women in London. She volunteered for duty in the Crimean War and took 38 nurses to Scutari in 1854. She organized the barracks hospital after the Battle of Inkerman and her rules of discipline and sanitation reduced the Crimean War hospital death rate from 42 per cent to two per cent. She founded the Nightingale School and Home for Nurses in London in 1856. She also devoted many years to the improvement of nursing and public health in India. In 1907 she was given the Order of Merit, the first woman to receive the honour.

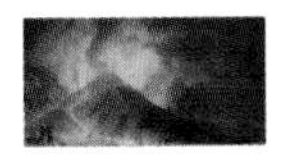

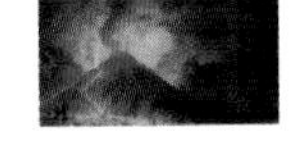

Pu Yi, the last emperor of China, who was crowned at the age of just two years old.

1908
PU YI BECOMES EMPEROR OF CHINA

Pu Yi was crowned in 1908 at the age of only two years – he was to be the last emperor of China. In 1911 revolution broke out and imperial rule ended with the infant being deposed. In 1912 a republic was formed and the ex-emperor was pensioned and sent to a summer palace near Beijing. He became known in the West as Henry Pu Yi, and in 1932 the Japanese set him up as a provincial dictator in Manzhouguo; he later held the title of Emperor Kangde from 1934 to 1945. In 1945 civil war resumed in China and he was imprisoned by the Russians and then the Chinese Communists. In 1949 the People's Republic of China was formed.

1908
THE FORD MODEL T

At first, motor cars were very expensive to own, but by 1908, Henry Ford (1863–1947) had started producing his Model T. It was designed to be affordable by the lay-person and, by 1927, 15 million had rolled out of his factories. In 1913, Ford had introduced the first conveyor belt assembly line and truly interchangeable parts, which revolutionized the car industry. After 1918 the motoring era took off; inspired by Ford, other car manufacturers followed suit. Petrol motor lorries and buses appeared in the 1890s but the diesel engine took over in the 1920s and 1930s.

The famous Ford Model T, designed to be a car for the masses.

Cartoon depicting Peary (left) and Scott arguing over who reached the North Pole first.

1909
REACHING THE NORTH POLE

A Norwegian scientist Fridtjof Nansen (1861–1930) was a principal polar explorer who completed the first expedition to the Greenland ice cap (1888–89). He then designed a ship capable of withstanding the pressure exerted by ice and embarked on an expedition across the Arctic Basin in 1893: by drifting with the ice instead of ramming it. After realizing the ship was not drifting towards the North Pole, he set off with a companion to reach it on specially designed sledges, but was forced to turn back 370 km (230 miles) from their objective. In 1909 American Robert Peary (1856–1920) claimed to have reached the North Pole with the help of Eskimos on sledges. The Japanese adventurer Naomi Uemura made the first solo trek to the North Pole in 1978.

25 JULY 1909
Flight Across the Channel

Louis Blériot achieves the first successful flight across the Channel in his Model XI Monoplane. He set off from Les Barques in France and landed near Dover castle in England. The 37.6-km (23 1/2 mile) crossing took him 36 1/2 minutes.

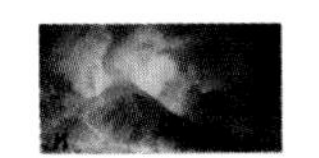

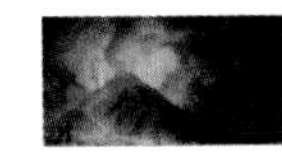

Chapter 2
1910–1919

1910
HENRI MATISSE PAINTS ***THE DANCE***

The French artist Henri Matisse (1869–1954) used colour as a means of expression rather than description and deliberately flouted the conventional rules of drawing and perspective. As a member of the Fauves, he developed his use of colour. By 1910, he had come to believe that enjoyment could be gained by studying a painting's essential lines with care. *The Dance*, a series of large canvases commissioned by Matisse's patron Shchukin in 1909, is an excellent illustration of this dictum, using just three colours to enhance the circle of dancers. Matisse's greatest accomplishment, apparent in all his work, was to liberate colour and utilize it as the foundation of a decorative art.

1910
CRIPPEN CAUGHT BY RADIO TELEGRAPHY

Telegraphy is the transmission of coded messages along wires by means of electronic signals and was devised by Charles Wheatstone and William Cooke in England in 1839. Marconi's later experiments in radio telegraphy

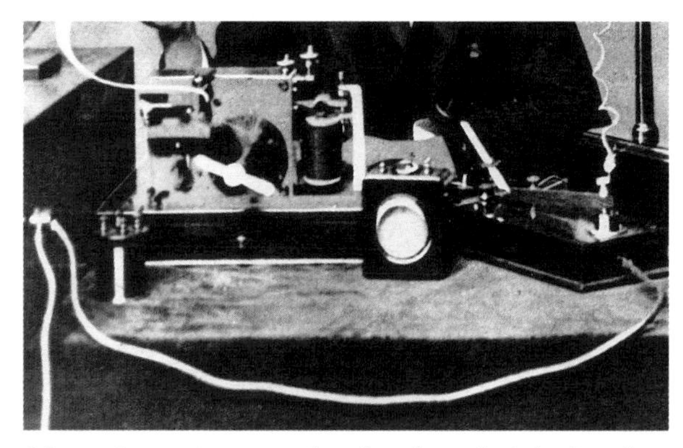

Marconi's experiments with radio telegraphy helped in the capture of the notorious murderer Dr Crippen.

helped open up the world. In 1910 the well-known criminal Hawley Harvey Crippen was attempting to flee the UK with his mistress Ethel le Neve. He had murdered his wife and buried her remains in the cellar of his London home. The captain of the Atlantic liner on which the couple were travelling became suspicious and contacted Scotland Yard by radio telegraphy (its first use for police purposes). A detective was dispatched in a faster boat and later arrested the couple. Crippen was tried, convicted and later executed at Pentonville prison in London.

Neon lighting, now a common sight all over the world particularly in advertizing, was first used to advertize the 1910 Paris Motor Show.

1910
MODERN LIGHTING

Neon lights were first used in 1910 as part of an advertising sign at the Paris Motor Show. The first successful fluorescent strip (or tube lighting) was made available in 1938, by General Electrics Co., America. Some fluorescent bulbs work by heating sodium vapour or neon gas until the atoms emit a glow of light. Others electrify mercury vapour, which gives off invisible ultra-violet light. This is then converted into visible light when it strikes a

The powers of the House of Lords were limited by the House of Commons in 1911.

phosphor coating on the inside of the glass. Fluorescent light is produced more efficiently than filament light, and the bulbs last longer because they do not produce destructive levels of heat. Tungsten filament lights are often used when very bright light is required, such as illuminating sports grounds or film sets.

1911
TAYLORISM AND THE RATIONALISATION OF MANAGEMENT

✹ Frederick Winslow Taylor (1856–1915) was the originator of 'scientific management', a means of rationalizing work in factories and maximizing efficiency. After a professional education, he chose to become a machine shop labourer in 1878, and soon progressed to the role of chief engineer. He believed that there was 'one best way' of doing each task and his time-motion studies involved analyzing, timing and improving every movement and action of production workers. His central work, *The Principles of Scientific Management*, was published in 1911. Critics of Taylorism saw the practice as turning craftsmen into robots and maximizing exploitation, while supporters claimed that Taylor had helped to increase the income of manual workers.

15 MAY 1911

Reform in Parliament

The House of Commons passes the Parliament Act which limits the powers of the House of Lords; members of the Lords will no longer be allowed to reverse legislation passed by the Commons.

Machu Picchu, the lost city of the Incas, rediscovered by Hiram Bingham in 1911.

1911
BINGHAM FINDS THE LOST CITY OF THE INCAS

Hiram Bingham taught Latin American history at Yale, but he was no armchair traveller. Reckless and adventurous by nature, he became an explorer. His obsession was to find 'the lost city in the clouds' – Machu Picchu, the last stronghold of the Incas after the Spanish conquest. It is perched high in the Andean Mountains, on a ridge 609 m (2,000 ft) above the rushing Urubamba River. Bingham crossed over a precarious wooden bridge – just a few logs lashed together – and followed a snake-infested trail until he suddenly found himself 'confronted with the walls of ruined houses built of the finest Inca stone'. Before him lay the abandoned terraces, temples and food-storage vaults of the sacred retreat of an ancient civilization.

1911
SUN YAT-SEN AND THE CHINESE REPUBLIC

Sun Yat-Sen was a western-educated politician who led the Chinese Revolution in 1911. The emperor, Pu Yi, abdicated in February 1912 and a republic was set up with Sun as president; an Assembly was then established with two houses. Sun, however, resigned almost immediately to allow Yuan Shih-k'ai to unite the country. Sun set up the Kuomintang, or Nationalist Party. In 1913 Yuan forced the Kuomintang members of the Assembly to leave and in 1914 dissolved the Assembly. In 1915 he declared himself emperor. Yuan's behaviour had important consequences in the long run. When the Kuomintang held its first national congress in 1924, Communists were admitted; these included Russian and German military advisers headed by Jiang-Jieshi, who had been trained in Japan. They set up a military academy and when Sun died in 1925, Jiang-Jieshi became the leader of the Kuomintang.

1911
AMUNDSEN REACHES THE SOUTH POLE

Antarctica was the last continent to be explored. In 1908 Ernest Shackleton's (1874–1922) British expedition set out on a 1,300-km (800-mile) trek to the South Pole, but food shortages forced them to turn back 160 km (100 miles) from their objective. The 'race' to

Robert Scott (right), who undertook the race to the South Pole against Norwegian Roald Amundsen.

the South Pole began in 1911 between a Norwegian team led by Roald Amundsen and a British one led by Robert Scott (1868–1912). Using Inuit survival skills, dog sledges and fur clothing, the Norwegians advanced faster than the mixture of horses, dogs and motor-sledges used by Scott. Amundsen took seven weeks to reach the pole in December 1911. Scott's team arrived in January 1912, but the entire team tragically perished on the return journey.

5 NOVEMBER 1912

Wilson Wins Presidency

The governor of New Jersey, Woodrow Wilson, wins the US presidential elections with 6.3 million votes, after a close-run campaign. He is the first Democrat to be elected for 20 years.

1912
THE DISESTABLISHMENT AND ABOLITION OF CONFUCIANISM

In 1912, the emperor of China was overthrown by the Chinese Republicans led by Sun Yat Sen. Confucianism, which put great emphasis upon loyalty to the emperor, was seen as a threat to the new regime and was disestablished,

Confucius, the founder of Confucianism, which was disestablished in China in 1912.

although it was allowed to continue. After another revolution in 1949, Confucian teachings were condemned by the Communists as élitist and reactionary, and the faith was abolished from the Republic of China. At the same time, all schools and colleges under the control of western missionaries were seized and nationalized. It is significant that the concept of an authoritarian state run for the welfare of the people has had much influence upon the contemporary government of China.

we shall stick it out to the end but we are getting weaker of course and the end cannot be far. It seems a pity but I do not think I can write more — R Scott

Last Entry
For Gods sake look after our people

A page from Robert Scott's diary after his failed expedition to the South Pole.

1912
DEATH OF CAPTAIN SCOTT

'Had we lived I should have a tale to tell of the hardihood endurance and courage of my companions.... These rough notes and our dead bodies must tell the tale.' On 16 January 1912, one of Scott's expedition party spotted a black marker flag left by the Norwegian explorer Roald Amundsen, and knew they had been beaten in their race to the South Pole. They turned and began the harsh journey back. Ill-equipped, suffering from frostbite and lack of food and warmth, they were trapped in the middle of a snowstorm and were unable to continue. The tent entombing their bodies was found eight months later by a search party from Cape Evans, although it was not until February 1913 that the news of the tragedy finally reached the British public.

1912
TITANIC SINKS ON MAIDEN VOYAGE

On 15 April 1912, the 'unsinkable' ship *Titanic* struck an iceberg off the coast of Newfoundland, and sank with a loss of over 1,500 passengers. The ship had been claimed unsinkable because of her 16 watertight compartments, but the collision opened too many of these, and she sank without trace, until 1985 when her wreck was discovered. The ship, the largest and most luxurious ever built, was on her maiden voyage from Southampton to New York, carrying more

*The **Titanic**, which sank on its maiden voyage, in one of the most famous disasters of all time.*

than 2,200 people – many of whom were rich and famous. The death toll was blamed on the shortage of lifeboats, many of which were sent away half-full, and the fact that many passengers opted to stay aboard the ship rather than risk their lives on the icy sea. A nearby unidentified liner failed to respond to the *Titanic's* distress calls.

14 FEBRUARY 1912

Expansion of the States

Arizona becomes the 48th state of the USA; this follows the admission of New Mexico as the 47th state of the union just a month ago.

1912
'PILTDOWN MAN' DISCOVERED

In 1912, a British lawyer and antiquarian, Charles Dawson, made an archeological find that was to puzzle scientists and anthropologists for the next 40 years. In a gravel pit on Piltdown Common in Sussex, he dug up portions of a human skull and jawbone. From the animal remains at the site, all indications were that the finds were over 500,000 years old. Strangely, however, the skull was of a modern type, though the jaw was similar to that of an ape. In 1953, chemical analysis revealed that *Eoanthropus Dawson* was an ingenious fraud. The skull was of a modern man; the jaw, that of an orang-utan. Both had been skilfully stained and aged. Another mystery of human evolution was solved and the need for the careful testing of fossil remains was emphasized.

1912
CARL GUSTAV JUNG PUBLISHES *SYMBOLS OF TRANSFORMATION*

A student of Freud, Carl Gustav Jung (1885–1961) rejected Freud's heavy emphasis upon sexuality as the principal driving force of unconscious thought. Jung focused instead upon the spiritual, and drew much inspiration from the study of the practices, beliefs and symbols of differing religions, publishing *Symbols of Transformation* in 1912. He felt that man's unconscious thoughts were not unique to each individual, reflecting personal thoughts and desires, but rather rose from a collective unconscious and therefore the symbols and thoughts that arose in dreams were timeless and universal archetypes. Jung reached these conclusions after noting similarities between patient's hallucinations or delusions, and finding that these could not always be linked to their personal experiences.

Carl Gustav Jung, one of the founders of psychoanalysis.

The New York Grand Central Station, which originally boasted 48 tracks on two levels.

1912
WOMEN'S FOOT-BINDING ABOLISHED IN CHINA

Foot-binding was a traditional Chinese custom in which the feet of young girls were tightly bound with strips of linen in order to discourage growth. The large toe was bent backwards over the top of the foot and the remaining toes were folded underneath and strapped. Foot-binding originated in the Song dynasty (AD 960–1279), after which the custom spread throughout all social classes in China – particularly the upper classes, who deemed it a mark of great beauty and gentility and proved that women were incapable of physical labour. Girls between the ages of five and 12 were selected to undergo this painful and debilitating procedure. In 1912 the Chinese government officially banned the custom.

1913
GRAND CENTRAL STATION OPENS

On 2 February 1913, Grand Central Station was officially opened in New York City at 42nd Street and Park Avenue, replacing a 41-year-old New York Central and New Haven train shed with the world's largest railway station. Grand Central, which had an impressive 31 tracks on its upper level and 17 on its lower level, was opened to commuters from October 1912. Far bigger than Penn Station, New York's second largest train station, Grand Central remained the city's largest and most important rail terminal for 78 years (until 1991), after which it became a strictly commuter terminal, Amtrak having rerouted its long-distance trains to Penn Station.

The Adolescents from Stravinsky's ***The Rite of Spring****, which paved the way for new forms and styles of music.*

1913
DEATH OF EMILY DAVISON

Suffragist Emily Davison, who had been imprisoned several times due to the militant nature of her campaigning efforts, was killed on 14 July 1913, when she ran in front of the king's horse at the Epsom Derby, and grabbed the reins. She was the first martyr of the British suffragette movement. Sylvia Pankhurst, founder of the WSPU (Women's Social and Political Union), was sentenced on 8 July of the same year to three months in prison. The suffragettes attended Davison's funeral in white, carrying wreaths and banners that pronounced 'Fight on and God will give the victory'. The demand for the national vote for women reached a peak in 1914; the suffragette movement also protested about a range of other gender inequalities.

1913
PREMIÈRE OF STRAVINSKY'S *THE RITE OF SPRING*

Igor Stravinsky has become one of the colossal figures of twentieth-century music. *The Rite of Spring* was at first a *succès de scandale*, causing a violent outcry when it premièred in Paris on 28 May 1913. The audience laughed and jeered at both the music and at Nijinsky's choreography for the ballet. Its new treatment of harmony, orchestration and structure, however, eventually made it one of the most influential works of the century. Its idiosyncratic rhythms, hard-edged and fast-pulsed, were its most outstanding feature, overturning the decorous romanticism of previous years. It was *The Rite of Spring*, with its 'scenes of pagan Russia', that made Stravinsky's name. The ballet began with a cluster of pan pipes and revolutionized the world of music with its fierce, primal rhythms and its beautifully inventive harmonies.

27 JANUARY 1913

Thorpe Stripped of Medals

US athlete Jim Thorpe is forced to relinquish the gold medals he won in Stockholm in 1912, after it is revealed he had received a fee for playing minor-league baseball, making him of professional status and thereby ineligible to compete in the Olympic Games.

Jim Thorpe of the USA at the Stockholm Olympics; he was later forced to reliquish his gold medals.

1913
PANAMA CANAL COMPLETED

President Wilson finally opened the Panama Canal in October 1913. It had been completed at a cost of £60 million and was described at the time as 'the greatest liberty man has ever taken with nature'. The project was managed by the autocratic engineer Colonel George Goethals. The US president

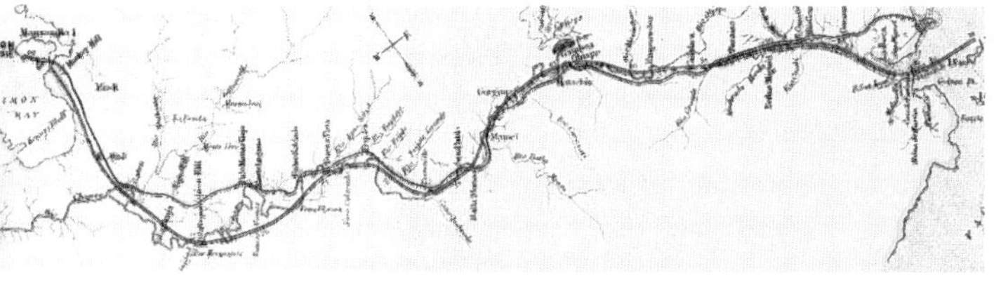

The Panama Canal, which was completed in 1913 after more than 10 years of construction.

formally completed the canal himself by detonating a 36,287-kg (40-ton) charge of explosives from the White House, some 6,400 km (4,000 miles) away. This charge removed the last obstacle. On 17 November, the steamship *Louise* successfully navigated the canal, passing into history as the first vessel to use the waterway. In January, in recognition of Goethals' contribution to the canal project, President Wilson offered the engineer the post of first governor of the Canal Zone.

1913
WASSILY KANDINSKY PAINTS *THE BLACK ARCH*

The Russian-born painter Wassily Kandinsky (1866–1944) is considered by many to be the founder of Abstract art. In 1907, he exhibited with the German Expressionist group Die Brücke, and in 1909 he founded the New Association of Munich Artists. In 1910, Kandinsky executed his first abstract painting and the following year, along with August Macke, Franz Marc and, later, Paul Klee, he founded the group known as Der Blaue Reiter. He wrote his famous theoretical study, *Concerning the Spiritual in Art*, in 1912. *The Black Arch*, painted in 1913, illustrates his abandoning of the tradition of spatial illusion, affirming the two-dimensional character of the canvas and the arbitrary nature of pictorial space. Kandinsky's painting later evolved from the expressionistic, highly coloured improvisations of his early period towards more precisely drawn and geometrically arranged compositions.

*Wassily Kandinsky's **Bindung**; he was considered by many to be the founder of Abstract art.*

1913
THE BEGINNINGS OF BEHAVIOURISM

Behaviourism is a school of psychology based on empirical science. It originated in about 1913, and was pioneered by J. B. Watson (1878–1958). He later outlined his theories in his book *Behaviourism* (1925). Behaviourists believed that the only valid form of psychology was the study of how animals and humans physically responded to stimuli, rather than concentrating on introspection. B. F. Skinner later stated the position in its purest form in his *Beyond Freedom and Dignity* (1971), in which he presented the mind as an automatic machine and rejected the idea of free will. He concluded, controversially, that people's minds should be scientifically programmed by psychologists to ensure socially beneficial behaviour.

10 FEBRUARY 1913

Robert Scott's Body Found

The search for the bodies of the ill-fated Antarctic exploration team led by Robert Scott is finally over. Scott's diary, found alongside his body in their tent, tells of their last few days, stuggling for survival in harsh and desperate conditions.

1913
CONVEYORS

Meat-processing factories in America had introduced conveyor cables for moving carcasses by the 1890s. In 1913, Henry Ford (1863–1947) introduced a conveyor to his assembly line for producing the famous Model T car. After that, conveyors became accepted as part of the route to achieving optimum efficiency in all kinds of industries. Many kinds of conveyor were developed for handling both unit and bulk materials, according to different process requirements. They include belt, roller, chain, bucket and carousel conveyors. Others have been invented for carrying people themselves: escalators, elevators and moving walkways are all conveying machines designed for saving the effort of walking or climbing.

Henry Ford, who introduced assembly lines into his factories in 1913.

Charlie Chaplin, the first true movie star.

1913
CHARLIE CHAPLIN

London's first specially-built cinema opened in 1912, but the first international movie star did not make his appearance until the following year – and he was British. Charlie Chaplin (1889–1977) was on a tour of the USA when his talent was recognized by the Keystone Studios; he made his first film with them in 1913, soon gaining his trademark bowler hat, moustache and walking stick. By 1918, Chaplin was internationally famous and instantly recognizable, and he was able to command a fee of $1 million for his performance in *Shoulder Arms*. He went on to be co-founder of United Artists. 'Chaplin means more to me than the idea of God,' said the French director François Truffaut (1932–84).

1 OCTOBER 1914
Global Warfare

Britain's entry into the war against Germany sees troops from every corner of the empire set out to support the cause. From the other side of the world, an Australian expeditionary force leaves to join the fight and the first troops from Canada, including many US volunteers, embark for England.

1914
MAHATMA GANDHI'S CAMPAIGN FOR FREEDOM

Mohandas Karamchand Gandhi (1869–1948) was born in Bombay. He studied law in England then, as a barrister, moved to South Africa. He first experienced the apartheid policy when he was thrown out of a first-class railway carriage at Pietermaritzburg in 1893. From this time he campaigned for justice using policies of non-violence (*ahimsa*), or what he called *satyagraha* ('truth force'). On returning to India in 1914, he dedicated himself to obtaining Indian independence from the British Empire through non-violent action. Protests such as the salt march – where 60,000 people were arrested for breaking a British ban on making salt – destroyed the credibility of British rule. With independence, the country underwent partition into Muslim Pakistan and largely Hindu India and over one million died in religious conflict. Hindu extremists, angered at his policies, assassinated Gandhi in 1948.

Mahatma Gandhi, who campaigned for justice in India through non-violent means.

The assassination of Austrian Archduke Franz Ferdinand was the spark that lit the flame of the First World War.

1914
ASSASINATION OF ARCHDUKE FRANZ FERDINAND

On 28 June 1914, Archduke Franz Ferdinand – the heir to the Austrian throne – and his wife were shot dead by Serbian terrorist Gavrilo Princip on a state visit to the country. Under normal circumstances this incident would have passed without major repercussions, but the build-up of alliances and the consequent heightening of tensions turned what was a political matter into an international tragedy. The Austrian government had been looking for an excuse to crush Serbia, which stood in their way in the Balkans. When Russia mobilized in support of the Serbs, Germany automatically became involved and this brought in France. By 12 August all the major European powers were involved in a catastrophic conflict, which would last for more than four years.

Tsar Nicholas II of Russia.

1914
RUSSIA UNDER NICHOLAS II

Tsar Nicholas II was an unintelligent family man who was completely unsuited to being the autocratic ruler of 140 million people. He was easily influenced by others and lacked the determination to carry out serious changes in Russia. He believed that it was his duty to pass on the power that he had inherited to his son, so he tended to side with his most conservative, even reactionary ministers. Nicholas allowed Russia to be rushed headlong into war in 1914, and when the Russian army was badly beaten by the Germans in the early battles, appointed himself commander-in-chief in August 1915 – a bad political move. As a result, and for the first time, Russians came to blame the tsar personally for Russian failures.

1914
LILLE FALLS

German troops took the cities of Lille and Ghent on 12 September 1914, following a fluid battle that saw the fall of Mons after a bitter struggle. The British Expeditionary Force (BEF) had landed in France only shortly before being forced into the line in Belgium. After suffering heavy casualties, the British pulled back, allowing the Germans to sweep across the Sambre and the Meuse rivers. On 5 September the Germans took Rheims and with it 12,000 prisoners. The major decisive battle on the western front was fought along the Marne River, where the French retaliated against the German attacks, driving them back to Aisne. This battle succeeded in saving the French capital.

The fallen city of Lille after the German invasion.

Scenes of destruction during the First Battle of Ypres, a site of conflict for the duration of the war.

1914

THE FIRST BATTLE OF YPRES

In November 1914, the German army attacked the Belgian town of Ypres and conducted a close-order frontal assault on prepared British trenches, losing hundreds of men and officers without having secured an inch of ground. Battles in the Ypres salient were to continue throughout the war. In February 1915, Germany began another series of offensives in the Soissons. The British then attacked in the Artois region and broke through at Neuve Chapelle, but were unable to exploit the advantage. The Germans soon closed the gap and, in April, successfully used gas for the first time on the western front at Ypres. These assaults also failed; resulting in 300,000 Allied casualties. The French then attempted another campaign against the German lines in the Champagne region, preceded by a lengthy artillery bombardment. After 250,000 casualties, the French commander Joffre called off the assaults.

25 DECEMBER 1914

Christmas Truce at the Front

Rumours are reported of a temporary truce between British and German soldiers on the Western Front; it is believed that soldiers from both sides walked and talked openly with one another and exchanged cigarettes in a reflection of seasonal goodwill.

1914
THE WAR EFFORT

To create and supply the armies of the First World War required overwhelming effort, enterprise and change. Supplies of raw materials had to be found for the manufacture of shells and guns. Labour was needed in armaments plants and other essential industries. Millions of men had to be trained and equipped before they went into the field and were then fed and supplied. The war effort was so great that soon there were shortages of supplies for civilians. People in many parts of Europe had to make do with too little clothing and food and in some areas non-essential products disappeared

The First World War saw women taking on many roles traditionally ascribed to men.

altogether. Many new armaments and weapons, such as tanks and poison gas, were used for the first time in this war.

1915
GALLIPOLI

The Allies had hoped both to capture Istanbul and join up with the Russians in a bold move against the Turks. Some 75,000 men under General Hamilton were landed on the Gallipoli Peninsula: 35,000 at Cape Helles

Soldiers in the trenches watching the effect of a catapult bomb at Gallipoli.

and a similar number further west. The Turks, under Colonel Kemal (later Kemal Ataturk), held their positions and by November 1916 the Allies decided to withdraw. The campaign was typified by the tremendous courage of the Empire troops (many Australian and New Zealanders took part in the Gallipoli campaign) and by the ineptitude of the allied commanders. The only success in the campaign was the bloodless withdrawal. Both the Allies and the Turks are believed to have lost in excess of 250,000 men.

5 APRIL 1915
Willard vs Johnson

Defending world heavyweight boxing champion Jack Johnson is defeated by Jess Willard in Cuba. Willard knocked the champion out to take the title in an epic slogging match lasting 26 rounds.

1915
RUPERT BROOKE, POET HERO

Following his untimely death in 1915, Rupert Brooke became the poet hero of the First World War. He was handsome, young, tall and blond – a 'golden boy'. He was a fellow at Cambridge University, and travelled in the United States and the South Pacific. When war broke out he enlisted as an officer. He died on a hospital ship, before he could witness the horror of the fighting. Brooke became a symbol of all the gifted youth killed in the conflict. He is best remembered for his patriotic poems, such as 'The Soldier' and 'Grantchester', where his romantic view of the war was reassuring to those not fighting at the front.

The great Jess Willard (left), who became the heavyweight Champion in 1915.

1916
BATTLE OF VERDUN

In February 1916 German General Falkenhayn launched the one million-strong 5th Army against the French-held city of Verdun. National pride forbade the French to lose the city despite the new policy of all-out attack against the Germans. The outer ring of French defenses fell, but accurate artillery fire checked the German attack. The village of Vaux fell on 6 June, but the main thrust on Verdun failed on 11 July. Up to this point the Germans had lost 280,000 men against the French casualties of 315,000. In October the French counter-attacked and took back much of the ground lost. By the end of the campaign the French losses were 542,000 compared with German losses of 434,000.

Scenes from the Battle of Verdun, in which the Germans launched an offensive against the French troops holding the city.

1916
THE EASTER RISING IN DUBLIN

Rebels proclaiming an Irish Republic rose up against the British in Dublin on 25 April. While rebels shot at sentries guarding Dublin Castle, others seized strategic parts of the city. The British responded by pouring troops into Dublin, under the charge of General Sir John Maxwell, swiftly regaining control and seizing

The first day of the Battle of the Somme saw the highest number of casualties ever recorded in warfare.

key leaders. By 11 May, 794 civilians had been killed along with 521 police and soldiers. Padraic Pearse, the rebel leader, was also dead along with five of the other seven rebel leaders. James Connolly, the last surviving rebel leader, was shot by a firing squad. Meanwhile, Sir Roger Casement, the former diplomat, was tried and executed for treason after attempting to smuggle German arms into Ireland.

1916
THE SOMME OFFENSIVE

On 1 July 1916, the British and French launched the Somme offensive. This brought them face to face with some of the heaviest German fortifications on the entire western front. The British general, Douglas Haig, resisted the idea, but French commander Joffre won the argument and the campaign began. The Somme saw the first use of tanks in war, and was preceded by the greatest artillery barrage of the war. Despite these advantages, the general slaughter of Allied troops that occurred is infamous, with the British suffering 65,000 casualties on the first day alone. When the October rains finally put an end to the prolonged carnage, 400,000 British, 200,000 French and 450,000 Germans had become casualties. The Allies only captured a few miles of ground, but the Germans responded by withdrawing to their new Hindenburg Line in early 1917.

1917
GERRIT THOMAS RIETVELD

In his search for the new, purer, mechanized furniture of the future, Rietveld (1888–1964) developed one of the most striking and far-reaching designs of the early twentieth century. Born in Utrecht, the son of a cabinet-maker, Rietveld started his own cabinet-making business in 1911; he was initially influenced by architectural drawings. In 1917, he started experimenting with design, producing the famous 'Red and Blue' chair (1917–18). The first prototype for this chair was constructed out of cheap wood and left unpainted. It was suggested to Rietveld that he might paint it, which he did using the simple primary colours of the De Stijl group. In so doing, he was able to emphasize the spatial characteristics of the chair, highlighting the ease of construction through standardized machined parts. Rietveld joined De Stijl following the publication of an article about his chair in the group's magazine.

> **7 DECEMBER 1916**
>
> ## Lloyd George as PM
>
> Prime minister Herbert Asquith resigns after criticism of his war policies; Liberal leader David Lloyd George is appointed by King George to take over the role, now complicated by antagonism from supporters of Asquith.

British prime minister David Lloyd George.

Revolution broke out in Russia in February 1917, eventually forcing the tsar, Nicholas II, to abdicate.

1917
THE FEBRUARY REVOLUTION

In February 1917, revolution broke out in Petrograd, the capital of Russia. It was not a planned uprising, but a series of protests against food shortages, inflation and rumours about the tsarina, Alexandra, who was believed to be a German spy. She was also suspected of having had an affair with Gregory Rasputin, a mysterious monk who had been murdered in December 1916. The protestors were joined by strikers from factories in Petrograd and by soldiers sent to deal with the demonstrators. Even some of the tsar's most loyal troops, the Cossacks, joined in. When Nicholas heard of the events, he tried to return to Petrograd from his headquarters, but his train was not allowed through. On 2 March 1917 the tsar of Russia finally abdicated.

1917
THE OCTOBER REVOLUTION

From March to October 1917, Russia was ruled by the Provisional Government. This had no legal standing, but was intended to govern until a general election could be held; this was planned for November. The Provisional Government gradually became more and more unpopular, partly because it decided to continue waging the war against Germany, but also because food shortages and inflation grew even worse. On 24–25 October the Bolsheviks overthrew the Provisional Government in a coup planned and led by Leon Trotsky, Lenin's second-in-command. A month later the general election was held. This was won by the Socialist-Revolutionary Party, but when the Assembly

Leon Trotsky, who led the Bolshevik coup in which the Provisional Government of Russia was overthrown.

met in January, Lenin dissolved it by force and began to rule as a dictator.

1918
THE YANKS ARE COMING

The British attacked at Arras on 9 April 1917, suffering 84,000 casualties, but achieved no breakthrough. Before this battle had ended, the new French commander, Nivelle, launched his own offensive from Soissons to Rheims. This offensive ground to a halt on its first day, and by the time the assault was finally over the French had suffered 220,000 casualties. Many French soldiers mutinied. In November, the British launched an attack toward Cambrai using hundreds of tanks. All three German lines were broken, but within days, German counter-attacks drove the British back to their starting positions. The last great German offensive was launched on 21 March 1918, with a 6,000-gun barrage and a heavy gas attack. The Allies suffered 350,000 casualties, but more troops were rushed in from across the Channel, and American troops began arriving for the first time.

12 NOVEMBER 1918

End of the Austrian Empire

Following the signing of the Armistice on 11 November, Charles I, the emperor of Austria, king of Hungary and last ruler of the Habsburg dynasty, resigns his position. Karl Renner becomes the first chancellor of the new Austrian Republic.

1918
BOLSHEVIK CIVIL WAR

In the summer of 1918, civil war broke out in Russia between the Bolsheviks and their opponents. At first it seemed inevitable that the Bolsheviks would be defeated as they were completely surrounded and had few effective forces. However, by the end of 1920 all the White Armies, as the Bolshevik's opponents became known, had been defeated. The Bolsheviks controlled the main centres of industry and the railway network. They were supported by many of the officers of the tsar's army and by some of the people of Russia. The Whites were disorganised and had few reserves or supplies, despite being supported by Britain and the USA. One by one, their armies were defeated and their commanders captured.

Celebrations in Britain after the Armistice was signed, marking the end of the 'Great War'.

Women worldwide had been struggling for emancipation since the turn of the century; the US granted them the vote in 1918.

1918
WOMEN IN THE US WIN THE VOTE

The US women's rights movement, which started as early as the 1830s and became involved with the struggle to abolish slavery, resulted in the proposal for the 19th Amendment (a move to allow women the vote), introduced in Congress in 1878. This amendment remained a controversial issue for over 40 years, during which the movement became strongly militant, conducting campaigns and demonstrations for congressional passage of the amendment and then for ratification by the states. This political action, reinforced by the service of women in industry during the First World War, resulted in the adoption of the amendment in 1918. The 19th Amendment, formally ratified in 1920, provided men and women with equal voting rights.

1919
MUSSOLINI

Benito Mussolini was the leader of the Fascist Party in Italy. He had fought in the First World War and was angry at the treatment Italy had received at the Treaty of Versailles. From 1919 he organised a propaganda campaign through his paper *Il Popolo d'Italia*. He made himself out to be a strong man who could solve Italy's problems. His supporters, known as the Blackshirts, were organised into Fascio di Combattimento; in some parts of Italy they were the main source of law and order. They punished criminals, broke up strikes and attacked Mussolini's opponents. In October 1922 Mussolini organised a 'March on Rome' by his Blackshirts. This was intended to put pressure on the government; in fact it led to Mussolini being appointed prime minister of Italy. He became the first dictator in western Europe.

Italian fascist dictator Benito Mussolini.

14 JUNE 1919

Flight Across the Atlantic

Captain John Alcock and his navigator Arthur Whitten Brown make the first non-stop flight across the Atlantic Ocean in their Vickers-Vimy biplane. The journey of nearly 3,200 km (2,000 miles) takes the Briton and the American 16 hours and 12 minutes.

1919
LEAGUE OF NATIONS FORMED

The League of Nations was suggested by US president Woodrow Wilson in 1917 as part of the peace settlement for the First World War. The League covenant was drawn up by the Paris Peace Conference in 1919 and was incorporated into the Versailles and other peace treaties. Its member states undertook to preserve the territorial rights of all and to bring international disputes before the League. It was established in Geneva, Switzerland, in 1920 and included representatives from states throughout the world. Its status was undermined, however, by the US decision not to join the League, and because it had no power to enforce its decisions. The League of Nations was dissolved in 1946.

1919
AMRITSAR MASSACRE

During the First World War, the imperial empires retained the co-operation of their colonial subjects, but the inter-war period exposed the fragility of their imperial control. Efforts to satisfy Arab aspirations in the Middle East led to Britain establishing the kingdoms of Iraq (declared independent in 1932) and Transjordan. Similar promises made to the Jews for a 'National Home' in Palestine created more complications and violence. The Indian independence movement proved a serious threat to British rule, with growing demands for Indian representation in central government. The 1919 Amritsar massacre of 400 Indians hardened nationalist campaigners and emergency powers were subsequently introduced to repress protests amid growing violence.

1919
NANCY ASTOR BECOMES BRITAIN'S FIRST WOMAN MP

Viscountess Nancy Astor (1879–1964) became the first woman to sit as a Member of Parliament (MP) in Britain. Born Nancy Witcher Langhorne, she married Waldorf Astor, a Conservative Member of Parliament in 1906. When he took over his father's title in 1919, entering the House of Lords, she won his seat in the House of Commons and held it until 1945. Lady Astor was outspoken but enormously popular, and she worked enthusiastically for temperance and for women's and children's welfare. In the 1930s, doubt was raised about her loyalty, when she was the focus of a group that favoured an appeasement policy towards Nazi Germany. When Britain declared war, however, she strongly supported the war effort.

Nancy Astor became the first female member of the British Parliament in 1919.

Chapter 3
1920–1929

1920s
KU KLUX KLAN REVIVED

The Ku Klux Klan (KKK) is the name of a group of American white racists who used violence and subversive methods to preserve white supremacy. From 1866 to 1872 they organized secret societies that terrorized local white and black Republican leaders and blacks whose behaviour violated old ideas of black subordination. Members wore white robes and masks and adopted the burning cross as their symbol. In the 1870s most Americans disclaimed the methods of the Ku Klux Klan but when the story of the KKK was popularized in Thomas B. Dixon's *The Clansman* (1905) and D. W. Griffith's movie *The Birth of a Nation* (1915), the problems increased. The movement reached its height of popularity in the 1920s, preaching anti-Catholic, anti-Jewish, anti-black, anti-socialist, and anti-labour-union 'Americanism'. At its peak, the Klan had more than two million members and exercised great political power in many states.

The white American racist group Ku Klux Klan, performing an initiation ceremony in 1923.

A new era of decadence dawned after the First World War, causing the decade to become known as the 'Roaring Twenties'.

1920s
THE ROARING TWENTIES

After the First World War, many young men and women tried to forget their grief for lost friends and relatives with thrills and pleasure. There were wild parties and new, provocative dances such as the 'Black Bottom'. Cars crammed with noisy young people headed for night clubs, from which many did not emerge until dawn. Young women in particular claimed new freedoms – to cut their hair short, wear 'indecently' short skirts above the knee, or drink and smoke – things which would never have been permitted to them only a short while before. This behaviour earned the decade the nickname the 'Roaring Twenties'.

1920
PROHIBITION BEGINS IN THE US

Prohibition officially began in 1920, when the 18th Amendment to the Constitution forbade the manufacture, sale and transportation of alcoholic beverages. Commonly called 'the Noble Experiment', national prohibition was the result of a reform movement that had campaigned for more than 100 years. Prohibitionists considered alcohol to be a dangerous drug that destroyed lives and disrupted families and communities, and they argued that it was the government's responsibility to free citizens from the temptation of drink by barring its sale. The law, which was enforced only sporadically, met with widespread opposition. Bootlegging, speakeasies (illegal saloons) and smuggling (known as rum-running) all flourished in a new black-market economy, run by gangsters. Opponents mounted a campaign to annul the law, and were finally successful in 1933, when the 21st Amendment repealed the 18th Amendment.

Cartoon depicting Uncle Sam and Prohibition, the ban on alcohol in the US that began in 1920.

10 DECEMBER 1920

Ireland Under Martial Law

In an attempt to control the escalating violence in Ireland over the issue of Home Rule, martial law is declared across the worst-affected areas of the country. The British army steps up its campaign to catch the terrorists who are causing devastation throughout Ireland.

Babe Ruth playing for the New York Yankees in 1926.

1920
BABE RUTH JOINS THE YANKEES

Ruth, universally referred to by his nickname 'Babe', started his professional career in 1915 with the Boston Red Sox, a team which had been founded in 1901 under another name as part of the new American League. After an erratic start, success came to the Sox at more or less the moment Babe Ruth joined the team. Although he had started out as a left-handed pitcher, by 1919 Ruth had been moved to the outfield because of his awesome talent with the bat. Throughout his tenure, the Red Sox enjoyed enormous success, winning both the league title and the World Series in 1915, 1916 and 1918. The American entry into the First World War led to disruption to the major teams. In 1916, the Red Sox had been bought by Hugh Ward and Harry Frazee, two theatrical entrepreneurs. By 1919, Ward and Frazee were in serious financial difficulty. Despite the fact that he scored a record 29 home runs that year, Babe Ruth was sold at the end of the season to the New York Yankees for $100,000 and a $300,000 loan, a record sum for its day. His departure marked the end of the Red Sox's winning streak and the start of their descent into the second division.

1921
THE YETI

The Tibetan Yeti is a mythical creature said to inhabit the mountainous regions well above the snow line; belief in the Yeti began when large footprints were discovered in the Himalayas. There have been numerous sightings of this so-called 'Abominable Snowman', said to be very similar in appearance to the North American 'Big Foot'. Yeti is the Sherpa name for 'bear man' and this may be the true nature of the beast. Apparently, when a bear moves along at a certain speed the hindfoot overprints the forefoot, making a large impression in the snow. The result looks like a large human footprint. Other prints have been attributed to snowfalls, but no one can explain the occasional sightings of the beast.

1921
PIET MONDRIAN PAINTS *COMPOSITION IN RED, YELLOW AND BLUE*

Piet Mondrian (1872–1944) was among the most prominent of the twentieth century's geometric painters, evolving an austere art of black lines and coloured rectangles placed against white backgrounds. He developed a style which banished the conventions of three-dimensional space and the curve. Mondrian moved these simple elements around the canvas until he found a perfectly

balanced composition. He aimed to create an objective, disciplined art whose laws would reflect the order of the universe. Having begun his career painting conventional Dutch landscapes, after 1908 Mondrian began to turn away from the imitation of nature. In 1911, he discovered the Cubist works of Picasso and Braque and was soon producing his own version of Cubism. In 1916, Mondrian and several other Dutch artists formed De Stijl. He believed that straight lines joined at right angles expressed perfect equilibrium; he used red, yellow, blue, black, white and grey because they are not found in their purest form in nature and were therefore the most abstract colours. *Composition in Red, Yellow and Blue*, painted in 1921, was Mondrian's expression of a spiritual and harmonious conception of the universe and of humanity's place in it.

25 OCTOBER 1921

Charles Marches on Budapest

The former emperor of Austria and king of Hungary, Charles I, attempts to regain the Hungarian throne by organizing a march on the capital city, backed by 12,000 troops. The leader, who has been exiled in Switzerland since his deposition, was defeated and captured outside Budapest.

The Hungarian capital of Budapest, where Charles I was defeated and captured in 1921.

1921
THE BEGINNINGS OF MODERN DRUGS

A significant breakthrough in modern medicine came in the field of hormones in 1921 when Frederick Banting (1891–1941) and Charles Best (1899–1978) discovered the role of insulin in treating diabetes. Since that time, work on hormones has seen impressive developments. Alexander Fleming (1881–1955) also made a significant contribution to medicine by discovering penicillin, which finally came into common use in 1941, in time to save the lives of many war wounded. This was the first of many antibiotics which have been developed since, and have changed the way people look at infection and illness. Drugs in general, for treating illnesses and for anesthetics, have seen a science built up around them throughout the twentieth century, as chemists and physicians have striven to perfect their work, aided by new technologies.

5 JANUARY 1922

Explorer Shackleton Dies

The renowned Antarctic explorer, Ernest Shackleton, dies of a heart attack. An adventurer to the last, Shackleton, who had trekked with Robert Scott before leading two further expeditions, was about to embark on his fourth journey to the inhospitable continent when he died.

1921
MARIE STOPES OPENS FIRST BIRTH-CONTROL CLINIC

After studying at University College, London, and taking her PhD in Munich, Marie Stopes made history by becoming the first female science lecturer at Manchester in 1904. Initially specializing in fossil plants and coal-mining, she changed direction after the annulment of her first marriage to R. Gates in 1916. She then turned her attention to marital unhappiness caused by ignorance and began a crusade to spread the word about contraception. In 1916 her book *0* caused a furore and was banned in the US. She married the aircraft

Marie Stopes' first mobile family planning clinic in North London.

British prime minister David Lloyd George, who signed the treaty establishing the Irish Free State.

manufacturer Humphrey Roe in 1918 and together they opened the first British birth-control clinic in North London in 1921.

1921
IRISH FREE STATE ESTABLISHED

On 7 December 1921, after David Lloyd George had threatened to put down the Irish rebellion by force, a treaty was signed that established the Irish Free State. The 26 southern counties became independent, the six Ulster counties remained part of the UK. A boundary commission was set up to decide upon the dividing line between north and south. The Irish Free State was seen as the end of '700 years of repression' by Ireland's leaders. It was hoped that differences regarding the status of some of the areas close to the new border could be settled and that a new parliament, based in Dublin, would take over control of the Free State in the near future. With this agreement, it was hoped that the violence and disagreements would end.

1922
BBC FORMED

American radio in the 1920s was commercial: advertisers paid the stations for air space, and all the listeners had to do was buy a wireless and tune in. Soon the airwaves were crammed with competing stations, fighting for a share of an audience of 13 million. British broadcasters were not impressed with the American system and formed a consortium, the British Broadcasting Corporation. They decided against advertizing; instead the company was to be financed by an annual licence fee, paid for by the listener. The BBC went on air in 1922 as a 'public service'. Because it had a monopoly over the airwaves, its attitude to programming was markedly different from the American system. It was to be a cultural oasis, representing 'the best of British'. Sports, popular music, comedy, vaudeville and entertainment were all broadcast, but the manner in which they were presented, such as the voices of the announcers, was upper middle class. The first newscasters had to wear dinner jackets when addressing the nation so that they would not slip into casual tones of voice when reporting on important matters. In the early years the BBC did not have regional diversity, but it provided entertainment and education at a very low cost.

Broadcasting House, the home of the BBC in its early days.

The magnificent funeral mask of Tutankhamen, discovered in his tomb in 1922.

1922
TUTANKHAMEN'S GRAVE DISCOVERED

Howard Carter had been searching for 15 years for the resting place of the Egyptian boy king, Tutankhamen. In November 1922, Carter and his patron, Lord Carnarvon, stood at the bottom of 16 steps in a tunnel in the Valley of the Kings. Before them was a sealed door that bore an ancient royal emblem of the Egyptian pharaohs. Carter picked up his hammer and chisel, chipped a small hole through the stone and plaster, and looked through. He wrote: 'At first I could see nothing, but presently details of the room emerged slowly from the mist, strange animals, statues and gold – everywhere the glint of gold.' After a long and dedicated search the tomb of Tutankhamen had been found.

1923
HYPERINFLATION IN GERMANY

Following the failure of the Allies to agree the level of reparations due from the defeated Germans after the War, the German currency began a disastrous collapse from June 1923. The currency fell from 20 marks to the pound to 20 trillion by November. A loaf of bread was valued at 200 billion marks. The German situation was further complicated by the French and Belgian occupation of the Rühr, its major source of coal. Trade unions demanded that the government seize all food and clothes in an attempt to ration them and ban the manufacture of all luxury goods. Only a loan from the USA in the following year to help pay for the reparations and stabilize the mark finally managed to control inflation and effectively re-value the currency.

The Ekco-Scophony Television Receiver, one of the earliest of its kind.

28 APRIL 1923
The White Horse Final

PC George Scorey and his horse Billy become unlikely heroes at the FA Cup Final between Bolton and West Ham, after an estimated 200,000 fans crowd into London's Wembley Stadium – nearly twice its capacity. Scorey and Billy play a significant role in controlling the fans and averting potential tragedy.

1923
EARLY TV PICTURES IN US

In 1873 it was discovered that the electrical properties of the element selenium varied according to the amount of light it received, making it possible to transmit pictures over a distance. The practical idea of television was born and in 1884 a system was patented by Paul Nipkow in Germany. Experimenters in the UK and US were working with the neon gas-discharge lamp produced by D. Moore in 1917 in the US. Using this, both John Logie Baird and Carl Jenkins experimented with mechanical methods. Jenkins showed the first television pictures in the US in 1923. In 1926 Baird gave the first demonstration of true television by electrically transmitting moving pictures in half-tones.

PC Scorey and his horse Billy controlling the crowds at the 1923 FA Cup Final.

Vladimir Ilych Lenin, leader of the Bolshevik revolution in Russia in 1917.

1924
DEATH OF LENIN

Vladimir Ilych Lenin was born in 1870. He was active in the 1905 revolution and had to leave Russia when it failed, settling in Switzerland in 1914. He returned to Russia after the February revolution of 1917 and led the Bolshevik revolution in October of that year. From the overthrowing of the Provisional Government in 1917, until his death in 1924, he effectively controlled Russia. He concluded the peace agreement with Germany, and organized a successful resistance to the pro-tsarist uprisings and foreign intervention in 1918–20. His modification of Marxist doctrines to fit the Russian conditions became known as Marxism-Leninism and became the basis of communist ideology.

1924
GEORGE GERSHWIN

In the 1920s the 'Jazz Age' was swinging and George Gershwin was right at its centre. He composed vibrant, witty songs that had syncopated rhythms and expressive harmonies. The tunes seemed to sparkle and they had 'that high attribute of making people fall in love with them'. In 1924, Gershwin bridged the gap between classical and popular music with 'Rhapsody in Blue', which captured the 'tempo of modern living with its speed and chaos and vitality' but was performed as a serious piece of music. In the same year he wrote 'Lady Be Good', to which witty lyrics, written by his brother Ira, were set. It marked the advent of the Gershwin musical.

1924
MALLORY AND IRVINE DIE IN EVEREST ATTEMPT

Everest is the highest mountain in the world, reaching up two-thirds of the way into the earth's atmosphere, where the oxygen is thin. Powerful winds and freezing temperatures make it difficult to climb. In 1922, George Mallory had struggled to within 975 m (3,200 ft) of the summit, and in 1924 he returned with Andrew Irvine to try again. They were less than 304 m (1,000 ft) from the summit and 'going strong for the top', when appalling weather came down and the support team lost sight of them as they disappeared into a swirling snowstorm. Before leaving for Nepal, Mallory was asked why he was so desperate to climb the world's highest mountain. He replied, 'Because it's there'.

1924
MALCOLM CAMPBELL BREAKS WORLD LAND SPEED RECORD

British Captain Malcolm Campbell (1885–1949) broke the world land speed record again and again over his illustrious and unprecedented career, using ever bigger and more powerful vehicles – most of which he called *Bluebird.* Campbell devoted his life to achieving and then holding the land speed

*Sir Malcolm Campbell and his **Bluebird** racing car, in which he broke the land speed record.*

30 JULY 1924
Olympic Triumph for Britain

Jewish Cambridge student Harold Abrahams becomes the first European to take the gold in the 100 metres event at the Paris Olympics. In doing so he defeats the two favourites from the US, Jackson Scholz and Charley Paddock.

record for Britain. He first broke the land speed record in 1924 at Pendine Sands, where he recorded 234.97 kph (146.01 mph) at a time when there had yet to be an official requirement for new records to exceed old by one per cent. He went on to set new records in 1927 at 280 kph (174 mph); 1928 at 332 kph (206 mph); 1931 at 394 kph (245 mph); 1932 at 407 kph (253 mph); 1933 at 440 kph (274 mph); and in 1935 at 444 kph (276 mph). Later that same year he broke the 300 mph barrier: clocking up 484.6 kph (301.1 mph). His son, Donald (1921–67), took over as world speed champion, carrying on the *Bluebird* name.

*Donald Campbell, continuing the work of his father in the record-breaking **Bluebird**.*

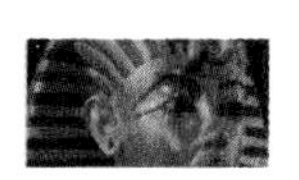

Joseph Stalin, who ordered severe persecution of religious groups in Russia.

1925
SOVIET PERSECUTION OF RELIGIOUS GROUPS

The Russian Bolshevik government considered all religion the 'opium of the people' and since 1918 the Church had been deprived of all rights including that of property ownership. In February 1922 the government decreed the confiscation of all valuable objects preserved in the churches.The head of the Orthodox Church, Tikhon, published a declaration that he 'was not the enemy of the Soviet government' but his conformity was to no avail. After his death in 1925 his successors were arrested. Under Joseph Stalin the Church suffered severe persecution that claimed thousands of victims. By 1939 only three bishops and 100 churches could officially function: the Church was practically suppressed.

1925
JOHN SCOPES TRIAL

In July 1925, high-school teacher John Scopes was charged with violating state law by teaching the theory of evolution in Tennessee. A recent Tennessee legislature had declared unlawful the teaching of any doctrine denying the divine creation of man as taught by the Bible. In the courtroom, fundamentalist literal belief confronted liberal interpretation of the scriptures. The judge ruled out any test of the law's constitutionality or argument on the validity of Darwin's theory, limiting the trial to the question of whether Scopes had taught evolution, which he admitted he had. He was convicted and fined $100. An appeal court acquitted Scopes on the technicality of an excessive fine but upheld the law's constitutionality.

John Scopes was convicted of violating state law by teaching Darwin's (above) theories of evolution in Tennessee.

1926
RUDOLF VALENTINO DIES

The death of Rudolf Valentino – the 'Great Lover' – in 1926, caused an unprecedented outpouring of public grief. Thousands wept and mourned; heaving crowds threatened to overwhelm his coffin as he was lying in state. The great male screen idol of his time, Valentino was sleek, graceful, and alluringly exotic. With his slicked-back hair and his flashing smile, he made villainy attractive. He had worked as a gardener in Central Park until he became a dancer in New York nightclubs. He played small parts in films but it wasn't until *Four Horsemen of the Apocalypse* that he became a star. His major role was in *The Sheikh.* As prince of the desert, his searing eyes cast such spells of seduction that women fainted in the cinema aisles.

1926
MICKEY MOUSE IS BORN

One of the world's biggest global media corporations was built with the help of a mouse. In 1926 things were shaky for Walt Disney, but they were about to change. He was travelling by train from New York to Hollywood, doodling on a drawing pad to pass the time. A shape began to appear on the page in front of him: 'out of trouble and confusion stood a mocking, merry, little figure; it grew and grew. And finally it arrived – a mouse. A romping, rollicking, little mouse'. He was named Mickey. The trouble was that while Mickey was spirited and funny, there was nothing particularly original about him. Disney decided that his cartoon would have synchronized sound, Mickey would talk, and he would be the very first cartoon character to do so. Disney came up with the idea of *Steamboat Willie*, the opening of which featured Mickey whistling as he recklessly steered across the water. The tune 'Turkey In The Straw' became a concert, using the livestock cargo as musical instruments. It worked beautifully; critics said: 'Clever is a mild word to use. It is a wow'. Disney capitalized on the success of Mickey Mouse, and within months hundreds of manufacturers were producing huge volumes of licensed Mickey merchandise. Things would only get bigger.

Mickey Mouse, the brainchild of Walt Disney, and the character that made him a household name.

13 MARCH 1926

No to Germany in the League

Following Germany's application to become a member of the League of Nations in February, the member states, sitting in Geneva, refuse to allow the country a permanent seat on the council.

Walter Gropius's designs for the new Bauhaus building, which moved from Weimar to Desau in 1925.

1926
WALTER GROPIUS, BAUHAUS

In 1915, during the First World War, Gropius (1883–1969) was appointed director of two schools of art and design, which, because of his belief in the unity of the disciplines, he combined under the name 'Bauhaus' in 1919. The school was based at Weimar until 1925, when a new site was found at Dessau, and the opportunity arose for Gropius to design a building consistent with his philosophy. His business partner, Adolf Meyer, assisted with the design, and students were given the opportunity to participate in the creation of the decoration and furnishings. The complex consisted of five main elements: a glazed, three-storey workshop block; a teaching block; social areas; a five-storey dormitory block; and offices spanning a roadway. The forms of these elements were derived from their different functions, but together they made a coherent composition. The general public took a great interest in what went on at the Bauhaus, condemning it for decadent and subversive tendencies. Gropius's design for the school was a perfect expression of Bauhaus theory, representing the first coherent work of the International Style.

1926
ROCKETS AND MISSILES

The first liquid fuel rocket was fired in America in 1926, by Robert H. Goddard. A German named Wernher von Braun developed the principle during the 1930s; he made the V2 liquid fuel rocket used by the Nazis between 1943–45. After the Second World War, von Braun travelled to America, where his work led to the series of Saturn rockets which launched the *Apollo* missions between

Space shuttles, such as the ***Columbia****, superseded the original rockets, first tested in the 1920s.*

1961–72. Space rockets were later superseded by Space shuttles, and new developments towards the end of the century have seen laser technology as the propellant force. Use of both liquid and solid fuel rockets has continued evolving in the realm of weaponry.

1926
GENERAL STRIKE IN THE UK

From 3 to 12 May 1926, Britain was crippled by a General Strike, in which three million workers rallied to the slogan 'Not a penny off the pay; not a minute on the day', in sympathy with coal-miners who refused to accept a pay cut averaging 13 per cent and an increased working day. Members of the Trades' Union Congress, including railwaymen, printing trade workers, building trade workers, truck drivers, dock workers, iron and steel workers, chemical industry employees and some power company workers, walked out in response to a strategy devised by Transport Workers' chief Ernest Bevin. Although the strike ground the nation to a halt, it actually failed, leading to the Trade Disputes and Trade Union Act of 1927, which limited unions' strike powers.

5 DECEMBER 1926
Claude Monet Dies

The French Impressionist artist, Claude Oscar Monet, dies at the age of 86; he continued painting right up until his death, despite failing eyesight. Monet, a prolific painter throughout his lifetime, became one of the most influential artists of his era.

Monet in his Floating Studio, by fellow-Impressionist Edouard Manet.

1926
BENNETT AND BYRD FLY TO THE NORTH POLE

On 9 May 1926, Admiral Richard E. Byrd (1888–1957) and Floyd Bennett (1890–1928) became the first men to fly to the North Pole by aeroplane. With the explorer Byrd as navigator, Bennett piloted a plane non-stop from Spitsbergen to the North Pole and back. Both men were awarded the Congressional Medal of Honor for their achievements. In 1928, on a flight to rescue stranded flyers in the Gulf of St Lawrence, Bennett was stricken with pneumonia, from which he later died in Quebec. In the same year, Byrd organized an expedition to Antarctica, establishing a base called Little America on the Ross Ice Shelf near Roosevelt Island, and a year later he flew with three companions to the South Pole and back.

Automobile pioneer Henry Ford, creator of the famous Model T Ford.

1927
LAST MODEL T CAR IS PRODUCED BY FORD IN THE US

Production of the famous Model T Ford, also called the 'Tin Lizzie' or the 'Flivver', ceased on 31 May 1927, when car number 15,007,003 rolled off the assembly line. The Model T Ford was introduced in 1908, designed by Henry Ford as the 'car for the great multitude', and it was an immediate success. It had a four-cylinder, 20-horsepower engine and a simple planetary transmission operated by foot pedals on the floor. To meet the demand for the new car, the Ford Motor Company introduced the moving assembly-line technique for mass production. By 1919 nearly 60 per cent of all US motor vehicles and half of those in the entire world were Model T Fords.

1927
MARTIN HEIDEGGER'S *BEING AND TIME*

Martin Heidegger (1889–1976) was responsible for an original exploration of the nature of being and of humankind's experience of existence. This was introduced in his *Being and Time*, published in 1927. He asserted that to be was not to exist like an object, but rather to choose who one is. He saw subject and object as two concepts derived from the single prior reality of existence – allowing him to be seen as one of the originators of existentialism. To the extent that humankind allows external events to determine our nature he felt we live inauthentically; to the extent that we create ourselves we live authentically. This concept was developed further later in the century by Jean-Paul Sartre.

1927
WALLACE CAROTHERS DEVELOPS PLASTICS, SYNTHETICS AND NYLON

American industrial chemist Wallace Hume Carothers taught at various universities before researching polymerization at the Du Pont

Company at Wilmington. Discovering that some polymers were fibre-forming, he produced the first successful synthetic rubber, Neoprene, in 1927, finding it to be much more resistant to light, heat, oxidation and petroleum than ordinary rubber. He followed this with the development of nylon and plastics. Nylon was the first all-synthesized fibre, made from petroleum, natural gas, air and water. It was found to be much stronger and more elastic than natural materials. Despite his achievements, however, he committed suicide in 1937, and the patent for nylon, awarded posthumously, was given to the Du Pont Company.

Synthetic materials and plastics were developed by American chemist Wallace Carothers.

3 MARCH 1927
Tribute to a Hero

John Godfrey Parry Thomas is killed when his car, Babs, overturns during his attempt to break the land speed record; he was travelling at an estimated 290 kph (180 mph). Thomas is the first man to die trying to break this record.

*Parry Thomas's car **Babs**, pulled from the sand after the accident that killed her owner.*

1927
FIRST SUBWAY SYSTEM OPENS IN TOKYO

In 1927, Tokyo's Chikatetsu subway was officially opened to the public. The Tokyo system would grow to have eight lines, with 165.6 km (102.9 miles) of track running to the far reaches of Tokyo's suburbs. From the 1960s, Tokyo lost most of its central city residents to the suburbs, following the trend of cities in most developed countries, and more than 85 per cent of Tokyo's commuters now use the subway system. The volume of commuter traffic on the lines is the highest in the world, and it is not uncommon for office workers in Tokyo to spend two hours or more each day in overcrowded commuter trains.

The crowded subway system in Tokyo, where the volume of human traffic is the highest in the world.

American president Herbert Hoover, who came to office in 1928.

1928
HOOVER BECOMES PRESIDENT

Herbert Hoover, born in 1874 to Quaker parents in Iowa, became the 31st US president in 1928. Supporting his family from an early age, following his father's premature death, he initially trained in mining. During the First World War he was closely associated with relief of distress in Europe. He became secretary of commerce under Harding. A Republican candidate, he defeated 'Al' Smith in the presidential election of 1928, but his opposition to government assistance for the unemployed after the world slump of 1929 made him unpopular and he lost to Roosevelt in 1932.

He assisted President Truman with the various American European economic relief programmes that followed the Second World War.

1928
THE FIVE-YEAR PLANS

In 1928, Stalin announced the first Five-Year Plan. This was an attempt to develop Soviet industry, which Stalin believed was 100 years behind the West. Every factory, coal-mine and industrial plant in the Soviet Union was set a series of targets which it had to meet over the following five years. The targets were worked out in Moscow by the state-planning agency, Gosplan. The first Five-Year Plan also included the collectivisation of all the farms in the Soviet Union. Farmers and peasants were forced to amalgamate their farms into large state farms. Second and third Five-Year Plans followed in the 1930s. Overall, industrial production increased by about 400 per cent, but the plans encouraged quantity not quality. Fifty per cent of tractors broke down and could not be repaired.

1928
FIRST ELECTRIC TRAFFIC SIGNALS INTRODUCED IN THE US

The first electric traffic signals were introduced in the US in 1928; they were a response to the extraordinary growth in motor-vehicle traffic. The system was a simple 'stop and go' scheme, and contributed to a significant decrease in traffic-related deaths. By the end of the century visual control systems were linked to pneumatic vehicle detectors and electronic queue detectors, and signals and television pictures were fed to a central computer control room with human managers, who could take charge in an emergency. Before the 1984 Summer Olympics, Los Angeles installed 3,200 computer-linked sensors in the intersections at 800 traffic signals in its central downtown area. A similar system was installed in New York City in the mid-1990s.

Portrait of Joseph Vyssarionovich Stalin.

10 NOVEMBER 1928

Hirohito Crowned

The regent of Japan, Hirohito, is crowned emperor in a lavish ceremony and amidst celebrations from the people. The emperor has been acting for his ill father since 1921 and is well-primed to be the head of the state he now inherits.

*LNER's **Flying Scotsman**, the first express train from London to Edinburgh.*

1928
EXPRESS SERVICE ON THE *FLYING SCOTSMAN*

In 1928, the London and North Eastern Railway offered a revolutionary service, running an express train non-stop from London to Edinburgh – a distance of 630 km (392 miles) – a landmark in the history of rail travel. Because of its superb speed, the train was nicknamed the *Flying Scotsman.* During the First World War the government took control, but not ownership, of the line, and in 1948 all the railways in Great Britain were nationalized and reorganized as British Railways. Increased competition from highway transport has resulted in the abandonment of many branch lines, but the original route of the *Flying Scotsman* is still home to a frequent, popular service.

1928
FLEMING DISCOVERS PENICILLIN

Scottish bacteriologist Alexander Fleming qualified as a surgeon at St Mary's Hospital in Paddington, London, where his career was spent. As a researcher, he became the first to use anti-typhoid vaccines on human beings and he pioneered the use of salvarsan against syphilis. As a medical officer in France during the First World War, he discovered the antiseptic powers of lysozyme, which is present in tears and mucus. In 1928 he made a chance exposure of a culture of *staphylococci* and noticed a curious mould, penicillin, which was found to inhibit the growth of bacteria and to have outstanding antibiotic properties. Unfortunately he had insufficient chemical knowledge to produce the drug alone and it was not until 1941 that penicillin came into general use.

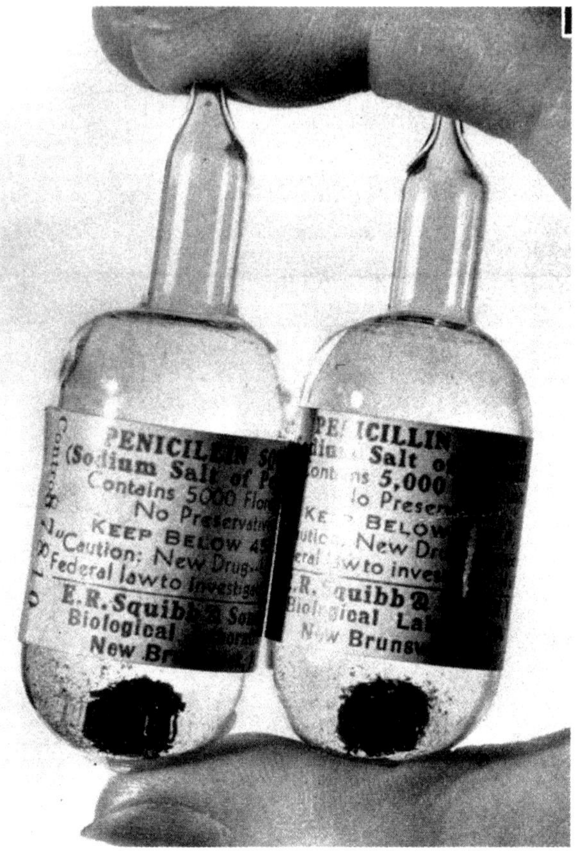

Although Fleming discovered penicillin in 1928, it was 11 years before a way was found to produce it as a drug.

14 JANUARY 1929
Revolt in Afghanistan

Forces in Afghanistan revolt against the king, Amnullah Khan, because of his policies of restriction towards the powers of religious leaders and his support for women's rights.

Mayan pyramids at Chichen Itza, first photographed by aviator Charles Lindbergh.

1929
CHARLES LINDBERGH PHOTOGRAPHS MAYAN RUINS

The American aviator Charles Lindbergh (1902–74) first achieved international fame in 1927 as the first person to fly alone across the Atlantic. He made the daring expedition in the *Spirit of St Louis*, his single-engine monoplane, travelling from New York to Paris in 33 1/2 hours. In 1929 he married Anne Spencer Morrow, daughter of the US ambassador to Mexico, and she became his co-pilot and navigator on many subsequent expeditions, including the 1929 flight over the Yucatán peninsula, during which he photographed Mayan ruins. His photographs made an important contribution to the study of the Mayas and to the field of archeology.

1929
STALIN COMES TO POWER

Joseph Stalin was born in 1879 and educated in the priesthood, but was expelled for Marxist propaganda. He joined the Social Democratic party in 1898 and then the Bolsheviks under Lenin in 1903. He was repeatedly exiled to Siberia between 1903–13. He became a member of the Communist Party's Politburo and sat on the commitee during the October Revolution. Stalin soon consolidated a powerful following and was appointed general secretary of the Communist Party in 1922. After Lenin died in 1924, Stalin sought to take over the reins and to create 'Socialism in one country', often clashing with Leon Trotsky, who thought Socialism in Russia impossible until there was revolution in western Europe. After the argument was won in 1927 a series of Five-Year Plans was launched to collectivize industry and agriculture and Trotsky was banished in 1928. Stalin controlled the USSR from 1929. As a dictator he soon disposed of all real and imagined enemies and he eliminated all opposition in the Great Purge of 1936–38. During the Second World War, Stalin intervened in the military direction of the campaigns against the Nazis, his role being denounced after his death by Krushchev and others in the Soviet regime. After the war Stalin maintained autocratic rule until his death in 1953.

Panic in the streets after the Wall Street Crash in October 1929.

1929
WALL STREET CRASH

Fear, confusion and panic triggered the frantic sale of 13 million shares in US companies on 24 October 1929. Thousands of small investors lost everything. Many companies had been overvalued, buoyed by the easy profits to be made and general overconfidence from investors and speculators. Eleven of the latter took their own lives when their fortunes were wiped out in minutes. Brokers, desperate to off-load overvalued shares, hunted for anyone who would buy. As the sheer volume of sales increased, the shares plummeted, reaching rock bottom before noon. Prices rallied after lunch but not before police riot squads had been called in to cope with the hysterical crowds in Wall Street. Governments throughout the world would have to cope with the horrors of economic depression over the next few years.

1929
ASHURBANIPAL LIBRARY DISCOVERED

The Assyrians, who first began to form a civilization after about 900 BC, were the first people to form a military state in the ancient world. They were not simply warriors, though; they took care to preserve the libraries they found in captured cities and Assyrian astronomers made observations of the Moon, recording them on circular clay discs. The knowledge that the Assyrians amassed was considerable. In 1929, the library of Ashurbanipal, who became king in about 626 BC, was discovered at his capital city of Nineveh; it contained over 20,000 clay tablets, inscribed with information on botany, mathematics, chemistry, medicine and history, offering an unprecedented insight into the knowledge and understanding of the Assyrians.

The notorious gangster Al Capone, who ran an illegal alcohol-smuggling operation during Prohibition in the US.

1929
ST VALENTINE'S DAY MASSACRE

Gangster Al Capone, in an attempt to protect his stake in illegal alcohol, extortion and prostitution rackets, had seven men gunned down, all members of a gang led by George 'Bugsy' Moran. This incident was the latest in what police commissioner William F. Russell described as 'a war to the finish'. Men dressed as police officers successfully passing themselves off as a raiding party, killed the seven victims. The men, armed with tommy-guns, lined them up against a wall at the back of a beer-house in Chicago and murdered them with a hail of bullets. The police commissioner was furious that the gangsters chose to dress up as policemen, particularly since half of his force was under investigation for corruption.

12 SEPTEMBER 1929

New Air-Speed Record

Flying Officer Waghorn pilots the winning Supermarine S6 plane at the Schneider Trophy competition on the Solent. In doing so he breaks every previous race record at 584.4 kph (370 mph). Despite this, the record is not officially ratified.

The Supermarine S6 plane which took the prize and the record at the Schneider Trophy in 1929.

Chapter 4
1930–1939

1930
SIR EDWIN LANDSEER LUTYENS DESIGNS THE VICEROY'S HOUSE

Larger than Versailles, the Viceroy's House, designed by Lutyens (1869–1944), was the jewel in the crown of the urban master plan for New Delhi. Following some debate about the appropriate architectural expression for the new capital of the Raj, Lutyens's design was chosen as a hybrid of Western classicism and Indian forms from different periods. As such, it was a great success in terms of diplomacy as well as architecture. Architectural references were made not only to Indian culture but also to local climate. So, for example, traditional wide stone ledges were used to shade internal spaces. Warm-coloured sandstone was also in keeping with tradition, although here it formed porticos which associated the building with Classical imperialism.

1930
THE FIRST WORLD CUP

Thirteen countries participated in the first soccer World Cup, with the South American teams almost certain to obliterate their European opponents. The Copa América tournament already held between these countries meant that they were more prepared for the concentration of games and the level of competition, while the Europeans had no equivalent. Preparation and training techniques fell far short of the South Americans. The hosts, Uruguay, were the hot favourites, and they didn't disappoint. Argentina beat the US in the semi-finals, while Uruguay smashed Yugoslavia 6–1. The head-to-head of the Final resulted in a 4–2 Uruguay win. It was followed by riots, the Uruguayan embassy in Argentina was stoned and the respective FAs fell out over the result. The tournament had been established as one of the most competitive and significant sporting events in the world.

The captains shake hands before the first World Cup in 1930.

1930
GANDHI ARRESTED

After returning to India in 1914, Gandhi took an increasing interest in the home rule movement (*Swaraj*), becoming master of the congress organization. He ran a civil disobedience campaign in 1920 which involved many violent disputes. From 1922 to 1924 he was jailed for conspiracy and then in 1930 he led a 200-km (124-mile) march to the sea to collect salt in symbolic defiance of the government monopoly. He was re-arrested, but on his release in 1931 he negotiated a truce between congress and the government and attended the London Round Table Conference on Indian constitutional reform. Once back in India , however, he renewed the civil disobedience campaign and was arrested yet again.

2 NOVEMBER 1930

Ras Tafari Crowned

Ras Tafari is crowned as the emperor of Ethiopia in a ceremony in the capital Addis Ababa, attended by world leaders as well as thousands of celebrating natives. He takes the title Haile Selassie for his new role.

Mahatma Gandhi, who was arrested in 1930 while conducting a demonstration in defiance of the government monopoly.

At the age of just 27, Amy Johnson became the first woman to fly halfway around the world.

1930
AMY JOHNSON FLIES TO AUSTRALIA

On 24 May, British aviator Amy Johnson (1904–41) became the first woman to fly solo from the UK to Australia; she was aged 27. She followed the 19 1/2 day flight with a record six-day solo flight from England to India, for which she received international acclaim. Johnson was one of the small, brave group of British women pilots who worked ferrying aircraft from the factory to the airfield during the Second World War, a mission that held great danger. Johnson was killed ferrying an aircraft in 1941.

1930
WILLIAM VAN ALEN DESIGNS THE CHRYSLER BUILDING

In complete contrast to contemporary socialist projects being built in Europe, the Chrysler Building, designed by van Alen (1888–1954) stands as a monument to capitalism. Very much a product of pre-Depression America, it was a celebration of the success of its client and of the free market. Until the early 1930s, the Chrysler Building was the tallest in the world at 259 m (850 ft). Tapering off as it reaches its zenith, its height is emphasized by a silvery reflective skin of grey bricks and windows, which rise in vertical shafts. The most distinctive feature is a stylized metal sunburst at the top, with the chevron patterns of the

Salvador Dalí's ***The Persistence of Memory****, showing his characteristic motif of melting clocks.*

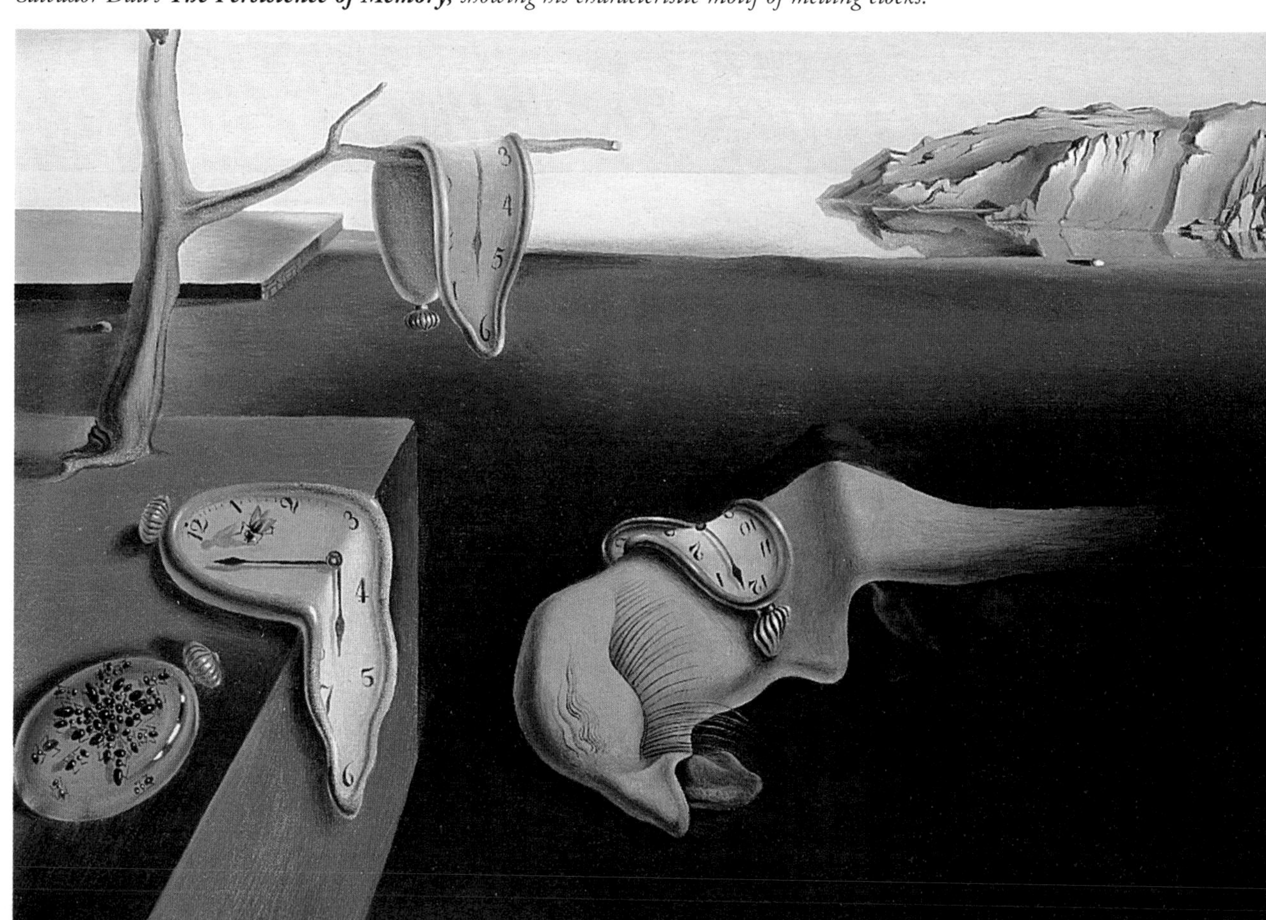

Chrysler logo. Other corporate symbols incorporated as decorations are metal radiator caps with wings, positioned at the corners of the 40th floor, and, alongside, a frieze of abstracted car wheels. Inside, luxuriant materials were intended to give visitors a sense of the wealth of the Chrysler company. The entrance lobby is clad in expensive marbles and red-tinted metals, with dramatic lighting to reinforce the effect, while the lifts are lined with wood and decorated with Chrysler logos.

18 OCTOBER 1931
Inventor Edison Dies

Thomas Edison, inventor of the gramophone and the electric light bulb, dies at the age of 84. His pioneering research and experiments led to his creating or contributing to numerous inventions that became part of everyday life. In all he patented over 1,000 ideas.

1931
SALVADOR DALÍ

Dalí (1904–1989), a Spanish artist, was associated with Cubism, Futurism and metaphysical painting before becoming one of the best-known Surrealists. He studied in Madrid, but moved in 1928 to Paris, where he was influenced by the works of Joan Miró and Picasso. He joined the Surrealists in 1929, fascinated by their interest in the subconscious, but soon developed his own techniques focusing on hallucinations and dreams. Dalí famously claimed that artists should develop their own paranoias and delusions in order to feed their work. His startling nightmare images were inspired by Freudian theory mixed with shocking photorealism. In *The Persistence of Memory*, painted in 1931, the melting clocks are characteristic motifs and were intended to create a sense of unease in the viewer.

Japanese and Chinese troops fighting at Manchuria; the Japanese eventually emerged the victors.

1931
THE OCCUPATION OF MANCHURIA

The links between Japan and the West developed with an alliance with Britain in 1904 and a declaration of war on Germany in 1914. In the 1920s, however, there was a revival of traditional Japanese ideas. The first reason for this was the failure of Japan to gain what it was expecting at the Treaty of Versailles at the end of the First World War. A second factor was the international reaction to the occupation of Manchuria in 1931. The Japanese army invaded Manchuria – which was part of China – and set up a puppet government. Despite international condemnation over this move, little else was done. In Japan, the government fell under the control of the army and the country began a period of territorial expansion on the mainland.

1 MARCH 1932

Lindbergh Baby Kidnapped

The 20-month-old son of the famous aviator Charles Lindbergh is kidnapped from their home in New Jersey, sparking a national manhunt. A ransom note, demanding $50,000 for the child's safe return, is found on the windowsill of the nursery.

1932
ELECTROSCOPES

In 1932, astronomer Karl Jansky (1905–50) detected the presence of 'radio noise' coming from outer space. This led to the development of radio telescopes, with the realization that radio waves, instead of light waves, could tell scientists a lot more about the universe. Radio waves have a much lower frequency than those of light, so a radio telescope is in the shape of a large dish, to catch enough information. The first scanning electron microscope (SEM) was developed by Max Knoll and Ernst Ruska between 1928–33. It worked by detecting electrons being bounced off the surface of objects being scanned, creating a visual image on a screen; it was able to magnify objects up to 200,000 times.

1933
HITLER SEIZES FULL POWER IN GERMANY

Adolf Hitler was born in 1889 in Austria and lived poorly for many years, dodging military service and emigrating to Munich in 1913. He volunteered for war service in 1914

Adolf Hitler fought in the First World War and became a member of the Nazi party in 1919; he soon rose to become its leader.

and rose to the rank of corporal. In 1919, while spying on the activities of small political parties, he joined one of them, changing its name to National Socialist German Workers' Party (Nazi Party), and provided it with a manifesto of nationalism and anti-Semitism. The party achieved little importance until the 1930 election; but by 1932, although Hitler was defeated by Hindenburg in the presidential elections, his party formed the largest group in the Reichstag, the German Parliament. Hitler became chancellor in a Nazi-Nationalist coalition in 1933.

1933
THE NEW DEAL

Franklin D. Roosevelt announced his 'New Deal' of 13 major measures to beat the Depression in the US in 1933. In the three months after his inauguration ceremony, the new president effectively took control of industry by regulating wages, working hours and production. Some $3 billion was ploughed into public works to boost the economy, the Prohibition laws were repealed and money was found to bail out penniless farmers and mortgage holders. By the end of the first 100 days, just under two million new jobs had been created. $75 million was allocated to feeding and clothing the poor over the winter. With over 3.5 million American families on welfare, another $700 million was found to provide federal relief. Without doubt, this rapid and effective programme was instrumental in ending the Depression.

President Franklin D. Roosevelt introduced the New Deal in an effort to relieve the Depression of the 1930s.

1933
LONDON UNDERGROUND MAP

By the late 1920s, the London Underground system had grown enormously, and the old-style map, originally created in 1908, had become a confusing mass of snaking lines. In 1933, Henry Beck (1903–74), an engineering draughtsman with London Underground, designed a new version and revolutionized the way the world saw railway maps. Rather than basing his map on geographical fact, he used the principles of electrical circuit diagrams to display the system, so that lines met only at right or 45-degree angles, with stations placed to give the central area more prominence in relation to outlying areas rather than showing their actual distance from one another. The pioneering Beck gave interchanges a distinct convention and used colour to identify the different lines. This type of clear diagrammatical map is now in use for transport systems all over the world.

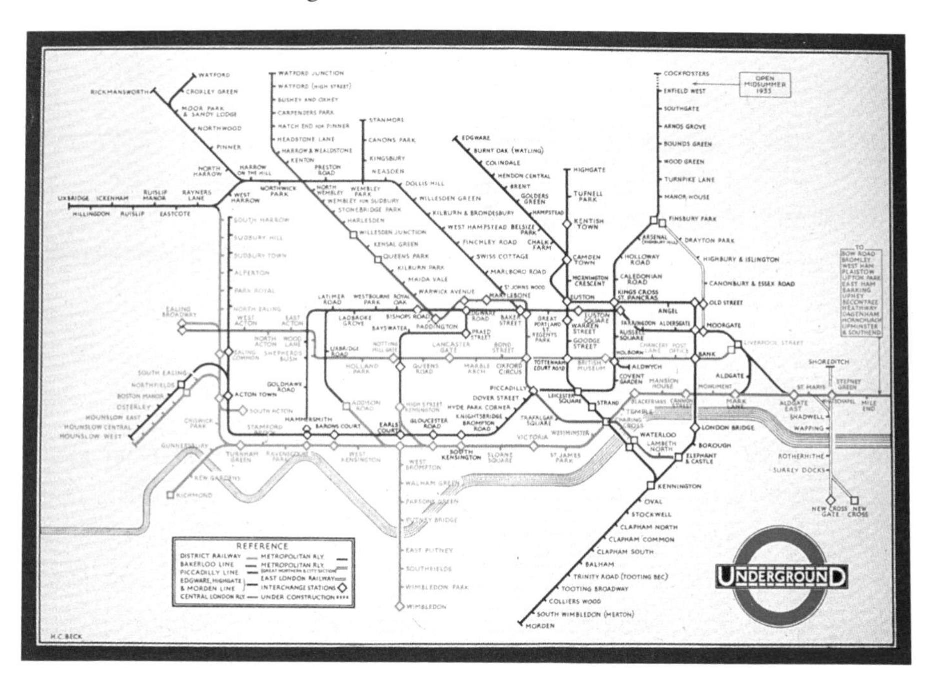

Henry Beck's map of the London Underground revolutionized railway maps the world over.

1934
THE PURGES

In 1934, Soviet leader Stalin began his most sinister use of power. He began to systematically eliminate anyone whom he suspected of opposing him throughout the Soviet Union. Other leaders of the Communist Party were put on trial and forced to confess to crimes that they could not possibly have committed. Generals and admirals were executed on suspicion of treason. Managers of state farms and factories were shot. Poets, musicians and scientists who did not agree with Stalin, were rounded up and sent to slave-labour camps, along with millions of others. The final total is unknown, but may have been as high as 20 million. Soviet citizens learnt to dread the arrival of the secret police in the early hours and the disappearance, without warning or explanation, of a member of the family, usually the husband or father.

Cartoon depicting Soviet leader Joseph Stalin.

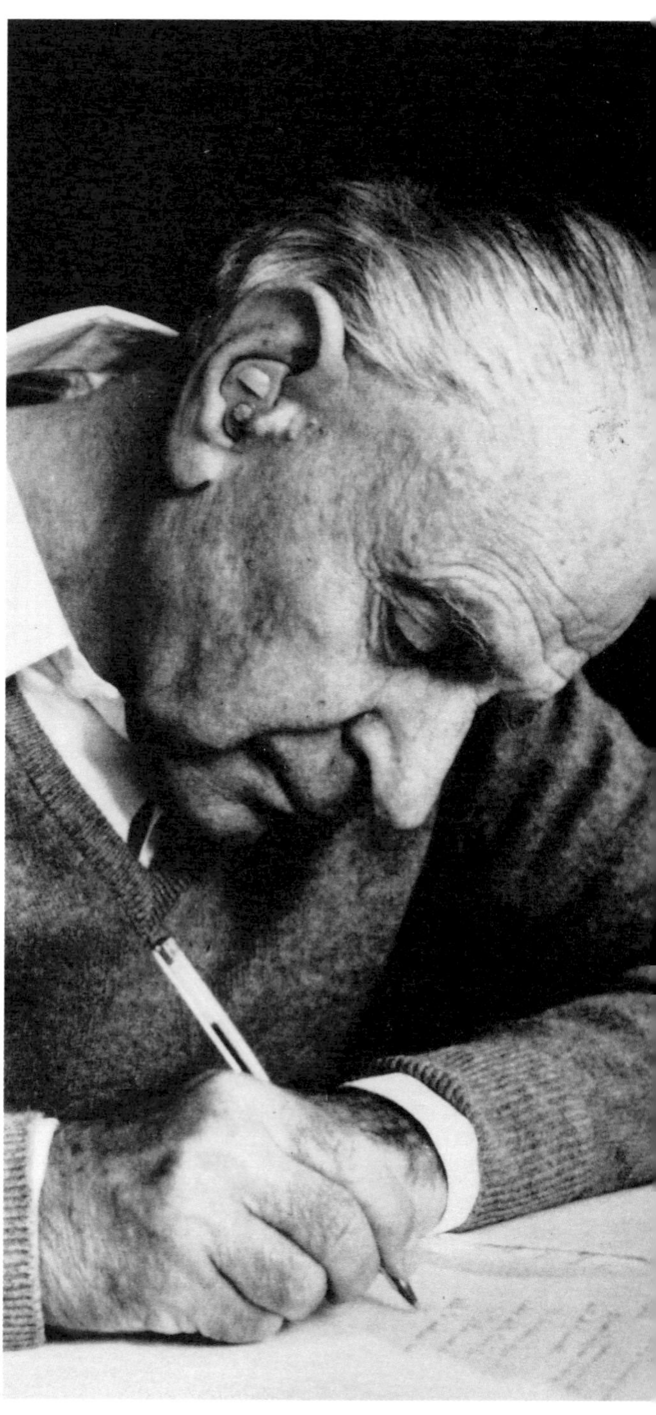

Sir Karl Popper, who expounded the theory that no scientific hypothesis could be proved.

1934
SIR KARL POPPER'S LOGIC

The Viennese philosopher, Karl Popper (1902–94), argued that it was never possible to have certain knowledge. In his *Logic of Scientific Discovery*, published in 1934, he

23 MAY 1934
The End for Bonnie and Clyde

The notorious criminal duo Bonnie and Clyde are killed by Texas Rangers, apparently working from a tip-off, in Louisiana; they are credited with the murder of at least 12 people across the American south-west.

showed that no scientific hypothesis could be proved – it could only be falsified. Indeed if it could never be falsified it would not be a scientific theory. Therefore, he suggested that every good scientific theory was simply a model that had yet to be disproved. His opposition to the concept of certainty led him, in his *The Open Society and its Enemies* (1945), to criticize authoritarian models of human society and historicism, such as those proposed by Plato and Karl Marx.

1934
STRIKES IN SPAIN

Coinciding with a violent national strike in Spain, called for by Socialists and the trade union movement, Catalonia attempted to declare itself an independent state. The strikes were in response to the appointment of three Catholic Popular Actionist ministers to the right-wing government. Martial law was pronounced and government troops clashed with strikers across the country. Troops were brought in from Morocco to quell the uprisings; garrisons were mobilized and the civil guard reinforced. For several days the fighting continued; shots were even fired at the home of the premier, Señor Lerroux. The smouldering discontent would soon ignite once more into full-scale civil war.

The Anglepoise lamp, created by George Carwardine, a car designer.

1934
PRODUCTION OF THE ANGLEPOISE LAMP

The Anglepoise lamp, designed in 1933 by the British designer George Carwardine, is the century's most successful and innovative desk lamp. Carwardine, an automobile designer, employed his engineering skills to produce a lamp which used hinges to mimic the elbow joint of the human arm. The hinge system, which allowed the lamp to hold any position and provided a wide range of possible adjustments over an extensive arc, was widely copied throughout the industry. The original Anglepoise, which was put into production by Herbert Terry & Sons in 1934, was chic, flexible and balanced, and the design is still produced today, by Anglepoise Ltd of Redditch, with only slight variations. The Anglepoise reflected the utilitarian and functional approach to office and domestic appliance design which characterized the late 1920s and early '30s.

1934
DIESEL POWER IN THE USA

The invention of the diesel locomotive made great increases in the operating efficiency of locomotive engines. The diesel engine had been invented in the 1890s, and the first diesel-electric locomotive was used by the Central Railroad of New Jersey for switching operations in New York City in the mid-1920s. In 1934, the Burlington and the Union Pacific both began using diesel power for their passenger trains, and the new *Burlington Zephyr* train went into service between Chicago and Denver. On 26 May, this streamlined passenger train hit a top speed of 181 kph (112.5 mph) and averaged 125 kph (77.6 mph) on a 1637-km (1017-mile) non-stop run between the two cities. This exciting development heralded the beginning of the end of steam locomotive use in the US.

A family prays for rain to relieve the drought that caused dust storms throughout the American Midwest.

1935
DUST STORMS SWEEP AMERICA'S MIDWEST

During the years 1933–35, the American mid-west states were hit by severe heatwaves and drought, with temperatures rising to 49°C (120.2°F). Strong winds raked up the unprotected soil, creating swirling dust storms which brought everything to a standstill. A bad storm could send topsoil whirling eight km

The concept of the helicopter only became a reality with the advent of the gasoline engine.

(five miles) into the air, making day as dark as night. The storm of March 1935 blew for 27 days without ceasing. Roads disappeared; houses were buried to window height; and roofs collapsed with the weight of soil. The worst-hit states were Dakota, Nebraska, Kansas, Oklahoma and Minnesota. In all, 70,000 refugees fled the dustbowl states, leaving areas with only 40 per cent of the previous population.

6 MAY 1935

King's Silver Jubilee

Crowds throng the streets of London in celebration of the king's Silver Jubilee; the king retained his popularity throughout the trials of the Great War, and the love and respect he earned in 25 years of rule is evident in the reception he and the queen receive as they journey to a ceremony at St Paul's Cathedral.

1935
THE FIRST HELICOPTER FLIGHT

Leonardo da Vinci is generally credited with sketching and describing a helicopter in 1483. But the helicopter – like aircraft of most descriptions – required a lightweight power source, which was not possible until the advent of the gasoline engine. Although modest flights had been made prior to this time, it was not until 1935 that a coaxial helicopter, constructed by Louis Bréguet and René Dorand in France, achieved flights of sustained duration. The helicopter was perfected between 1936 and 1941. With the completion of the single-rotor type by Igor Sikorsky in the United States, between 1939 and 1941, the helicopter became a practical aircraft capable of carrying a useful load and performing diverse commercial, military and emergency functions.

Parade of officers of the Third Reich at the Nurnberg Party Day rally in 1933.

1935
REARMAMENT

One of Hitler's main aims after his rise to power, was to re-establish Germany as a major force in Europe and to overturn the Treaty of Versailles. To do this he needed military strength. From 1935, he began to build up the German armed forces, by first introducing conscription and then producing warships and military aircraft. In 1936 he reoccupied the Rhineland, and in 1938 he occupied Austria and then demanded – and was given – the Sudetenland, the German-speaking part of Czechoslovakia. All these acts had been banned by the Treaty of Versailles, but apart from a few protests by the British and French governments, little was done to stop him. It was only when the remainder of Czechoslovakia was occupied in March 1939 that Britain agreed to defend Poland if it was attacked.

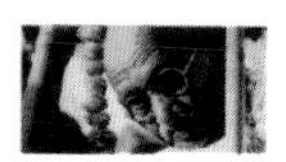

John Maynard Keynes, who revolutionized theories of employment and economics.

1935
RADAR AND SONAR

Radar, an acronym of Radio Direction and Ranging, was invented in 1935 by Robert Watson-Watt (1892–1973), as a method of locating enemy aircraft. It worked by emitting radio waves at regular intervals, which bounced back if an object was within range. A receiver translated the returning radio waves into a visual location dot on a screen. Sonar is an acronym for Sound Navigation and Ranging. It worked in a similar way to radar, except that it used ultrasonic waves, because radio waves could not travel through water. Sonar served the equivalent purpose to radar, but in a marine environment. It had been invented by

28 JANUARY 1936

A Nation Mourns

Thousands of British subjects take to the streets to pay their respects to their king, George V, who died on 20 January. The funeral procession winds its way from Westminster, where the body lay in state, to Paddington Station, from where it is taken to Windsor, to be buried.

Frenchman Paul Langevin (1872–1946) in 1914, for detecting German U-Boats in the First World War.

1936
THE GENERAL THEORY OF EMPLOYMENT, INTEREST AND MONEY

British economist and pioneer of the theory of full employment, John Maynard Keynes, was greatly influenced by the cycles of unemployment he witnessed. Although his *General Theory*, published in 1936, initiated a revolution in economic thought, he went on to write two other major texts that support his reputation. Arguing that full employment was not an automatic condition, he strongly disagreed with successive governments' policies. Unemployment was curable, he suggested, if the government fine-tuned its monetary and fiscal policies to suit the circumstances. Keynes not only influenced the British government, but his theories were also incorporated into Roosevelt's New Deal in the US. He was also instrumental in setting up the International Monetary Fund and the International Bank for Reconstruction and Development. The 30-year boom in western industry after the Second World War has often been referred to as the 'Age of Keynes'.

1936
EDWARD VIII ABDICATES

Edward VIII was born in 1894. He was the eldest son of George V and was appointed Prince of Wales in 1910. During the First World War, he served in the navy and the army and achieved considerable popularity. He became Edward VIII when he succeeded to the throne following the death of his father on 20 January 1936. On 16 November, however, a constitutional crisis arose when Edward declared that he wished to marry Mrs Wallis Warfield Simpson, an American divorcee he had met in 1930. Mrs Simpson had already been divorced from her first husband, US Navy Lieutenant E. Spencer, in 1927, and the divorce from her second husband, Ernest Simpson, an American-born Englishman, came through during 1936. The king made it clear to prime minister Stanley Baldwin and his government that he was determined to marry her even if it meant giving up his title. The marriage of the 'supreme governor' of the Church of England to a divorced person was considered totally unacceptable and so the king renounced the throne and finally abdicated on 11 December. He left for voluntary exile in France, where he married Mrs Simpson on 3 June 1937.

Edward VIII, who abdicated when the government would not allow him to marry twice-divorced Mrs Simpson.

The first Volkswagen, the 'people's car', that would eventually become one of the most popular in the world.

1936
HITLER LAUNCHES VOLKSWAGEN

Designed by Ferdinand Porsche in the 1930s as the German 'people's car' – a small automobile that would be inexpensive enough for the average family – the Volkswagen, with its air-cooled rear engine, was assembled by hand in Nazi Germany. The cornerstone for the first Volkswagen factory was dedicated on 26 May 1936, at Wolfsurb on the Mittelland Canal. The low-cost 'Beetle' was commissioned by Adolf Hitler and launched by him in 1936; it would not go into mass production for more than 10 years, but more than 18 million of the 'Beetles' would eventually be sold, exceeding the Model T Ford's record. Volkswagen's decision was to concentrate on a single model, to avoid annual model changes.

1936
CIRCUIT BOARDS AND MICROPROCESSORS

In 1936, an Austrian named Paul Eisler, living in England, decided that it would be a good idea to incorporate the workings of his home-made radio on to a board. Having invented the circuit board, he attempted for some years to sell the idea of printed circuit boards to electronics companies. Necessity in warfare eventually created a need for the rapid reproduction of electronic circuits, which were used to control the proximity fuses for the anti-aircraft shells. After the war the Americans embraced the printed circuit board, which revolutionized a burgeoning electronics industry. By the 1950s America was developing miniature circuit boards using silicon as a semiconductor. These became known as silicon chips, and could comprise many thousands of components all scaled down into a microprocessor.

1936
SPANISH CIVIL WAR

Political unrest and a lack of direction prompted right-wing military factions in Spain to revolt against the government. General Sanjurjo, who was to lead the uprising, died in a plane crash, leaving General Francisco Franco to take command. After seizing Morocco, he landed in Cadiz at the head of Spanish foreign

A propaganda postcard from the Spanish Civil War.

legionaries. After a series of sharp clashes, the rebels moved on Madrid. By 1937, with the capital still under siege, many European countries had become entangled in the war. Although the Nationalists continued to enjoy popular support, the better-trained Republicans continually outfought them. Spain provided a useful training ground for many European troops.

1936
JESSE OWENS'S OLYMPICS

Jesse Owens's finest hour was at the 1936 Berlin Olympics, where he won four gold medals, triumphing in the 100 and 200 m, the 4x100-m relay, and the long jump. Nazi leader Adolf Hitler, however, refused to shake Owens's hand or present him with his medals because he was black. Trying to qualify for the long-jump final, Owens had trouble with his run-up and fouled his first two attempts. In a supreme act of sportsmanship, his main rival, the German Carl Ludwig 'Luz' Long, offered to place his towel in front of the foul line for Owens to use as a marker. Owens did, qualified for the final, and went on to win the event with Long taking the silver. Afterwards, in an act of bravery considering that Hitler was looking on, Long walked past the Nazi leader's box arm-in-arm with a man portrayed as a 'black auxiliary' by German propaganda.

18 JANUARY 1936
Death of Kipling

The much-beloved British author of the Jungle Book tales, Rudyard Kipling, dies at the age of 71; the novelist, poet and children's story writer had been awarded the Nobel Prize for Literature in 1906.

US athlete Jesse Owens, star of the 1936 Olympics held in Nazi Germany.

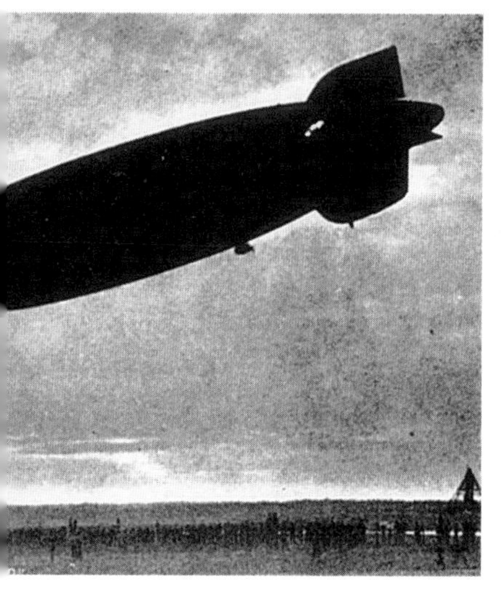

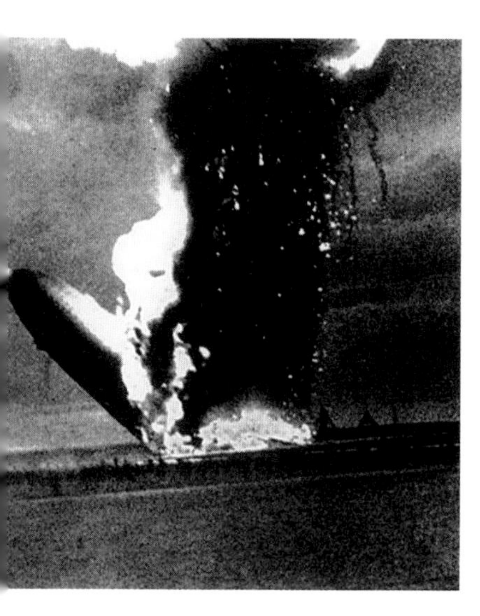

The airship ***Hindenburg*** *was torn apart by an explosion over New Jersey.*

1936–37
GENERAL MOTORS STRIKE IN DETROIT

Although Ford established the first car-production plants in the city, the emergence of mass-production techniques attracted many other companies to Detroit. The car industry suffered greatly during the Depression, but began to recover quickly. The labour movement became far more active than before and numerous strikes at the huge General Motors plants in Flint, 1936–1937, resulted in the recognition of the United Automobile Workers of America. This industrial action was by far the most significant of all strikes in the twentieth century. Over the course of the dispute thousands of car workers across the US were affetcted. During the Second World War, the city was called 'Arsenal of Democracy' for its production contributions to the armed forces.

1937
THE *HINDENBURG* TRAGEDY

On 6 May 1937, the giant dirigible *Hindenburg*, which had cost £380,000 to build, exploded in flames, killing 33 people. The *Hindenburg* had already made 10 successful trips across the Atlantic when it came to grief in New Jersey. The most plausible reason for the explosion seems to be the fact that a thunderstorm had placed static electricity in the mooring mast and when the *Hindenburg* came alongside it ignited the hydrogen gas. The *Hindenburg*, which had journeyed from Frankfurt, was delayed by strong headwinds over Canada. The airship, circling the mast waiting for a lull in the storm, was at about 90 m (300 ft) when the disaster occurred.

1937
JAPAN VS CHINA

In July 1937 the Japanese army invaded northern China. The following month two Japanese sailors were killed at a Chinese aerodrome in Shanghai. This led to the landing of a Japanese army, which captured and then forced its way inland. The Japanese airforce was used to bomb Chinese cities into submission. Within a year Nanking, the capital, Tsingtao, Canton and Hankow had all been taken. Britain and the US gave large loans to the Kuomintang government of China, but the Japanese government began to demand that Britain and the other western countries should give up supporting China and co-operate with Japan in establishing a 'new order' in the Far East.

3 JUNE 1937

Duke of Windsor's Wedding

The Duke of Windsor, who abdicated the British throne in 1936 after Baldwin's government issued him with an ultimatum, marries the twice-divorced Mrs Wallis Simpson, bringing to an end the months of crisis and speculation.

Edward VIII, who finally married Mrs Wallis Simpson, after abdicating the British throne.

The Guggenheim Museum, another of Frank Lloyd Wright's major architectural success stories.

1937
FRANK LLOYD WRIGHT BUILDS FALLING WATER

Falling Water, a country house built by Wright (1869–1959) for the millionaire Edgar Kaufman, would have been impossible without twentieth-century materials and engineering skills. The site – above a waterfall – demanded a radical approach to take advantage of the view and dramatic forces of nature. Wright's solution was to cantilever a series of horizontal concrete trays from a core which seemed to merge with an outcrop of rocks above the waterfall. Falling Water had the low horizontality of Wright's earlier Prairie-Style houses, such as the Robie House in Chicago (1910), but that style was given a new meaning and function. The horizontal layers both acted as shelter and allowed the walls to take the form of almost invisible glass screens, set back from the edge. The balconies also formed a backdrop against which the surrounding birch trees cast their shadows. The chimney, in roughly hewn local stone, contrasted with the smooth finish of the concrete balconies, reflecting the contrast between human and natural forms. Wright thought that modern architecture could bring about the close relationship with nature which he believed was the key to freedom.

1938
BOMBING OF GUANGZHOU

In late May and early June 1938, the Japanese began a 10-day bombing of the Chinese city of Guangzhou (Canton). The death toll ran into tens of thousands as the

Japanese attempted to bomb the Chinese into submission. With few anti-aircraft guns and no fighter aircraft, the Chinese could only hope for salvation. Even when an unarmed passenger aircraft attempted to leave the city it was shot down. By 21 October the city had been occupied. Some 3,000 Japanese, led by tanks, moved in after a 160-km (100-mile) push through Chinese lines. The Chinese, led by Jiang Jieshi, fled inland, attempting to destroy anything that was of use to the Japanese before the city was occupied.

1938
CHAMBERLAIN SIGNS ANGLO-GERMAN ACCORD

Disorder in Czechoslovakia, instigated by Sudeten Nazis, gave Hitler the excuse to demand the protection of the German population of 3.5 million. Faced with the prospect of war over the issue, Chamberlain flew to Germany and signed the Munich Agreement with Hitler, giving the Nazis control over the region. At the time, it was believed that this 'peace with honour' would mean that war had been averted. Chamberlain was roundly criticized for caving in to Hitler and many thought that he had been fooled. On 5 October 1938, the Germans occupied parts of Czechoslovakia, other areas were taken by Poland and Hungary. The Czechs received nothing from the deal.

1938
PHOTOCOPIER AND FAX

Before 1938, techniques for duplicating documents were messy and too slow to be economically viable. Chester Carlson managed to solve this problem in 1938 by inventing the xerographic copier. It used an electromagnetic plate to attract powder ink to the paper, which was then fixed. The photocopier was born, achieved by a quick dry process. A small company bought the rights to produce and market the machine, which resulted in the Xerox Corporation. It was also the Xerox corporation who manufactured the first fax machine, in 1966, for office and domestic use via a telephone line. It was called the Magnafax Telecopier.

Adolf Hitler signed the Anglo-German Accord with Neville Chamberlain, an act that unfortunately did not prevent the outbreak of war the following year.

28 MARCH 1938

Electric Shocks to Treat Schizophrenia

Italian psychiatrists Ugo Cerletti and Lucio Bini demonstrate the use of electric shock therapy for the first time, inducing convulsions or fits believed to be beneficial in treating those suffering from mental illnesses.

The aftermath of Kristallnacht: shops were wrecked and synagogues all over Germany were destroyed in anti-Semitic riots.

1938
KRISTALLNACHT

Kristallnacht ('night of broken glass') was a night of supreme violence against Jewish people and property carried out by the German Storm Troopers on 9–10 November 1938 in Austria and Germany. It followed the assassination of a German diplomat, Ernst vom Rath, in Paris by a Polish Jewish youth. In all, 91 Jews were killed, hundreds seriously injured and thousands more terrorized. About 7,500 businesses were gutted and around 177 synagogues were burnt or demolished. Subsequent measures included legislation preventing Jews from owning businesses or property in Germany and restrictions on schooling, use of public parks and leaving the country. Kristallnacht marked a major escalation in the Nazi programme of Jewish persecution.

1938
BETTE DAVIS WINS ACADEMY AWARD FOR *JEZEBEL*

Bette Davis was given her role in *Jezebel* as a consolation prize for not getting the part of Scarlett O'Hara in *Gone With the Wind.* In the film she plays Julie, a perverse Southern belle, who ruins her own chances in love, as well as shaking up America's Old South. It is the Lupas Ball in New Orleans in 1852, and Julie turns up in a scarlet dress, while all the other unmarried women are dressed in pristine white. As she walks across the dance floor, couples shrink away from her. Her defiance threatens all the social conventions. The dress seems fiery red despite the film being shot in black and white, and Davis won an academy award for her colourful performance.

1938
RELEASE OF *SNOW WHITE*

Snow White was called 'Walt Disney's folly'. He was determined to make the first feature-length cartoon, but nobody thought it would work. Disney, however, managed to entrance his animators with his vision of the Grimms' fairy tale, and before long thousands of sketches and watercolours were being produced to make the creation that is so famous now. Disney wanted the characters to be individual, and Snow White to move as a realistic human figure. Everything was discussed in the minutest detail. The film was a masterpiece of imagination and innovation, scary and magical. It made Disney 'a hatful of money' and charmed cinema audiences when it was released in 1938.

1939
GERMANY ATTACKS POLAND

At 6 a.m. on Friday, 1 September 1939, German troops crossed the Polish border. The 1.25 million men, spearheaded by tank divisions, swept all resistance before them. Within

Snow White *was the pioneering feature-length cartoon that started Disney on the road to movie success.*

hours, the Polish air force had ceased to exist and the railway system was in tatters. This new form of warfare, called 'Blitzkrieg', was seen as a determined attempt to avoid the trench warfare stalemates of the previous war. The Germans claimed the port of Danzig and the Polish Corridor, and peaceful attempts to resolve the situation failed. Britain and France declared war on 3 September and by 8 September the Germans were at the gates of Warsaw. On 17 September, following a pre-agreed plan, the Russians invaded Poland. The partition of Poland was complete by 30 September, the Germans taking the west of the country and the Russians absorbing the east. Over 60,000 Polish troops died and 200,000 were wounded. The Germans also captured 700,000 prisoners. Although the League of Nations and most states around the world condemned the action, it had little effect and Poland ceased to exist. Poland would suffer many indignities over the next six years and beyond. If nothing else, this 'lightning war' should have proved to be ample warning to the western allies: a similar fate would face France within a year.

24 APRIL 1939

New PM for Australia

Robert Menzies succeeds Joseph Lyons as prime minister of Australia after his death earlier in the month; Menzies had served as attorney-general in Lyons' coalition government and was noted for his tough approach to party policies.

German troops invading Polish territory in 1939.

31 AUGUST 1939

Evacuation Begins in Britain

The first evacuations take place in Britain, as children are removed from the impending threat of war on the home front in the cities, and moved to the relative safety of the countryside.

Second World War field radio and map showing safe escape routes to the coast.

1939
SCHINDLER'S AND OTHER LISTS

During the Second World War, many Nazi concentration camps served as reservoirs of forced labour. Inmates were worked to death in industries such as the I. G. Farben chemicals works and the V-2 rocket factories. From 1939 Oskar Schindler (1908–74) ran an enamelware factory in Krakow, which became a haven for the predominantly Jewish workforce. When the Krakow ghetto was destroyed in 1943, he constructed his own for his workers; later (1944), in the face of the Russian advance, he succeeded – by bluff and bribery – in moving factory and workers to Czechoslovakia. Schindler's factory, supposedly producing munitions for the war effort, in fact made almost nothing usable. Instead, Schindler bought goods cheaply on the black market, sold them to the Nazis and maintained his staff with the profits.

1939
GONE WITH THE WIND RELEASED

Scarlett O'Hara was the role that every actress wanted. *Gone With the Wind's* producer, David O. Selznick, used it to launch a publicity blitz of a kind never witnessed before. He created the illusion that any woman in America could win the part of the wilful heroine of Margaret Mitchell's best-selling Civil War novel. He organized talent contests and screen tests throughout the land, mostly to create public interest in his project, with the part always likely to go to one of Hollywood's established stars. After two years of searching, the part finally went to little-known English actress Vivien Leigh. She turned out to be an inspired choice – playing the impetuous, resilient, selfish Scarlett beautifully. The whole production was star-studded: with Clark Gable as the handsome, gambling Rhett Butler, Leslie Howard as Ashley and Olivia de Havilland as Melanie. The set pieces were theatrical and tremendous: the burning of Atlanta, the carnage at the railway station, full of smoke, fire and wounded bodies. The film lasted nearly four hours, and took a year of filming, editing and scoring before it reached movie screens in 1939. It had cost almost $4 million, and audiences flocked to it. It won nine Oscars and remains one of the biggest cinema hits of all time.

Poster for the Oscar-winning film ***Gone With the Wind****.*

Chapter 5

1940–1949

The house of noted architect-designer Charles Eames, best known for his utilitarian, mass-produced furniture.

1940
CHARLES EAMES

The most significant contribution made by Charles Eames (1907–78) to the history of furniture design was his unswerving desire to solve problems of mass production. In 1940, he collaborated with Eero Sarrinen to produce a series of chairs using plywood and new techniques of manufacture, including a method of bonding metal to a wooden shell with a rubber weld joint, for the Museum of Modern Art's 'Organic Design in Home Furnishings' competition. In 1948, at another MOMA competition, Eames won second prize for his designs for low-cost furniture with his proposal for a moulded fibreglass chair, which became the first piece of mass-produced furniture. Eames joined the firm of Herman Miller, one of the two largest and most innovative American furniture manufacturers, and this association brought both parties worldwide renown and acclaim.

Children in Warsaw watch the German bombers fly overhead.

A British battleship lying wrecked after the evacuation of Dunkirk.

1940
CONQUERORS AND CONQUERED

Between April and June 1940, Nazi Germany overran Norway, Denmark, France, Belgium and the Netherlands and, in 1941, parts of Russia. Poland had already been conquered in 1939. These countries were now forced to live under foreign and often retributive domination, as the Nazi conquest brought curfews, shortages and savage punishments for disobedience. This produced several reactions: most people simply tried to survive as best they could and keep out of trouble; others risked everything to form resistance movements, and were not always helped by their compatriots who thought it best to keep their heads down. Some collaborated with the Germans, seeking safety by fraternizing with the winning side. Their punishment after the war was savage.

1940
THE BATTLE OF BRITAIN

As a prelude to Operation Sealion – the proposed invasion of Britain – the Germans pounded Channel shipping from 10 July 1940. The RAF had just 600 fighters against the 3,000 mustered by the Germans. The Germans switched their attacks to the Channel ports and airfields in the south of England, reaching a peak on 15 August with a 940-bomber attack. The last week in August and the first of September were the most critical, with the RAF losing 25 per cent of their strength and the Germans losing 50 per cent of theirs. Unable to defeat the RAF, the Germans switched to daylight terror raids on British cities. The Battle of Britain is said to have ended on 12 October when Hitler cancelled Operation Sealion. The RAF had given the Germans their first defeat at a cost of 915 aircraft and 481 pilots. The Germans admitted losing 1,733 aircraft, while the British claimed the figure was closer to 2,698. Churchill is credited with two of the most memorable quotations of the period. On 20 August at the height of the battle he said of the RAF, 'Never in the field of human conflict was so much owed by so many to so few.' After the cancellation of the invasion he taunted the Germans with, 'We are waiting for the long-promised invasion. So are the fishes.'

10 MAY 1940
Chamberlain Resigns

British prime minister Neville Chamberlain resigns after wartime disasters cause disillusionment to sweep through the country; former lord of the admiralty and key player in the First World War, Winston Churchill, takes over, with the intention of forming a coalition government.

The Blitz by the German Luftwaffe left many parts of London in ruins, particularly the East End.

1940
THE BLITZ

Some 900 German aircraft, followed by another 250, launched a series of raids against London on 7 September 1940. The massive daylight raids reached a peak on 15 September when Herman Goering sent over 400 bombers. He lost 60 of these to the RAF and flak guns. The Germans were forced to resort to night attacks and for 57 nights, an average of 200 bombers appeared over the capital. On 15 October, 400 bombers dropped 380 tons of explosives and 70,000 incendiaries; Fighter Command responded, supported by 2,000 mobile flak guns. The Luftwaffe attacks continued into 1941 on a diminished scale, the last big raid occurring on 10 May just before Barbarossa.

1940
RATIONING

Because of its island location, rationing was essential in wartime Britain. Luxuries, and certain foodstuffs, especially from distant countries, such as oranges, and for a time,

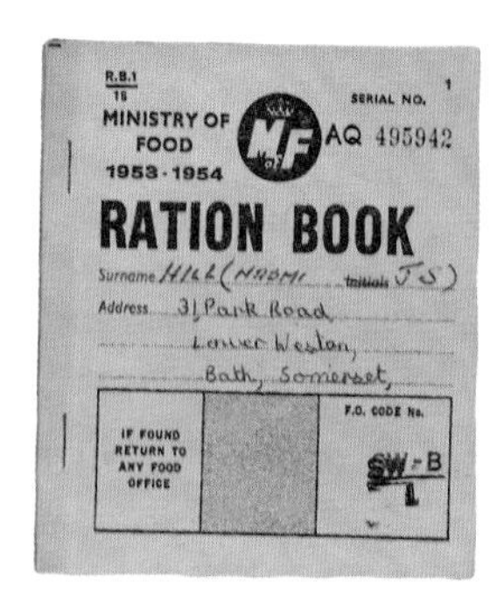

Rationing was introduced in Britain shortly after the beginning of the Second World War.

chocolate, virtually disappeared. Essentials – butter, eggs, meat, fish, clothing – were strictly apportioned through ration books containing coupons. It was a well-considered system and in fact provided some Britons with better nutrition than they had had in peacetime, when poor families relied too much on carbohydrates and not enough on vital proteins. The radio and newspapers carried regular hints on how to make the most of the rations, but there were, of course, black marketeers and many were willing to buy from them. Others, who told the police about blackmarketing activities, could be ostracized.

1940
ALAN TURING CRACKS THE ENIGMA CODE

Alan Turing was a brilliant English mathematician and logician. In 1936 he described a 'universal computing machine' that could theoretically be programmed to solve any problem capable of solution. This concept, now called the 'Turing Machine', foreshadowed the computer. During the Second World War he worked with the Government Code and Cypher School at Bletchley Park, where he played a significant role in cracking the German 'Enigma' codes. After the war he worked in the construction of early computers and the development of programming techniques. He also championed the idea that computers would eventually be capable of human thought (Artificial Intelligence) and he suggested the Turing test to assess this capability.

1940
ROCK PAINTINGS DISCOVERED AT LASCAUX

The now well-known rock paintings and engravings at Lascaux were discovered accidentally in 1940. A group of boys searching for their dog stumbled on some underground chambers connected by passageways. The decorated areas were deep within the caves and stone lamps were probably used to illuminate the area where the artist worked. The paintings were coloured in red, yellow, brown and black, made from ochre ground into powder and mixed with fat. The animal drawings were vivid and beautiful. Bison, rhinos, horses, wolves and deer were shown running and grazing. Several animals were shown in groups or herds. Some of them had spears or arrows embedded in them, a reminder of their importance as a food source to the artist.

21 AUGUST 1940

Trotsky Assassinated

The Soviet Bolshevik leader Leon Trotsky dies in Mexico City after an assassin attacks him with an axe; rumours spread that the assassin, Ramon Mercador, was acting on the orders of Joseph Stalin. Trotsky was in exile after being sentenced to death for treason.

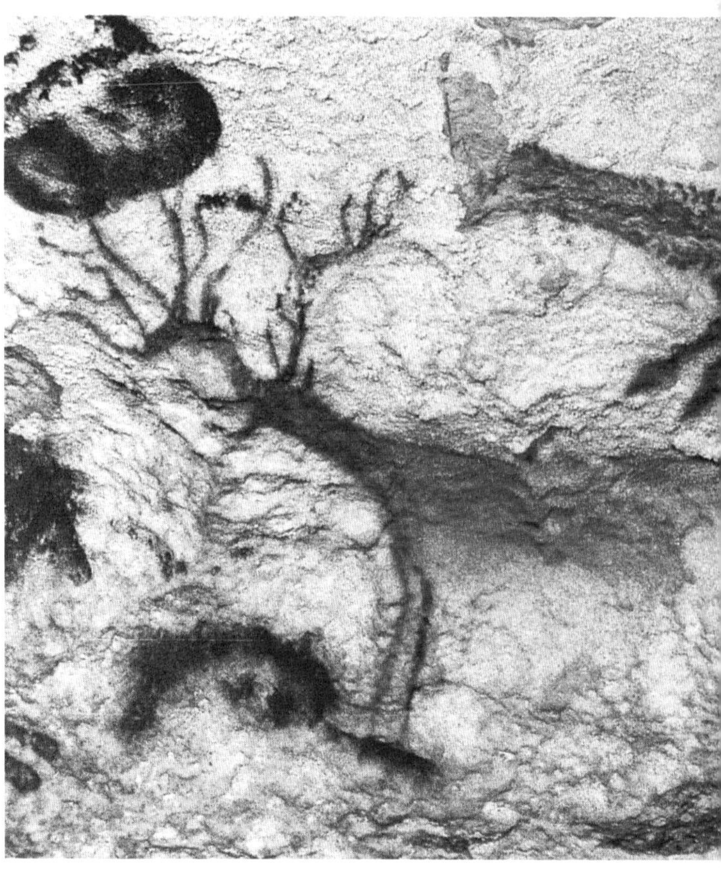

The wall paintings, showing animals such as horses and bison, were discovered in 1940.

LA DOMENICA DEL CORRIERE

Si pubblica a Milano ogni settimana
Supplemento illustrato del «Corriere della Sera»
Spedizione in abbonamento postale - Gruppo 2

Uffici del giornale:
Via Solferino, 28 - Milano

Anno 43 — N. 50 | 14 Dicembre 1941 XX | Centesimi 50 la copia

Il Giappone in guerra. Un attacco in massa di aeroplani nipponici sopra una base americana nell'Oceano Pacifico: una nave da battaglia degli Stati Uniti viene colpita e incendiata.

(Disegno di A. Beltrame)

The Japanese bombing of Pearl Harbor brought the US into the Second World War.

1941
JAPANESE BOMB PEARL HARBOR

With Britain largely occupied elsewhere, the Japanese only had to deal with the US Pacific Fleet based in Hawaii to leave the zone open to their territorial ambitions. In 1941, an armada of 350 aircraft launched from the Japanese carrier fleet hit the ill-prepared American base at Pearl Harbor. Despite the loss of several battleships and other warships, the Americans were fortunate that their own aircraft carriers were out on exercises and thus survived the attack. It was to be the move that finally brought the US officially into the war. America declared war on the Japanese and later on the Axis. The American lack of battleships in the Pacific caused them to centre much of their operations on the carriers, which proved to be the undoing of the Japanese.

1941
FIRST USE OF ANTIBIOTICS

After Fleming's discovery of penicillin it took 11 years before two brilliant experimentalists, Howard Florey and Ernst Chain, managed to perfect a method of producing the volatile drug. The three of them shared the Nobel Prize for Medicine for the discovery in 1945. The first antibiotics, all derived from penicillin, came into use from 1941 and were

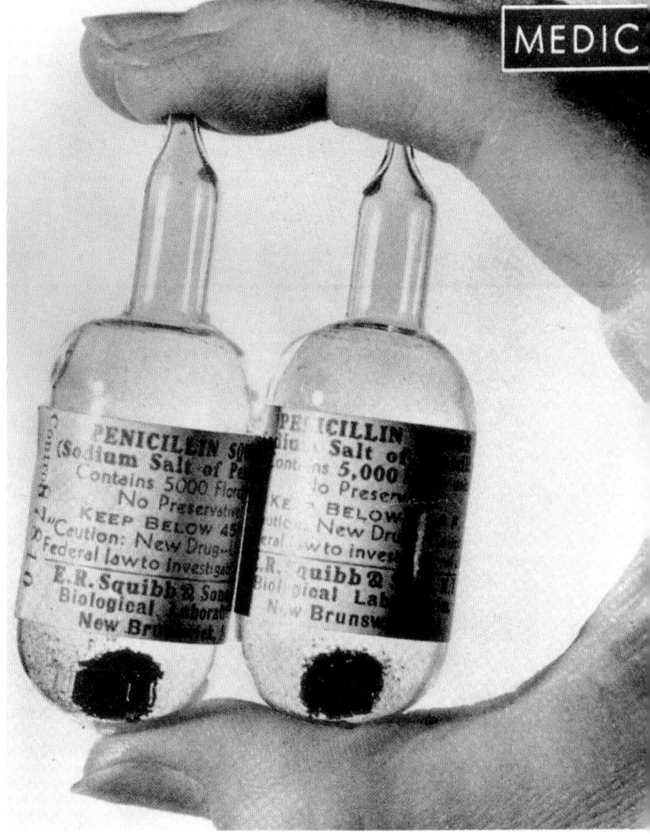

Howard Florey and Ernst Chain finally created a drug from Fleming's penicillin that could be marketed.

quickly joined by chloramphenicol, the cephalosporins, erythromycins, tetracyclines and aminoglycosides. Each type of antibiotic acts in a different way and is active against varying types of disease-causing agents. Unfortunately bacteria have the ability to

develop immunity following repeated doses of antibiotics, so more advanced antibiotics must constantly be discovered to overcome them.

1941
VIRGINIA WOOLF COMMITS SUICIDE

On the day of her death in 1941, Virginia Woolf dressed herself in a bulky fur coat. She walked along by the Ouse River, put a large stone in her pocket and stepped into the water. It was the end of a life's work of sensitive, beautifully crafted novels and a struggle with mental illness. Her writing was based on the world of women, and she created a poetic language to explore their lives. Her non-fiction – *A Room of One's Own* and *Three Guineas* – are powerful comments on women's need for financial independence. Woolf was an important figure in the Bloomsbury Group. With her husband Leonard, she founded the Hogarth Press, which published new and innovative fiction. She was in her late fifties when she died.

1942
BATTLE OF MIDWAY

On the afternoon of 3 June 1942, a patrol plane sighted a Japanese force approaching Midway in the Pacific. The next day 100 Japanese bombers took off from their carriers and headed for Midway. In wait for the invaders was a strong force of American torpedo planes and fighters. The US aircraft launched off the carriers Hornet, Yorktown and Enterprise and sank four Japanese carriers. Within four days Japanese losses, in addition to the four aircraft carriers, included two heavy cruisers and three destroyers badly damaged, and 322 aircraft. The Americans lost the carrier Yorktown, a destroyer and 147 aircraft. Midway remained in American hands, and the Japanese fleet was so severely damaged that Japan's war effort changed from an offensive thrust to a holding operation.

5 JANUARY 1941

Amy Johnson Dies

Amy Johnson, the first woman to fly solo from England to Australia, is killed after her aircraft crashes in the Thames Estuary; the wreckage of the plane is found, but there is no sign of the body. Johnson was working for the war transport service, flying aircraft from factories to airforce bases.

Amy Johnson, the first woman to fly solo to Australia was killed while ferrying aircraft to RAF bases.

9 JUNE 1942

Czechs Pay for Heydrich Murder

The Germans massacre the village of Lidice in Czecholslovakia in a retaliatory move after the assassination of high-ranking Gestapo officer Reinhard Heydrich by two Czech soldiers. All the men in the village are slaughtered and the women and children taken to concentration camps.

1942
THE SIEGE OF STALINGRAD

Stalingrad was the site of a critical Soviet victory that reversed Germany's advance to the east. The first phase of the battle lasted from 17 July to 18 November 1942, when the German 6th Army under Friedrich von Paulus closed in on the heart of the city, which was being tenaciously defended by General Vasily Chuikov's 62nd Army. On 19 November, Soviet forces under General Georgy Zhukov attacked north and south of the city, encircling the Germans, who finally surrendered on 2 February 1943. Soviet losses numbered 750,000, whereas Germany and its allies lost 850,000. Coupled with the defeat of Rommel at El Alamein in Egypt at the hands of a British army under General Montgomery the month previously, the end of 1942 saw the turning point of the war.

1943
WAKSMAN DISCOVERS TUBERCULOSIS TREATMENT

Russian biochemist Selman Abraham Waksman became a US national in 1915 and professor of microbiology at Rutgers University in 1930. While researching the process of breaking down organic substances by micro-organisms and antibiotics he discovered streptomycin, an antibiotic drug derived from a soil bacterium, in 1943. He coined the word antibiotic to describe bacteria-destroying chemicals derived from microorganisms. Streptomycin was found to be useful in treating tuberculosis, influenzal meningitis and other infections unaffected by penicillin. Tuberculosis is an infectious disease where

The Soviet forces finally won the day in the Siege of Stalingrad, forcing the German surrender in a turning point of the war.

inflammation and abscesses can rapidly spread through the lungs and into the bloodstream and brain. Waksman was awarded the Nobel Prize for Medicine for this discovery in 1952.

Betty Grable, the 'Forces' Sweetheart'.

1943
BETTY GRABLE

One of the most enduring images of Betty Grable is as the 'forces' favourite', looking back over her shoulder in a white swimming costume, and displaying her 'million dollar legs' – the amount that Lloyds of London insured them for. She was trained at Hollywood Professional School from the age of 12, and was in chorus lines before she was 14. She got her break at Fox, where she starred in 18 musicals, high on gloss and Technicolor. *Coney Island* is typical of them: 95 minutes of Betty singing and dancing, with *Coney island* as a background and the story of two guys after the same girl to link the routines.

1943
WAR IN THE EAST

On the eastern front, the situation had changed slightly in Germany's favour since Stalingrad. They had shortened their lines, while the Soviet troops were stretched over a massive front with a bulge westward around Kursk. On 5 July 1943 the Germans, using their new Tiger and Panther tanks, struck at this Soviet salient. Hitler committed more than 1,000 planes against the Red Army's enormous concentration of troops, artillery pieces and tanks. The encounter developed into one of the largest and most vicious armour battles ever fought. More than 3,000 tanks were engaged on the grasslands. On 12 July 1943, the Soviets moved in fresh tank divisions and the advantage finally swung to the Russians. Manstein, having lost 70,000 men, half his tanks and more than 1,000 planes, was forced to withdraw.

The Russians and the Germans both employed tank warfare on the eastern front.

1943
JEAN-PAUL SARTRE'S
BEING AND NOTHINGNESS

'Existence precedes essence' and 'man makes himself'; these phrases encapsulate the atheist existentialism of the French philosopher Jean-Paul Sartre (1905–80). In the absence of a God who created us with a purpose, he pointed out, we arrive in the world with nothing but our own existence. This problem is explored in his *Being and Nothingness*, published in 1943. In this he argued that people had no choice but to decide for themselves who they were – they must invent their own essence. The self is not an entity but a project, not something that has being but something that is forever becoming. Whoever defines themselves by their current role in life lives in 'bad faith'. It is a philosophy that gives each person an enormous responsibility, but also complete freedom.

Cartoon of Jean-Paul Sartre, one of the central figures in the Existentialist movement.

1944
GLENN MILLER DISAPPEARS

Mystery surrounds musician Glenn Miller's death. Colonel Miller and two companions were passengers on a routine flight to France in 1944. While in the air their plane vanished, no distress call was made and no wreckage sighted. The passengers were declared missing, and no further information about this strange occurrence was ever discovered. Miller's music, however, lives on. He dedicated himself to writing and arranging his own compositions. The sweet swing melodies of his 'Little Brown Jug' and 'Moonlight Serenade' have a distinctive reed section, with the sound of the clarinet sweeping out over four saxophones. His signed up for active service in the US. His army band played in the war zones of the Pacific and Europe as a morale booster for the troops.

1944
D-DAY

On 6 June 1944, the Allies finally opened the long-awaited second front against the Germans. Landing on a 48-km (30-mile) stretch of the Normandy coast, they established a bridgehead with 10 divisions. Up until the last minute, the Germans had been fooled into believing that the invasion would be targeted at Calais and several key German divisions sat out the early stages of the invasion in the belief that Normandy was just a diversion. Airborne landings protected the five beaches: Omaha, Utah, Gold, Silver and Juno. At Omaha, the Americans suffered 3,000 casualties on the first day and penetrated just 1.6 km (one mile). To the east, the British and Canadians took Arromanches and Bayeux against strong German opposition. The British on Sword Beach failed to take their main objective of Caen, but the Canadians from Juno swept 11 km (7 miles) inland. The Germans reacted slowly, hindered by the allies' parachutists and superior air cover, not to mention

Allied forces coming ashore at Normandy during the D-Day landings.

the widespread activities of the French resistance. Hitler released his panzers too late and by the afternoon of the 7th the battle for Normandy had been won. By 12 June the bridgehead had expanded to 130 x 16 km (80 x 10 miles). D-Day still ranks as the greatest amphibious landing in history.

12 SEPTEMBER 1943

Mussolini Rescued

The Italian dictator Benito Mussolini is rescued from his imprisonment by a Nazi parachute operation; this daring rescue comes after Mussolini was deposed by Victor Emmanuel, the king of Italy, in July. He is believed to have been transported to a safe location in the north of Italy.

Italian fascist dictator Benito Mussolini.

The organic farming movement excluded the use of synthetically produced fertilizers, pesticides and growth regulators.

1944
ORGANIC FARMING

The organic farming movement, known also as biological, regenerative or sustainable farming, was started by Lady Eve Balfour. Not only a talented jazz trombonist and pilot, Lady Balfour was an assiduous agricultural researcher and, in 1944, published *The Living Soil.* Two years later the Soil Association was formed. Organic farming as much as possible excluded the use of synthetically produced fertilizers, pesticides, feed additives and growth regulators. Preferred farming methods therefore included crop rotation, the use of green and animal manures and biological pest and weed control. Organic farming methods are sometimes the only option in under-developed areas, and those that are developing. In developed countries organic farming is gaining ground, often as a reaction against intensive or factory farming or scares about food safety.

4 JUNE 1944
Allies Take Rome

Allied forces enter Rome and begin a campaign to seize control of Italy; they meet with little resistance in this, the first of the Axis capitals to be taken. At last an end can be seen, with victory for the Allies.

1944
BRETTON WOODS, THE IMF AND THE IBRD

The Bretton Woods Conference was convened in July 1944 to plan currency stabilization and credit in the post-war era. Representatives of 44 nations took part. Out of Bretton Woods was created the International Monetary Fund (IMF) to support economic development, promote international monetary co-operation, flatten out exchange-rate fluctuations, facilitate international trade and payments and provide short-term credit. The International Bank for Reconstruction and Development (IBRD, the World Bank) was also set up at Bretton Woods to provide loan capital for specific projects in member nations. It has proved particularly valuable in financing projects in health, education and other non-profit-making areas. The Conference also proposed an informal system for maintaining stable exchange rates between currencies.

1945
TUPPERWARE

The name Tupperware, developed in 1945 by the American Earl Tupper, has become synonymous with plastic storage containers of every description. Designed from polyethylene, with air-tight seals to keep contents fresh for long periods of time, Tupperware revolutionized the storage of food in the home. The functional Tupperware design was produced in a variety of forms and translucent colours which are being constantly updated. Tupperware was flexible but durable; in 1947, the range was featured in an article in the American magazine *House Beautiful* under the title 'Fine Art for 39 cents'. Part of the commercial success of Tupperware was due to the unique ploy of home-party selling, which was introduced in the USA in 1946 and in the UK and Europe in 1960.

Delegates at the Yalta Conference in 1945.

1945
YALTA CONFERENCE

Winston Churchill, Franklin D. Roosevelt and Joseph Stalin met in the Crimea for eight days in February to decide the fate of the world after the war. They agreed on the strategies to finish off Germany and how they would deal with Japan. It was decided that Germany should be partitioned between the US, USSR, Britain and France. With Russia's enormous gains on the eastern front, they were in a strong position to make territorial claims. With the allies advancing on all fronts against the Germans and the Japanese, it would not be long until these agreements came into force.

1945
MUSSOLINI AND HITLER DIE

By 1945 things were falling apart for Mussolini and Hitler. Italian leader Benito Mussolini had resigned on 25 July 1943 and had been arrested, only to be rescued by German parachutists in September. Vainly seeking to regain what he had lost, he set up a 'Republican Fascist' government in northern Italy. Mussolini, his mistress Clara Petacci and other Fascists were caught by Italians at Dongo on Lake Como trying to make it through the Swiss border. After some form of trial they were shot on 28 April 1945 and their bodies were taken to Milan and hung upside-down in a public square. In Germany, Rundstedt's counter-offensive against the Allies in the Ardennes in December 1944 under Hitler's direction had failed and Germany had been invaded. Hitler was living out his fantasies commanding non-existent armies from his bunker, the air-raid shelter beneath the chancellery building in Berlin. On 29 April 1945, with the Russians only several hundred metres away, he married his mistress Eva Braun in the presence of the Goebbels family. All available evidence suggests that Hitler and Braun committed suicide on the following day and had their bodies cremated. Hitler's beloved Third Reich, which was to have endured forever, had ended ingloriously.

1945
ALLIES DISCOVER THE HORRORS OF THE HOLOCAUST

On 30 April British troops entered the Buchenwald concentration camp. In it they discovered 40,000 emaciated prisoners, many beyond help. Huge heaps of rotting bodies were found everywhere; it was believed that 30,000 had died there in the last few months. American troops liberated Belsen, finding another 20,000 prisoners there, including 900 boys under the age of 14. Many SS guards were executed on the spot. The Russians made further discoveries, confirming that the German 'Final Solution' was

Auschwitz, one of many concentration camps where millions of people were executed by the Germans.

well advanced. Victory had come too late for so many in Europe. In June 1945, many Germans would be forced to witness the reality of the Nazi regime and the mass murders in the camps.

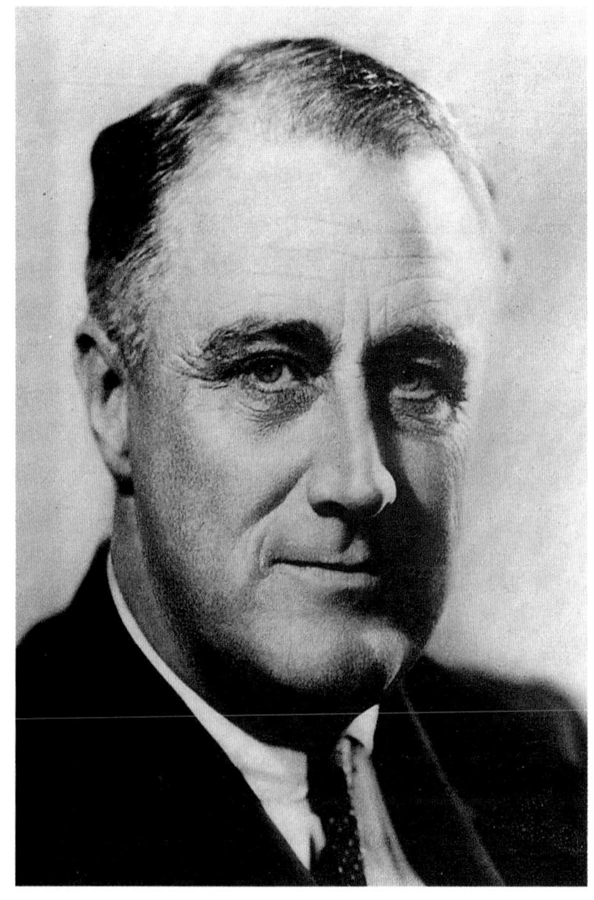

US president Franklin D. Roosevelt.

20 JANUARY 1945

Roosevelt Stays

US president Franklin D. Roosevelt is inaugurated for his fourth term in office, the first time a president has been re-elected this number of times. Roosevelt has maintained his pre-war popularity through the difficult recent years.

Devastation after the dropping of the bomb on Hiroshima.

1945
HIROSHIMA

Working in intense secrecy, thousands of American scientists finally realized what they had been labouring towards. On 6 August 1945 the first atomic bomb was dropped on Hiroshima; the second, on the 9th, obliterated the city of Nagasaki. 'If Japan does not surrender,' President Truman threatened, 'atomic bombs will be dropped on her war industries. A rain of ruin from the air, the like of which the world has never seen.' The Hiroshima bomb was dropped by the US bomber *Enola Gay.* The Nagasaki bomb alone killed 70,000 people outright. Many thousands more would die of their injuries and radiation sickness over the next few months. The Japanese had no choice but to surrender unconditionally. The bomb, created by the German scientist Otto Hahn, produced a massive explosion following the splitting of uranium 235 atoms. Churchill was prompted to say, 'By God's mercy British and American science outpaced all German efforts. The possession of these powers by the Germans at any time might have altered the result of the war.' On 19 August the formal occupation of Japan began and General MacArthur accepted the surrender of Japanese forces on the deck of the US carrier *Missouri* in Tokyo Bay.

The Berlin Wall was just part of the Iron Curtain that stretched for 1,000 miles across Europe.

1945
THE IRON CURTAIN

In 1945 and 1946, Stalin built the Iron Curtain across Europe. It was a barrier that ran for 1,000 miles from the Baltic to the Adriatic, cutting Europe in two. Its purpose was to prevent any western influence from reaching the eastern European countries controlled by Stalin. In particular, it cut Germany into sections, the Soviet zone and the three western zones. The Iron Curtain received a very hostile reception in the West, which surprised Stalin. At Yalta and later at Potsdam he had agreed that the West could do as it liked in western Europe and he assumed therefore, that he could do as he liked in the East. As always, Stalin's main preoccupation was security, and the Iron Curtain seemed to him a natural step. To the West it correctly suggested the beginning of another form of dictatorship.

1945
DIARY OF ANNE FRANK DISCOVERED

Anne Frank (1929–45), was a young Jewish girl who hid with her family in occupied Amsterdam between 1942 and 1944. She kept a diary while hiding from Nazi persecution, living in a secret apartment for two years before being discovered. Anne and her family were betrayed to the Gestapo on 4 August 1944, and deported with eight others in the last convoy of cattle trucks to the extermination camp at Auschwitz. Anne was shipped on

The diary of Anne Frank became one of the most revealing insights into Jewish persecution in the Second World War.

to the Bergen-Belsen concentration camp, and died there in March 1945. Her three notebooks, left behind at 263 Prinsengracht in Amsterdam, contained her diary, chronicling the period in which she and her family hid from the Gestapo. Her moving diary was abridged in 1947 and became an international bestseller, acting as a poignant reminder of the plight of the Jews during the Holocaust.

1946
THE SOVIET UNION'S FIVE-YEAR PLAN

On 9 February 1946 Stalin announced his fourth Five-Year Plan since taking power. Previous plans had covered 1928–32, 1933–37 and the wartime 1938–42. By regulation, control and planning Stalin used these plans to carry forward his own programme of socialism. He collectivized agriculture, forcing up the crop yield, developed industrialism and made Russia a manufacturing state. He was keen to eradicate illiteracy and was a strong supporter of the sciences. Within the confines of the state apparatus, a wealthy and privileged new class emerged, bound to the state by virtue of their office and power. His plans were not always successful, but in many cases they proved to be the right policy for Russia.

13 JUNE 1946

Republic in Italy

King Umberto II of Italy abdicates and goes into exile in Portugal. The move follows a vote by the Italian public to abolish the monarchy and establish a rebublic. King Umberto had succeeded his father Victor Emmanuel only one month previously.

1946
ECKERT AND MAUCHLY PRODUCE ENIAC

The very first electronic digital computer, known as the ABC computer, was built by J. Atanasoff and C. Berry between 1937 and 1942. A special purpose-built computer with vacuum tubes was built independently at Bletchley Park; it was known as the Colossus and was designed to decipher the 'Enigma' code during the Second World War. The major breakthrough in computing came in 1946, when J. Mauchly and P. Eckert in Pennsylvania built the high-speed electronic digital computer known as the ENIAC (Electronic Numerical Integrator and Computer). In primitive form the ENIAC contained virtually all the circuitry used in present-day high-speed computers. It was used by the US army for military calculations.

The first high-speed computer, known as ENIAC.

Jackson Pollock created his works by dripping, pouring and hurling paint on to the canvas, as in this, ***Frieze.***

1946
OPERATION HIGHJUMP

In 1946, Admiral Richard Byrd (1888–1957) returned to Antarctica to lead the largest expedition ever mounted to that inhospitable continent. Operation Highjump involved a fleet of 13 ships and 4,700 men. Highjump charted a large extent of the coastline of the ice pack covering the pole. Expeditions such as these were considered highly prestigious in the ideological war between the United States and the Soviet Union. The scientists involved, however, preferred activities such as the International Geophysical Year (1957–58). Some 12 nations participated in this, involved in projects such as the causes of earthquakes, oceanography, the study of the weather and the crossing of the Antarctic.

1947
THE MARSHALL PLAN

The Marshall Plan was proposed in July 1947 by the US secretary of state George Marshall. It set up a European Recovery Programme, that offered money to countries in Europe to help them rebuild after the war. All countries in Europe were invited to apply for aid and at first the Soviet Union and the countries of eastern Europe were involved. However, when they discovered that Marshall Aid would involve membership of the Organisation for European Economic Co-operation, Stalin the Soviet leader, withdrew. Even so, Poland and Czechoslovakia still tried to obtain aid until Stalin banned their applications. Altogether about $13.5 billion was given out in aid from 1948 to 1951.

1947
JACKSON POLLOCK PAINTS *FRIEZE*

The controversial painter Jackson Pollock (1912–56) was a central figure of American Abstract Expressionism, producing art which was both intensely personal and violently emotional and anarchic. By the mid-1930s, he had developed a dark style which he used while working on the Federal Art Project between 1938 and 1942. Pollock's first solo show included paintings representative of his increasingly vivid style, such as *The She Wolf* (1943). By 1947, he was relying on a type of painting that was expressive in form, but with imagery derived from the unconscious or from myth. Gradually, the surface of these paintings became more homogeneous as the figures became less easily separated from the grounds. Pollock perfected new techniques of application, dripping paint from tins and pouring and hurling it on to unstretched canvases placed on the floor, as in *Frieze.*

1947
GATT

The General Agreement on Tariffs and Trade (GATT) was signed in Geneva in 1947

by representatives of 23 non-communist nations. By 1988 the agreement had 96 members. GATT created an international forum dedicated to the expansion of multi-lateral trade and the settlement of trade disputes. Members agreed to treat all other members equally – the most-favoured-nation policy. In theory this represented a desire to abolish all non-tariff barriers to trade. The eighth round of trade negotiations, the Uruguay Round, continued from 1986 to 1996, and the final agreements resulted in the creation of the World Trade Organisation (WTO).

1948
BERLIN AIRLIFT

After walking out of the Allied Control Council meeting in March, the Russians clearly intended to make a military move against Berlin. In the following month the Russians began checking all rail and road movements into Berlin. By June, over 200 aircraft a day were flying into Berlin to prevent the city's population from starving. It was estimated that around 2,350,000 kg (2,300 tons) of food a day was required. In September this had risen to 895 aircraft per day carrying over 6,450,000 kg (6,350 tons). On 18 September US pilots flew in 651 times carrying over 4,570,000 kg (4,500 tons) of coal. The Berlin blockade ended in May 1949, after costing the allies $200 million. The Russians had installed a communist government in the east of Germany and had accepted the creation of West Germany.

US pilots flew food and supplies to Berlin after the Russians blockaded the railways and roads.

14 OCTOBER 1947

Breaking the Sound Barrier

Captain Charles 'Chuck' Yeager becomes the first man to travel faster then the speed of sound in his aircraft the Bell XI. Flying at an altitude of 27,430 m (42,000 ft), Captain Yeager reaches a speed of Mach 1.015 or 1,078 kph (670 mph).

The American Bell XI, the first aircraft to break the sound barrier.

1948
MAHATMA GANDHI ASSASSINATED

♲ In May 1947 Gandhi had at last realized his dream. Since 1946 he had been negotiating with the British government over constitutional reform, and finally India had been granted independence. He hailed the decision as 'the noblest act of the British nation'. Things were darkened in his last few months by communal strife between Hindus and Muslims, but his fasts to shame the instigators helped to avert the situation to some extent. He was assassinated in Delhi by a Hindu fanatic on 30 January 1948, just 10 days after a previous attempt on his life. He is now venerated as a moral teacher, a pacifist reformer and a dedicated patriot.

Mahatma Gandhi, who was assassinated by a Hindu fanatic in 1948.

1948
THOR HEYERDAHL PUBLISHES ***THE KON-TIKI EXPEDITION***

Thor Heyerdahl set out to prove that a voyage across the vast seas from America to Polynesia was possible centuries before motorized travel. With the help of an engineer, he built a raft, made from nine huge balsa-wood logs bound together with rope, and named it the *Kon-Tiki*. On 28 April 1947, he and five companions set off from Callao Harbour, in Peru. For nearly 100 days they were buffeted by the sea and followed by sharks and whales, but eventually their craft was carried by the trade winds on to a palm-covered island, across the Pacific Ocean. His popular account of the voyage of *Kon-Tiki* was published in 1948, and a documentary film won an Academy Award in 1951.

The Jewish Star of David was adopted for the flag of Israel when the state was founded in 1948.

1948
ISRAEL FOUNDED

The new independent state of Israel came into being at 4 p.m. on 14 May 1948. The former Jewish Agency leader, David Ben-Gurion, became the first prime minister. The Jewish leaders had finally agreed to a ceasefire in April after the Palestinian government had threatened them with military action by the British. It was this act that temporarily defused the situation. The fact that the new state of Israel did not have clearly defined borders was to be the cause of many conflicts in the future. It was hoped that the Israelis and the Arabs could agree. The reaction to the forming of the new state was predictable: the Israelis mobilized their Haganah army of 30,000, while the Egyptians massed on the southern border. Meanwhile in Amman, the king of Transjordan pledged to support any Arab move with his own troops, the Arab Legion. The rest of the year saw conflict on all fronts, with the UN and the British getting involved. Despite the shooting down of five RAF reconnaissance aircraft in January 1949, the British government recognized the state of Israel on the 29th. After 42 days of talks a truce was signed between Israel and Egypt on 24 February.

1948
FANNY BLANKERS-KOEN TAKES LONDON BY STORM

Rarely can victories in the Olympics have proved as emotional as Fanny Blankers-Koen's quadruple success in the London Olympics in 1948. To win her four gold medals, she overcame press derision in her native Holland, sexism, and homesickness for the Netherlands and her two small children. In fact, so painful was the last that Blankers-Koen threatened to quit the Olympics after having won her first two golds. But she was persuaded to stay and became the first-ever woman to win four gold medals at one Olympics, emulating her hero Jesse Owens. Blankers-Koen won gold in the 100 m, 200 m, 80-m hurdles, and 4x100-m relay. Incredibly, she opted not to take part in two other events, the long jump and the high jump, in which she held the world records.

23 DECEMBER 1948

General Tojo Hanged

The former Japanese prime minister Hideki Tojo, and six other wartime leaders, are hanged for crimes perpetrated during the Second World War. The seven men were convicted during a war crimes trial held in Tokyo in November.

IBM became one of the dominant formats and languages of computers.

1948
COMPUTER PROCESSORS

The first computer with an electronic memory was built by Tom Kilburn and Fred Williams at Manchester University in 1948. The floppy disc was invented two years later, by Yoshiro Nakamats, for IBM. By 1969, computers had become fully transistorised and featured the microprocessor, invented by American, Edward Hoff. The personal and microcomputer were refined during the 1970s and the first laptop appeared in 1983. By the 1990s, computers had evolved in a few directions according to application, but the two dominant formats or languages were IBM and Apple Macintosh.

1949
THE PEOPLE'S REPUBLIC OF CHINA ESTABLISHED

Mao Zedong (1893–1976), Chinese Communist leader was chairman of the Communist Party of China and the principal founder of the People's Republic of China. Mao helped found the Chinese Communist Party in Shanghai in 1921. In 1927, their then-allies launched a military campaign against the Communists, who retreated to rural areas where they gained the support of the peasants. After Nationalist forces surrounded them in 1934 the Red Army retreated 6,000 miles to the north-west in the Long

Cartoon showing the people's admiration for Mao Zedong after he formed the People's Republic of China.

The symbol of the North Atlantic Treaty Organization.

March. In 1949 they eventually captured most of China and declared the People's Republic. Chairman Mao promoted rural development, equality and the pursuit of economic self-reliance in the villages, but his government was extremely authoritarian and up to 100 million dissidents may have died in his labour camps.

1949
NATO

NATO (the North Atlantic Treaty Organization) was set up in 1949 after the Berlin Blockade. It was a military alliance involving countries on either side of the North Atlantic. It changed relations between East and West by uniting the countries, leading to the stationing of US forces in western Europe for the first time. The most important clause in the treaty was that an attack on one country would be considered an attack on all of them; so the East could not pick off democratic countries without the risk of a war with NATO. The Soviet Union did not react until West Germany was admitted as a member in 1955. It then set up the Warsaw Pact, a military alliance between the Communist countries of eastern Europe.

2 MARCH 1949

First Flight Around the World

The B-50 bomber Lucky Lady II lands at Carswell Air Force base in Texas, completing the first non-stop flight around the world. The plane, carrying 13 crew members, set off from the base on 27 February, completing the journey in 94 hours.

Chapter 6
1950–1959

1950
KOREA

At the end of the Second World War, Korea had been divided into a Communist North and a non-Communist South. In 1950 North Korea invaded the South and quickly overran all but the very southern-most tip of the peninsula. The US took the matter to the United Nations Security Council, which agreed to send a UN force to support South Korea. UN forces landed in the south and also behind North Korean lines at Inchon. The North Koreans were forced back and retreated almost to the Chinese border. However, the Chinese army invaded to support them and the UN forces were forced to retreat. A cease-fire was finally agreed in 1953. The border between the North and the South was then fixed at exactly the same point as it had been when the war began.

Memorial to those who died in the Korean War.

1 NOVEMBER 1950

Truman Murder Attempt

Two Puerto Ricans make an assassination attempt on US president Harry S. Truman at his residence Blair House in Washington. In the attack one guard and one of the assassins were killed. It is believed the men were nationalists.

1950
THE SCHUMAN PLAN

The Schuman Plan was proposed by the French foreign minister, Robert Schuman, in May 1950. It was a plan to integrate the coal and steel industries of western Europe. In April 1951 the plan was put into effect when France, West Germany, Italy, Belgium, the Netherlands and Luxembourg signed a treaty setting up a single market for coal and steel. This became known as the European Coal and Steel Community, which met for the first time in August 1952. The Community was the prototype for the European Economic Community, which the members began to discuss almost immediately in 1953. These discussions continued for three years and resulted in the drawing up of the terms of the Treaty of Rome in 1957.

1950
CHRISTIAN DIOR

The 'New Look' caused a sensation. In the war years women had been dressing in utility clothing: short, drab and uncluttered in style. Material was rationed and suits and frocks

President Harry S. Truman, who survived an assassination attempt in 1950.

were asexual. And then Dior appeared. He said: 'I designed clothes for flower-like women, with rounded shoulders, full feminine busts and hand-span waists.' His dresses used metres of fabric and had hems rustling near the floor. The look was opulent and uncomfortable to wear, but a sunburst after years of practicality. Women were enraptured and rushed to buy them. In England, senior politicians were outraged at the thwarting of fabric restrictions, but soon Princess Margaret was wearing the 'New Look' everywhere.

1950
TOLLUND MAN FOUND

A Tollund Man was found in an Iron Age bog on Tollund Fen in Denmark in 1950. His body was well preserved – and naked except for a well-made leather cap on his head and a hide belt around his waist. Looped around his neck was a leather thong, by which he had met his death, from being hanged or strangled. Radio-carbon dating established that he lived around 210 BC. Analysis of his stomach contents revealed that he had eaten his last meal 12 to 24 hours before his death, a sort of gruel, made from seeds and plants. He had also shaved two or three days before he died. It was less clear why he was killed.

The yards of fabric used in Dior's New Look were a reaction to wartime rationing.

1950
JACQUES-YVES COUSTEAU COMMANDS RESEARCH SHIP *CALYPSO*

Jacques-Yves Cousteau (1910–97), the French ocean explorer and pioneer in underwater research, became the foremost authority on oceanography and exploration, inventing (with Emile Gagnan), in 1943, the first scuba-diving device, which he called Aqualung. He commanded the prestigious research ship *Calypso* from 1950, and subsequently wrote a book about his findings, *The Calypso Log.* In 1957 he became head of the Conshelf Saturation Dive Program experiments, in which people live and work for extended periods in deep water along the continental shelves. He also conducted archeological research, exploring submerged shipwrecks.

Advertizement for the 1951 Festival of Britain.

1 SEPTEMBER 1951

ANZUS Treaty Signed

Representatives of Australia, New Zealand and the United States sign the ANZUS Treaty, or Pacific Security Treaty, forming an alliance in which each of the three countries guarantees aid to each of the others in case of attack from foreign powers.

1951
FESTIVAL OF BRITAIN

In the post-war years Britain was in trouble: almost bankrupt and faced with shortages and continued rationing. It was a gloomy and austere time, but a ray of hope shone out in the Festival of Britain in 1951. It was a nationwide celebration of the country's achievements and potential. In London the main exhibition took place in the blitzed-out spaces between Waterloo and Westminster Bridges. The Festival Hall was the first building to be completed, and the areas surrounding it were transformed with temporary pavilions, restaurants and a Dome of Discovery. It was cheerful by day, and by night it became 'a floodlit dream world breathing music'.

Poster for the classic Technicolor film ***Singin' in the Rain.***

1952
GENE KELLY'S *SINGIN' IN THE RAIN*

Singin' in the Rain had everything – colour, pace, elegance and above all Gene Kelly's dancing. It was set during the Roaring Twenties, when sound was introduced to movies. The songs were catchy – the vibrant 'Gotta Dance', or the witty 'Moses Supposes' – but it was the choreography that captivated contemporary audiences, with Gene Kelly swinging through rain-drenched streets, spinning around lamp-posts and jumping for love. In the 'Broadway Ballet', co-star Cyd Charisse's 'crazy veil', a 7-m (25-ft), white, silk scarf streamed about her, kept airborne by three aeroplane motors whirring in the wings. The scene took a month to rehearse and two weeks to shoot, and cost one-fifth of the film's overall budget.

1952
ALBERT SCHWEITZER AWARDED NOBEL PEACE PRIZE

The German theologian and missionary Albert Schweitzer was awarded the Nobel Peace Prize in 1952 for his humanitarian activities. He had founded a hospital in the French colony of Gabon in 1913 and had spent much of his life there tending to the needs of the inhabitants of the area. He managed to raise considerable sums of money to fund his medical work by giving organ recitals and writing books. His publications of particular note include *Life of Bach* (1905), *The Quest of the Historical Jesus* (1906), *On the Edge of the Primeval Forest* (1921) and *My Life and Thought* (1931). He was also awarded the Order of Merit in 1955. He died in 1965.

1952
TORNADO HITS THE STATES

Over 700 tornadoes lash the US each year, travelling at between 48 kph (30 mph) and 64 kph (40 mph). When a tornado hit the Midwest on 22 March 1952, it left several states devastated, 2,000 people dead and a further 2,500 injured. Tornadoes tend to hit the US east of the Rocky Mountains, especially in the Mississippi basin, with around 150 each year in that area alone. The most destructive tornado occurred on 11 April 1965: it killed 271 people and caused damage in excess of $30 billion. An earlier tornado hit Missouri, Illinois and Indiana in 1925, the death toll this time reaching 689. Tornadoes are violent cyclonic storms with a relatively small diameter. It is the updraft from these that causes the destruction.

Tornadoes hit the American Midwest in 1952, killing more than 2,000 people.

A ball of fire resulting from the first test of the H-bomb, at Enewetak in November 1952.

1952
MAU MAU FREEDOM MOVEMENT

The secret and sinister Mau Mau movement began to assert itself in 1951, but little was known about its purpose or origins. By April 1952, Kenya was on the verge of chaos as the Mau Mau openly intimidated and murdered people who refused to support them. In November the movement began an open rebellion against the British. Murdering and intimidation intensified, white settlers began to arm themselves and the British sent in troops. Many Mau Mau were killed and thousands of suspects rounded up. Jomo 'Burning Spear' Kenyatta was jailed for seven years in April 1953 for masterminding the Mau Mau plot. He would later become the leader of his country.

1952
H-BOMB TESTED

The H-bomb, or hydrogen bomb, works on the principle of nuclear fusion. A large-scale explosion results from the thermonuclear release of energy when hydrogen nuclei are fused to form helium nuclei. Edward Teller, a Hungarian-born US physicist, is known as the

23 SEPTEMBER 1952

Rocky Takes the Title

Defending world heavyweight boxing champion Jersey Joe Walcott meets Rocky Marciano, nearly 10 years his junior, in an incredible showdown. Marciano finally throws one of the most debilitating punches in the history of the sport in the 13th round, knocking the champion out cold. Marciano's total now stands at 50 wins from 50 matches.

father of the hydrogen bomb. He worked on the H-bomb after taking part in the atom-bomb project at the Los Alamos research centre in New Mexico between 1946 and 1952. The H-bomb was first tested at Enewetak atoll on 1 November 1952. The USSR first tested a hydrogen bomb on 12 August 1953, followed by the UK in May 1957, China in 1967 and France in 1968.

1953
DEATH OF STALIN

In March 1953 the infamous Soviet leader Joseph Stalin died; after a period of rivalry he was replaced by Nikita Khrushchev, who immediately brought about a change in East-West relations, by introducing the policy of Coexistence. Khrushchev believed that there was nothing to be gained by trying to destroy the West; the Soviet Union had to accept that it existed and had to try to compete with it and prove that the Soviet system was better. One form of this competition was the 'Space Race', which the Soviet Union won with the first satellite in 1957, and the first man in space in 1961. Soviet athletes also began to dominate the Olympic Games from 1956. Khrushchev was a lively character who made a point of travelling and meeting people. He set out to hit the headlines and produce a popular image for Communism.

Rocky Marciano, showing his undefeated fists.

LA DOMENICA DEL CORRIERE

Supplemento settimanale illustrato del nuovo CORRIERE DELLA SERA - Abbonamenti: Italia, anno L. 1400, sem. L. 750 - Estero, anno L. 2000, sem. L. 1050

Anno 55 — N. 24 | 14 Giugno 1953 | L. 30.—

Conquistata la vetta del mondo. Una cordata della spedizione britannica, composta dal neozelandese Hillary e dalla guida nepalese Tensing, ha raggiunto, con l'aiuto di apparecchi respiratori ad ossigeno, la vetta dell'Everest (m. 8888) la massima elevazione della Terra, che aveva finora respinto dieci tentativi. Sulla cima sono state spiegate al vento tre piccole bandiere: della Gran Bretagna, delle Nazioni Unite e del Nepal. (Disegno di Walter Molino)

Sir Edmund Hillary reaching the top of Mount Everest, the first person to conquer this inhospitable mountain.

1953
EVEREST CONQUERED BY SIR EDMUND HILLARY

Edmund Hillary was a beekeeper who climbed to the top of the world. In 1953, Hillary and the Nepalese explorer Tenzing Norgay achieved the 8,848-m (29,028-ft) summit of Everest. An earlier attempt had been foiled by fierce winds; but on 29 May 1953 at 11.30 a.m. the two men stepped on to the 'symmetrical, beautiful snow cone summit'. They spent 15 minutes taking photographs and eating mint cake, before leaving the Union Jack, the Nepalese national flag and the United Nations flag, as well as sweets and biscuits as a Buddhist offering from Tenzing Norgay. Their success was a triumph of scientific planning and lightweight equipment. Hillary was knighted for his achievement, and Tenzing was awarded the George Cross.

1953
QUEEN ELIZABETH II CROWNED

Princess Elizabeth was born in London on 21 April 1926. During the Second World War she served in the Auxiliary Territorial Service and by an amendment to the Regency Act she became a state counsellor at the age of 18. She married her third cousin, Philip, who became Duke of Edinburgh, in November 1947. She was proclaimed Queen Elizabeth II when her father, George VI, died on 6 February 1952 and was crowned on 2 June 1953 with millions watching the televised coronation. Philip became Prince Philip in 1957 and together they had four children, Charles, Anne, Andrew and Edward. Despite criticisms of the monarchy in the later decades of the twentieth century she maintains her position as a powerful ambassador for the UK.

1953
JACQUELINE BOUVIER MARRIES JOHN KENNEDY

On 14 September 1953 John Fitzgerald Kennedy married Jacqueline Lee Bouvier. Kennedy had been a PT boat commander during the Second World War, and had survived the boat's sinking by the Japanese in

11 MAY 1953
Waco Tornado

A tornado hits Waco in Texas, leaving a trail of destruction in its path. Over 100 are killed and 600 more injured, as the tornado passes through almost without warning in the middle of the day. Property damage reaches an estimated $40 million.

1943. JFK traded his naval career for politics in 1946 when he won a seat in the House of Representatives. A Harvard graduate, Kennedy was the son of the former US ambassador to London. By the time he married he had just won a Senate seat in Massachusetts after beating Henry Cabot Lodge. He would become president in 1960, but would die tragically in Dallas in 1963 at the hands of an assassin.

The coronation of Elizabeth II.

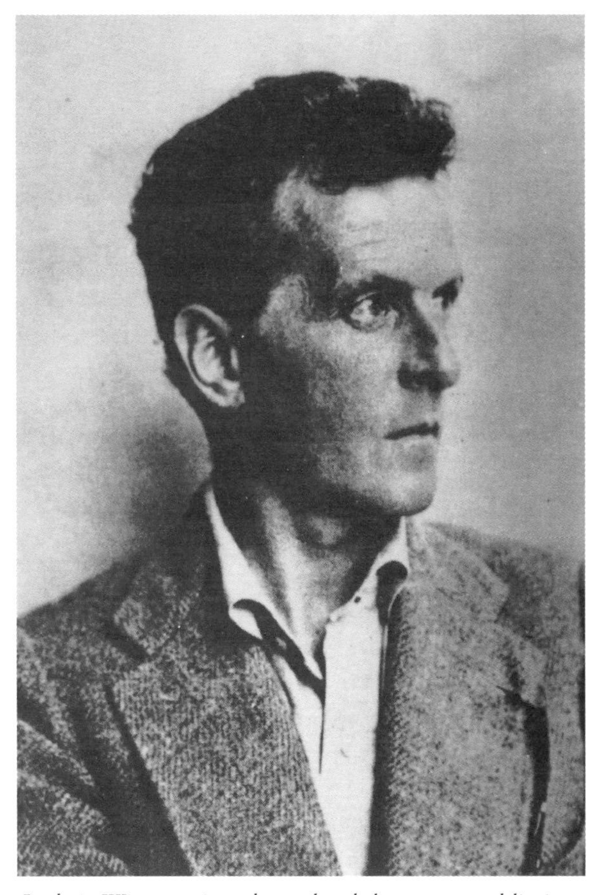

Ludwig Wittgenstein, who explored the nature and limits of language and thought.

1953
LUDWIG WITTGENSTEIN'S *PHILOSOPHIES*

Ludwig Wittgenstein (1889–1951) was Professor of Philosophy at Cambridge University between 1939 and 1947. His two very different books, *Tractatus Logico-Philosophicus* (1922) and *Philosophical Investigations* (1953) explored the nature and limits of language and thought. In them, he argued that factual language was nothing but a way of creating pictures of the world, that all logical statements were, by their own definition, true (that is, tautologies) and that language was in itself incapable of communicating aesthetic, ethical or religious insights. He showed, therefore, that thought and language were not about describing objective reality but rather about constructing coherent, meaningful and shared models of the world.

12 FEBRUARY 1954

Smoking Linked to Cancer

The first suggestion that cancer could be linked to smoking is put forward after a study by the British Standing Advisory Committee. The carcinogenic ingredient remains undiscovered and tobacco companies call for further evidence.

1954
A DOUBLE FIRST AT THE DERBY

On 2 June 1954, 18-year-old Lester Piggott rode the American-bred Never Say Die to a spectacular victory in the Epsom Derby. He was the youngest jockey to win in the history of the race, and Never Say Die was the first American-bred horse to take the title since Iroquoise had won in 1881, in a race from which he had very nearly been scratched.

Never Say Die, with odds of 33–1, earned Piggott the Blue Riband, and the jockey went on to become the new king of racing, notching up four more classics by the end of a decade in which he was rarely out of the headlines.

1954
THE DOMINO ERA

Communists were frequently involved in the highest councils of independence movements, which therefore became suspect in the eyes of the United States. The worst offenders, from this perspective, were the Indochinese Communists, led by Ho Chi Minh (1890–1969). When the French finally agreed to the independence of Indochina, the United States supported an anti-Communist regime in its own state in the south. The war continued because political leaders in the United States had adopted a strategy of containment. Friendly governments were established in states bordering the Communist bloc, and linked by means of military alliances such as the Baghdad Pact of 1955 between Turkey, Iraq, Iran and Pakistan. The strategy was publicized under the less aggressive name of the 'Domino theory'.

Lester Piggot rides into the unsaddling enclosure after winning the Derby.

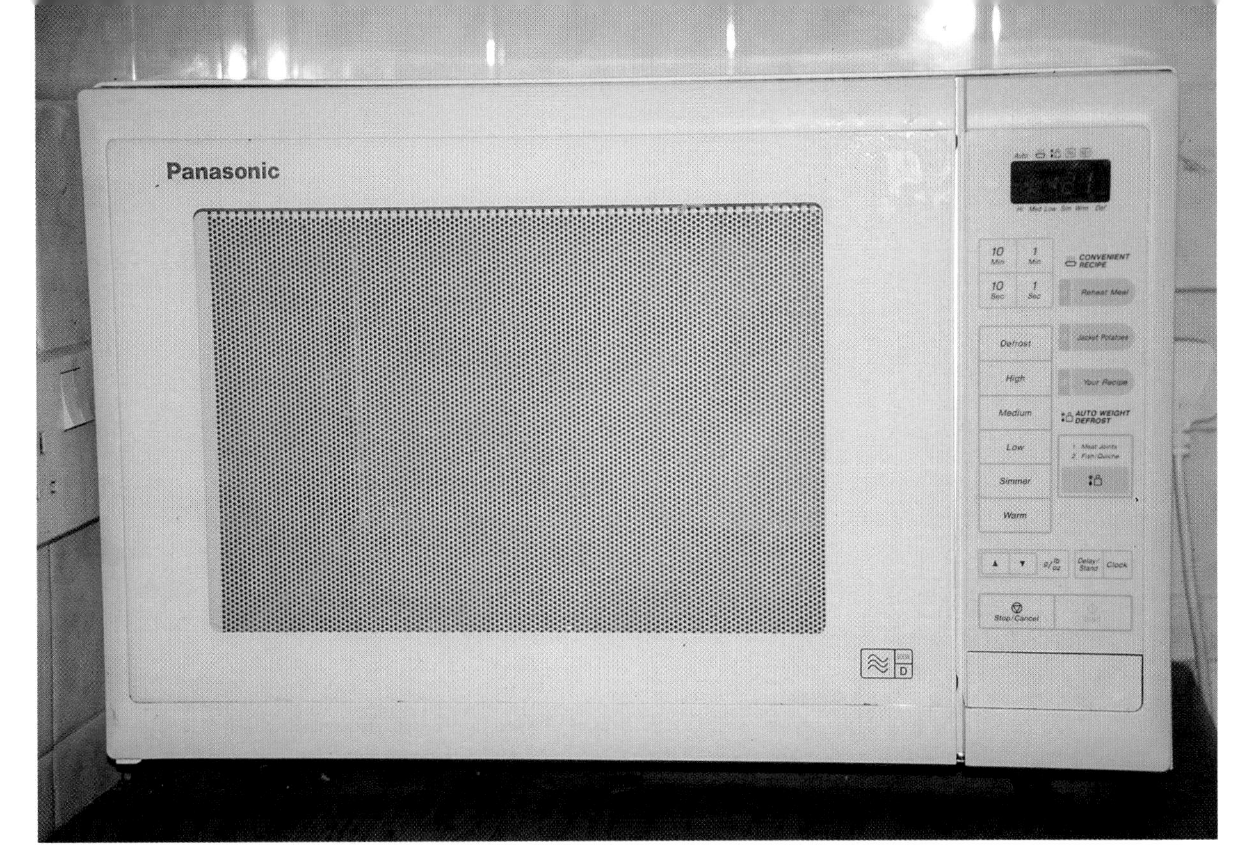

The microwave oven is just one of many uses for the high-frequency microwave amplifier.

1954
MASER INVENTED

Maser is an acronym for 'microwave amplification by simulated emission of radiation'. It is a high-frequency microwave amplifier or oscillator in which the signal to be amplified is used to stimulate unstable atoms into emitting energy at the same frequency. Atoms or molecules are raised to a higher energy level, then allowed to lose this energy by radiation at a precise frequency. This amplifier can be used for such diverse purposes as cooking food in a microwave or as a receiver for satellite communications and radio astronomy. The ammonia-gas maser was suggested by Charles Townes, and independently by Nikolai Basov and Alexsandr Prokhorov in the USSR in 1954.

1954
BILL HALEY INTRODUCES ROCK 'N' ROLL

Bill Haley was an unlikely rock 'n' roller, with his kiss-curled hair and staid image. But he changed pop music for ever in 1954 with the single 'Rock Around the Clock'. It was released as a 'novelty foxtrot', but its fast pulse and snapping beat had teenagers jiving in the aisles, and ripping out cinema seats when it featured in the film *The Blackboard Jungle.* The music fizzed with energy; a boogied-up rhythm and blues slapped out by his backing band The Comets, with Bill Haley's dance-call vocals over the top. They had a quick uccession of hits, before Elvis became King, and the Comets were seen as old pretenders to his rock'n'roll throne.

Communist leader Ho Chi Minh (left).

Roger Bannister breaking the winning rope after 3 minutes, 59.4 seconds.

1954
BANNISTER'S DREAM MILE

Although athletes had dreamt about it for years, the first sub-four-minute mile was close to becoming a reality in the early to mid-1950s. However, Roger Bannister, a 1.85-m (6-ft 1-in), 25-year-old medical student at St Mary's Hospital, London, was by no means assured of being the man to make history. The world record of four minutes 1.4 seconds had been set nine years earlier by Sweden's Gundar Haegg. Now a group of runners bunched on the verge of history. Bannister lined up with colleagues Chris Brasher and Chris Chataway. What was to follow looked distinctly implausible given the windy conditions and the threat of rain. Brasher and Chataway set the pace. Brasher took the trio along for the first two laps, but then dropped back. Chataway took over and led at the bell. Bannister, though, was the stronger and by the end of the race had opened up a 50-yd lead. His split times were 57.7 seconds for the first lap, 60.6 for the second, 62.4 for the third, and 58.7 for the final lap.

1954
OUTBREAK OF ANTI-FRENCH VIOLENCE IN ALGERIA

Algerian Nationalists orchestrated an effective series of attacks against key French targets in the Aurès district of the country on 1 November 1954. The Nationalist leader,

19 OCTOBER 1954

Britain to Withdraw from Suez

Representatives from Great Britain and Egypt sign a treaty in which Britain agrees to withdraw from The Suez Canal Zone over a period of 20 months. British troops have occupied the Zone for more than 70 years.

Chanel's suit design became a classic of the 1950s.

Ahmed Ben Bella, had begun his campaign to rid the country of the French. For their part, the French were seriously under-manned in the country as military and police targets were hit and were powerless to respond. On the 12th the French Interior Minister, François Mitterrand, decided to send French troops to Algeria and later proposed integrating Algeria with France. The writing was on the wall for the French colonial possessions in Africa. Within 10 years little would be left.

1954
CHANEL SUIT

Although the classic Chanel suit had been around since the 1920s, it was not until the designer's return to fashion in 1954 that it became the suit we recognize today: a three-piece uniform of soft tweeds, collarless cardigan jackets and weighted pockets and blouses made to match the inner lining of the jackets themselves; skirts were always below the knee. Chanel's (1883–1971) tailoring was always masterful and masculine. Her heyday was the 1920s, her associations with names like Picasso and Le Corbusier putting her in touch with a 'less is more' aesthetic she made her own. Chanel adopted beige as her favourite colour; borrowed from the functionality of sportswear to put her women in trousers and designed skirts with 'walking pleats' to facilitate greater movement. She also gave us the fashion beret, the cloche hat, costume jewellery as an acceptable accessory, and the strapless, backless, bias-cut evening dress. In 1939, accused of aiding the Nazis, Chanel retreated to Switzerland, but in 1954 she returned to the rue Cambon in Paris to run her couture house, where she continued to design and refine her look until her death.

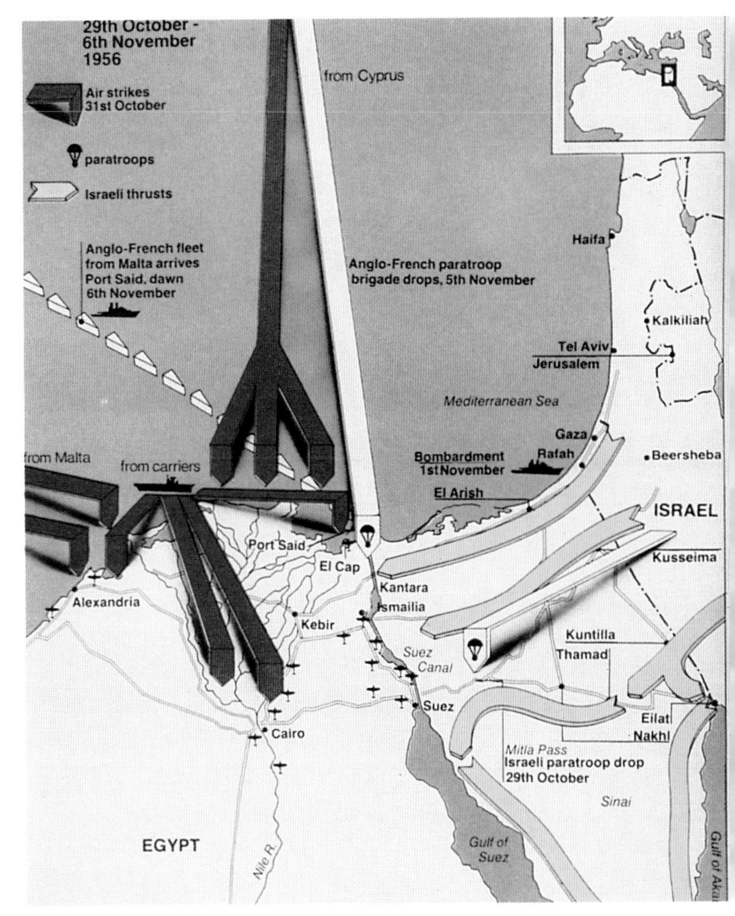

In 1954, British troops agreed to withdraw from the Suez Canal Zone.

Soviet president Kruschev planned to take advantage of the inexperience of the young US president John F. Kennedy.

1955
DISNEYLAND OPENS

Disneyland was designed as a place 'where the parents and the children could have fun together'. A 160-acre site was bought in Anaheim, Orange County, for the ambitious project. The park had mechanically operated figures, fairground rides, waterways and themed sections: Fantasy Land, Frontier Land and Adventure Land. Disney was warned that it would be 'a spectacular failure' – and the opening day almost was. Food and drink ran out, rides broke down and women's stiletto heels sank into the melting asphalt. But things improved rapidly – just seven weeks after opening, Disneyland welcomed its millionth customer, and within a year over five million people had visited the magical kingdom.

1955
FIBRE OPTICS DEMONSTRATED

An optical fibre is a strand of glass with a mirrored cladding, which can convey coded messages sent through it as light pulses. It was first demonstrated in 1955 by Narinder Kapany. The first fibre-optic telephone cables were finally put into service in America in 1977 by the General Telephone Company; one fibre could carry 24 simultaneous calls. By 1988 the first transatlantic cable had been laid; its six fibres could convey 40,000 simultaneous calls.

1955
SUMMITS

From 1955, the leaders of the USA, the USSR, Britain and France began to meet regularly; the meetings were called Summits. Very little ever came of these meetings in terms of actual agreements, but they were a sign that relations between East and West were improving. In fact, the Soviet prime minister, Nikita Khrushchev, used the meetings as a means of

Disneyland was opened in 1955, and has been a popular holiday destination ever since, attracting millions of visitors each year.

winning popular support throughout the world. When he visited Britain in 1957 he broke with protocol and shook hands with workers at a factory. He also decided, after a meeting with the US president Kennedy at Vienna in 1961, that he could take advantage of the younger man's political inexperience.

1955
ALBERT EINSTEIN DIES

Albert Einstein was born in Bavaria in 1879. He later became a Swiss citizen and was appointed an inspector of patents in Berne. He published theoretical papers on physics and achieved fame with his special and general theories of relativity (1905 and 1916). His theories attempted to rationalize many unexplained aspects of physics, showing that in the case of rapid relative motion involving velocities approaching the speed of light, phenomena such as decreased size and mass are to be expected. He received the Nobel Prize for Physics in 1921. After Hitler's rise he emigrated to the US (1933). He died in 1955 before he could complete his unified field theory.

Albert Einstein, whose theories of relativity changed people's perception of physics and the world around them.

8 MAY 1956

Look Back in Anger Premières

John Osborne's play Look Back in Anger opens at the Royal Court Theatre in London's West End. The play meets with a mixed reception, some finding the 'angry young man' hero, Jimmy Porter, a bleak representation of his generation, others seeing truth in Osborne's portrayal of post-war, middle-class England.

1956
BRITISH POWER IN FLUX

With little colonial reform in Africa, independence campaigns arose across the country. The first major incident to expose imperial vulnerability was the Kenyan Mau-Mau guerrilla war (1952–56). Nations such as Britain became increasingly aware that decolonisation would not disrupt overseas economic interests, but would relieve them of imperial defence and administration. The 1956 Suez Crisis, in which France and Britain were forced to make a humiliating withdrawal from Egypt under US pressure, undermined the credibility of the colonial powers and revealed their declining global status. A major review of Britain's imperial position resulted in Ghana becoming the first independent 'black' nation in Africa (1957). By 1964 British prime minister Harold Macmillan (1894–1986) spoke of a 'wind of change', as decolonisation spread through Africa and the Caribbean.

Despite admirable defence by the Hungarians, the Russians finally succeeded in taking the capital, Budapest.

1956
GRACE KELLY MARRIES PRINCE RAINIER III OF MONACO

The marriage of an American movie queen to Europe's sole absolute monarch was the media sensation of the 1950s. Grace Kelly was blonde, cool and sophisticated. She came from a wealthy family, went to good schools and was determined to prove that she could work. She modelled, did some work in commercials and acted in a few Broadway plays before Hollywood beckoned. Her icy regality was spotted by Alfred Hitchcock who cast her with exquisite taste, in *Dial M for Murder*, and opposite James Stewart in *Rear Window*. While working on her third Hitchcock film, *To Catch a Thief*, she met Prince Rainier III, the ruler of the small principality of Monaco. A year later, in 1956, she married the Prince in spectacular ceremony and left Tinsel Town for a royal palace.

1956
HUNGARIAN UPRISING

On 23 October 1956 demonstrations called for Hungarian independence and a withdrawal of Russian forces from the country. Within three days, the demonstrations had developed into a full-scale revolt, with Hungarian nationalists openly defying the Russians and engaging in running battles in the cities. In the first few days an estimated 3,000 people died in their attempts to fight the tanks of the Soviet army. The prime minister, Imre Nagy,

19 OCTOBER 1956
Japan and USSR Make Peace

The state of war, which has existed between Japan and the USSR since the Second World War, is finally ended with a peace treaty. The terms of the agreement include an opening up of trade between the two nations and the way is now clear for Japan's admission to the United Nations.

promised that once the revolt had been suppressed he would enter into negotiations with the Russians for a withdrawal of troops. His words fell on deaf ears and it was the Russian troops who would settle the situation. By 5 November the Soviets had crushed the rebellion with a concerted operation against key points in the country. Hungarian soldiers had vainly attempted to bar the way into Budapest but against thousands of Russian troops backed by over 1,000 tanks they had little hope. The Defence Ministry and the Parliament fell at 9.00 a.m. and the last words heard from the prime minister over Radio Budapest were at 5.15 p.m. At 8.10 p.m. the radio station fell silent after desperate cries of 'Help Hungary'. The West, despite their concerns, seemed unwilling or unable to assist the Hungarians or to stop the Russians. The Russians would not allow dissent at any cost in their eastern European possessions.

1956–58
THE SEAGRAM BUILDING

The German architect Ludwig Mies van der Rohe (1886–1969), one of the principal founders of modern architecture and design, created a number of starkly beautiful glass and steel buildings which have made his name synonymous with the functionalist aesthetic of twentieth-century design. Perhaps the most spectacular of all Mies's high-rise structures is the Seagram Building in New York City (built between 1956 and 1958), a 38-storey tower clad in bronze and bronze-tinted glass, which he designed in collaboration with the distinguised American architect Philip Johnson. The Seagram Building is recognized as a masterpiece of American corporate architecture and design. The interiors were designed to complete the overall vision, with the external features repeated in the glass and bronze furnishings and decorative scheme.

The Seagram Building in New York, designed by Ludwig Mies van der Rohe.

1957
BORIS PASTERNAK PUBLISHES *DOCTOR ZHIVAGO*

Doctor Zhivago was a novel on an epic scale. It swept across three decades of Russian history, including the revolutions of 1905 and 1917 and their violent aftermath. But it was not all blood and guts; threaded through the narrative was a poetic beauty. Pasternak's descriptions of nature and human love, his religious imagery and philosophical reflections celebrated the human spirit and the value of compassion. It was hailed by western writers as a work of genius and awarded the Nobel Prize for Literature. Pasternak was overjoyed. Unfortunately, in Pasternak's homeland, *Doctor Zhivago* was not the unmitigated success it had been in the West. The author was labelled a 'traitor' by the Soviet Writers' Union on account of his hero's thoughts of disillusionment. Within a week of winning the prize, he had been expelled from the Union; as a result, he felt he could not accept the honour.

Pasternak's epic and revolutionary novel, ***Doctor Zhivago.***

14 JANUARY 1957
Movie Legend Dies

US film star Humphrey Bogart dies from cancer at the age of 57. Bogart had made his name playing tender-hearted tough-guys in films such as The African Queen (for which he won an Oscar), The Big Sleep and Casablanca.

1957
THE TREATY OF ROME

The Treaty of Rome, establishing the European Economic Community, was signed in March 1957. There were six member countries at first: France, West Germany, Italy, Belgium, the Netherlands and Luxembourg. These countries had been the members of the European Coal and Steel Community. The EEC came into effect on 1 January 1958; at the same time, the European Atomic Community was set up. Delegates from the six countries met in the European Economic Assembly in March 1958, under the presidency of Robert Schuman. At first the EEC, or the Common Market as it became known, was a strictly economic body. It encouraged trade between the members and set tariffs on imports from outside. The Treaty of Rome, however, contained clauses, which allowed for political union at some future date.

1957
MALAYAN INDEPENDENCE

After 170 years of British rule the largest of the Asian colonies gained its independence on 30 August 1957. In the capital, Kuala Lumpur, the chief minister Tunku Abdul

Rahman, proclaimed that this was the greatest day in the history of Malaya. The country had a rich ethnic mix of native Malays, Chinese, Indians, Eurasians and Europeans. He went on to praise the efforts of the British in suppressing the communist uprising that so nearly tore the country apart. Since the nineteenth century, Malaya had occupied a key position in the British Empire. It was a dangerous battleground during the Second World War, but the Japanese were finally defeated by the British, ably assisted by loyal Malays.

Cuban communist leader, Fidel Castro.

American movie legend, Humphrey Bogart, who died in 1957.

1957
THE HIGH WATERMARK OF COMMUNISM

In October 1957, the Soviet Union's considerable investment of resources into rocket technology paid off, with the launch into space of an unmanned satellite called *Sputnik* into space. Politicians and military leaders in the United States were alarmed. The United States had, in 1955, openly declared its intention of launching a space satellite in 1958 as part of International Geophysical Year. The Soviets had kept quiet, and beaten the United States to it. The advantage that the Soviets had in rocket technology enabled them to repeat the feat of beating the United States in what had been christened 'the Space Race'. In 1959, a Cuban civil war ended with the victory of Fidel Castro (b. 1927), a man who openly welcomed the support of Cuba's Communists for his regime.

6 FEBRUARY 1958

Munich Air Crash

One of the best football teams of the decade is decimated in a tragic air crash. The Manchester United team were on a flight to Munich after a game in Belgrade when the plane crashed on landing and ploughed into the airport building; seven players were killed outright. Matt Busby is one of the survivors.

1957
LARGEST RADIO TELESCOPE UNVEILED

After the Second World War, the British astronomer Alfred Lovell began working at the University of Manchester's botanical site at Jodrell Bank with war-surplus radar equipment. Researching into radio and radar astronomy, he began to construct what became known as the Lovell telescope: a fully steerable radio telescope with a reflector that measures 76 m (250 ft) in diameter. Operation began in 1957 shortly before the launch of *Sputnik I*, and the satellite's carrier rocket was tracked at Jodrell Bank. Most operational time at the site is devoted to astronomy rather than tracking and communication, but the telescope has been part of the tracking network for the US programme of space exploration and monitored most of the Soviet accomplishments.

1957
SPUTNIK 1 LAUNCHED

Sputnik I, the first satellite launched by man, was an 83-kg (184-lb) capsule. It was launched by the Soviet Union on 4 October 1957 and so heralded the Space Age. It achieved an Earth orbit with an apogee (farthest point from Earth) of 934 km (584 miles) and a perigee (nearest point) of 230 km (143 miles), circling the earth every 96 minutes and staying in orbit until 1958, when it fell back and burnt up in the Earth's atmosphere. A month later, on 3 November, the Soviets launched *Sputnik II*, weighing 508 kg (1,121 lb) and carrying the dog Laika, the first living creature put into space orbit. The flight proved that animals could exist in weightless conditions for an extended period of time, and placed the Soviet Union at the forefront of the international race to develop a space programme that included human flight. Eight further *Sputnik* missions with similar satellites carried out experiments on a variety of animals to test spacecraft life-support systems.

Members of Matt Busby's Manchester United team boarding the plane to Belgrade; the return journey would end in tragedy.

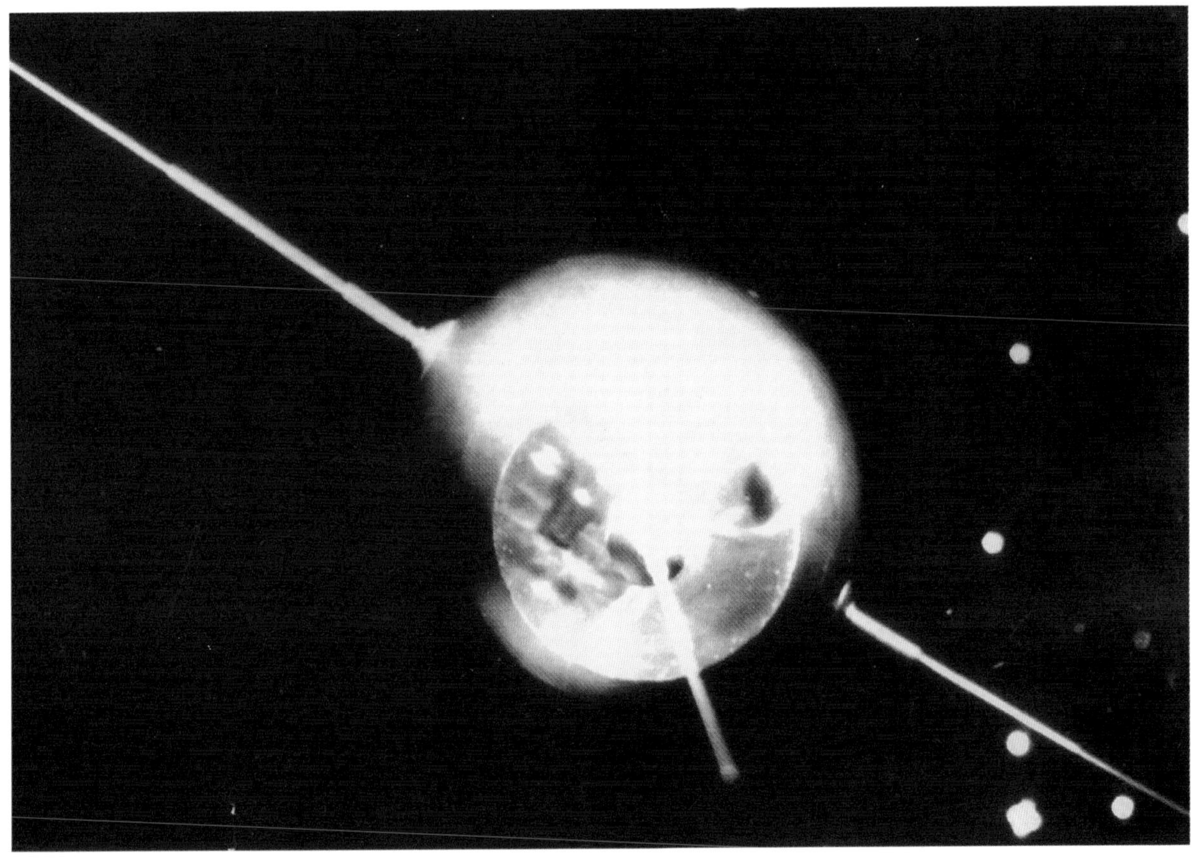

The Soviet Earth satellite ***Sputnik****, the first step towards the new 'space age'.*

1958
ESCALATING VIOLENCE IN CYPRUS

Smouldering discontent flared into violent rioting in Cyprus in January 1958. On the 28th, a British army vehicle drove through a Turkish demonstration and sparked off a series of riots that would leave seven dead and hundreds injured. The leader of the minority Turkish community, Rauf Denktash, managed to defuse the situation after a public appeal. Two Turks were killed and over 100 injured during the rioting. Violence flared again in June, claiming four more lives. A curfew was imposed on the 20th after Archbishop Makarios, the leader of the Greek-Cypriot community, rejected a peace plan. A further week of violence in July led to 31 more deaths.

1959
CUBA

Until 1959 Cuba was governed by a pro-American dictator, Batistá, but in 1959 he was overthrown by a group of rebels led by Fidel Castro. The USA cut off all aid to Cuba, and Castro in turn nationalized all US assets and property in Cuba. Soviet leader Khrushchev took advantage of the situation by agreeing to buy one million tonnes of Cuban sugar every year at inflated prices. This brought Cuba Soviet influence and Castro set up a Communist regime. Many US citizens were horrified. Communism now existed only 70 miles off the coast of Florida. Eisenhower, the US president, authorized an attempt to overthrow Castro by landing a force of Cuban exiles at the Bay of Pigs. The landing actually took place in April 1961, after Eisenhower had left office and was a disaster. The 1,500 Cubans were all killed or captured.

1959
MONKEYS IN SPACE

The first animals to travel in space and return alive were two monkeys. The *Jupiter Missile Cone*, in which they travelled 2,736 km (1,700 miles) and reached a height of 579 km (360 miles), was picked up from the Atlantic by the US navy. Able, a 3-kg (7-lb) rhesus monkey, and Baker, a slight, half-kg (one-pound) squirrel monkey were carefully monitored from the ground to see how they were affected by the stresses of space flight, particularly the weightlessness and the severe acceleration of the launch and then re-entry into the earth's atmosphere. Their performance of trained tasks was also closely observed. The tests were essential preliminaries to the manned space flights which were already in research and development. Seven human astronauts had already been selected.

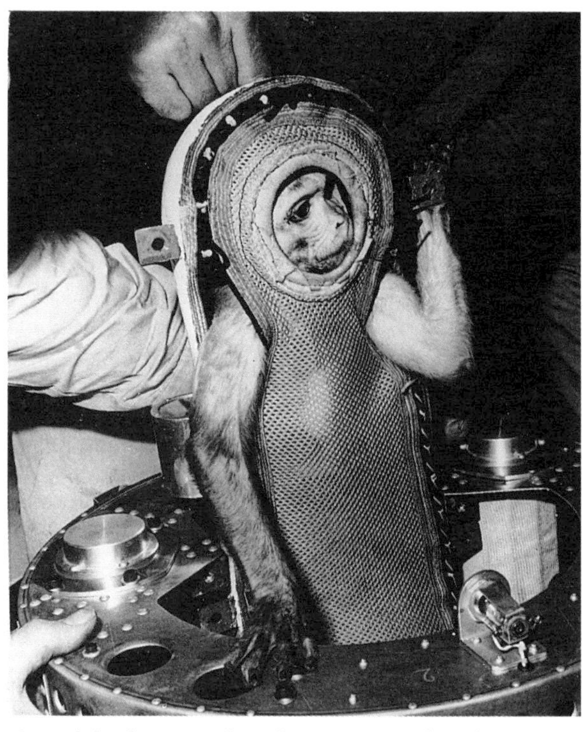

One of the rhesus monkeys that participated in the successful space-travel experiment.

The hovercraft prototype began life on a very humble scale, created from kitchen implements and a hair dryer.

1959
HOVERCRAFT TESTED

The first air-cushion vehicle, or hovercraft, stemmed from work done in the 1950s by the British electronics engineer Sir Christopher Cockerell. He constructed a model from two coffee tins and a hair dryer and measured its lift with kitchen scales. The idea was patented in 1955, and in 1959 the first full-scale ACV, the SR.N1, was successfully tested at Cowes, England. One of the largest of today's ACVs is the SR.N4, a class of vehicle that is used for ferry service across the English Channel. Hovercrafts cruise at up to 143 kph (77 knots), making them the fastest class of sea-worthy vehicles in the world.

The spiritual and temporal leader of Tibet, the 14th Dalai lama.

3 FEBRUARY 1959
The Day the Music Died

A plane carrying rock star Buddy Holly, together with the Big Bopper and Richie Valens crashes, killing all three. They were on their way from a concert at Clearwater to North Dakota and had decided to charter a plane at the last minute to avoid the long bus journey. Holly was only 22.

1959
DALAI LAMA GOES INTO EXILE

The 14th incarnation of the Dalai lama, the spiritual and temporal head of the Tibetan state, was born in 1935. Tibetan Buddhists believe each Dalai Lama is a reincarnation of his predecessor and also of Avalokitesvara. Enthroned in 1940, he temporarily fled in 1950–51 when the Chinese overran Tibet. In March 1959 he went into exile in protest at the Chinese annexation of Tibet; he escaped from Lhasa to India, and eventually settled at Dharmsala. The Chinese offered to remove a ban on his return providing he would no longer call for Tibet's independence. He was awarded the Nobel Peace Prize in 1989 for his commitment to the non-violent liberation of Tibet.

Chapter 7
1960–1969

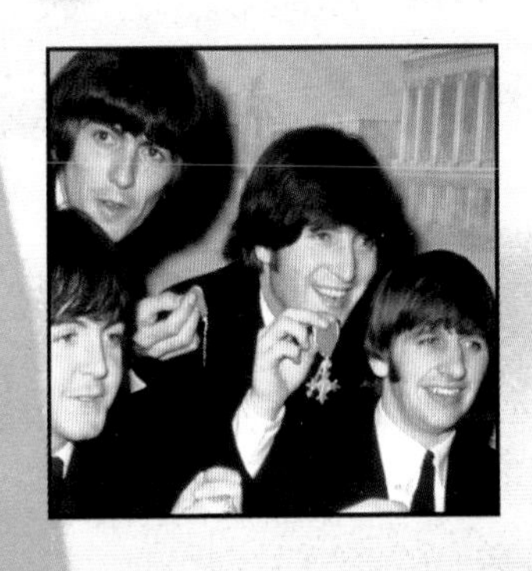

A coal mine in Wales; the Green Revolution stressed the importance of preserving non-renewable energy sources.

1960s
THE GREEN REVOLUTION

The Green Revolution is the term used since the 1960s to describe the effort to increase and diversify crop yields in developing countries. The American agricultural scientist Norman E. Borlaug is often considered the founder of the Green Revolution. Many countries have taken steps to implement Borlaug's programme for achieving agricultural efficiency. The programme stressed the need to abandon local, traditional strains of plants and breeds of animals in favour of new strains and breeds; conduct research to enable new procedures to be adapted to local conditions; obtain long-term support from local government to apply and extend knowledge; and achieve changes in the infrastructure in order to stabilize the numbers of people in a society and to enhance the quality of their lives.

1960s
R. D. LAING AND ANTI-PSYCHIATRY

R. D. Laing (1927–89) was one of the most radical critics of psychiatric practice of the twentieth century. In his books *The Divided Self* (1960) and *Sanity, Madness and the Family* (1964) he rejected the orthodox view that schizophrenia was simply an illness and saw it instead as a normal response to an impossible social situation. He therefore favoured group therapies and attacked chemical therapies and electric shock treatments. He also viewed madness not as a sign of mental decline, but as a phase through which the mind needs to pass whilst healing itself. This led him to see the therapist as a companion on a journey through madness.

R. D. Laing, who favoured electric shock treatment for mental illnesses such as schizophrenia and depression.

1960s
BAN THE BOMB!

Protest soon became the virtual symbol of the 1960s, with rallies, marches, demonstrations and clashes with the police. The Nuclear Age which followed the atomic bombing of Japan in 1945, produced rowdy, vociferous

Malcolm X used violent means in his campaign for civil rights in the United States.

demonstrations in Britain, France and Germany, demanding that the government eschew atomic weapons. The war in Vietnam, too, roused fury at what young Americans, British and French saw as an immoral conflict. Some Americans went to Canada to avoid being drafted: they were dubbed cowards by some, but heroes by others. In America, too, Martin Luther King (1929–68) used peaceful, but determined, methods to promote black equality. Malcolm X (Malcolm Little, 1926–65) preferred more violent ways to achieve the same object. Both were assassinated.

1960
PICCARD AND WALSH DIVE TO BOTTOM OF PACIFIC

On 23 January 1960, Jacques Piccard and navy lieutenant Donald Walsh descended 10,912 m (35,800 ft) into the Mariana Trench of the Pacific Ocean. This is the deepest known point on the Earth's surface, located about 320 km (200 miles) east of the Mariana Islands. The trench contains a steep-sided gorge called Challenger Deep, into which the two men descended in the bathyscaphe *Trieste*, a pioneering form of submersible craft, invented by Piccard's father Auguste. This was able to withstand the intense pressures of the sea and was capable of measuring currents, temperature and salinity of the water. It consisted of a compressible, petrol-filled tank, with a small, pressure-resistant sphere to hold a crew of two. The bathyscaphe undertook a series of record-setting dives, which have proved enduring.

9 NOVEMBER 1960

Kennedy for President

John Fitzgerald Kennedy narrowly beats his Republican opponent, vice-president Richard Nixon, to the presidency. He is the youngest man ever to hold this office (43) – and the first Roman Catholic.

1960
SHARPEVILLE MASSACRE

On 21 March 1960, South African police opened fire on a large crowd of black Africans demonstrating outside the police station in Sharpeville, a township on the outskirts of Johannesburg. The newly formed Pan Africanist Congress (PAC) had called for a nationwide day of protest against one of the fundamental policies of apartheid – the ruling that all blacks had to carry papers or 'passes'. All over South Africa, supporters of the PAC gathered at local police stations without their passes. In Sharpeville some 20,000 demonstrators assembled, and the police started shooting. Sixty-seven peaceful demonstrators were killed and another 178 were wounded. Hendrik Verwoerd's Nationalist government declared a state of emergency and banned both the PAC and the African National Congress. The massacre inspired widespread international condemnation, and trade embargoes ensued. A year later South Africa was expelled from the Commonwealth of Nations.

Protestors demonstrating about the apartheid policy of the enforced carrying of papers or 'passes' were shot at by South African police in March 1960.

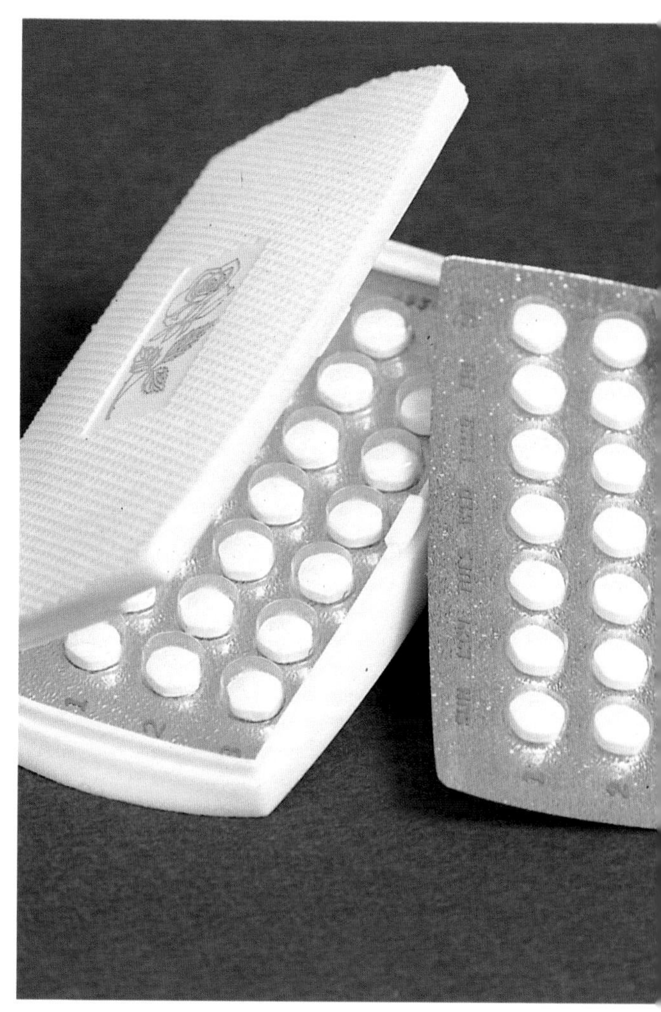

The female contraceptive pill, launched in 1961.

1960
FIRST LASERS DEMONSTRATED

Laser is an acronym for 'light amplification by stimulated emission of radiation'. Lasers are devices for producing a narrow beam of light, capable of travelling over vast distances without dispersion, and of being focused to give enormous power densities. The laser operates on a principle similar to that of a maser and was invented by US physicists Charles Townes and Arthur Schawlow in 1958. The demonstration of the world's first practical laser was by the US physicist Theodore Maiman in 1960. The use of lasers includes communication (a laser beam is capable of carrying more information than radio waves), cutting, drilling, welding, satellite tracking, medical and biological research and surgery.

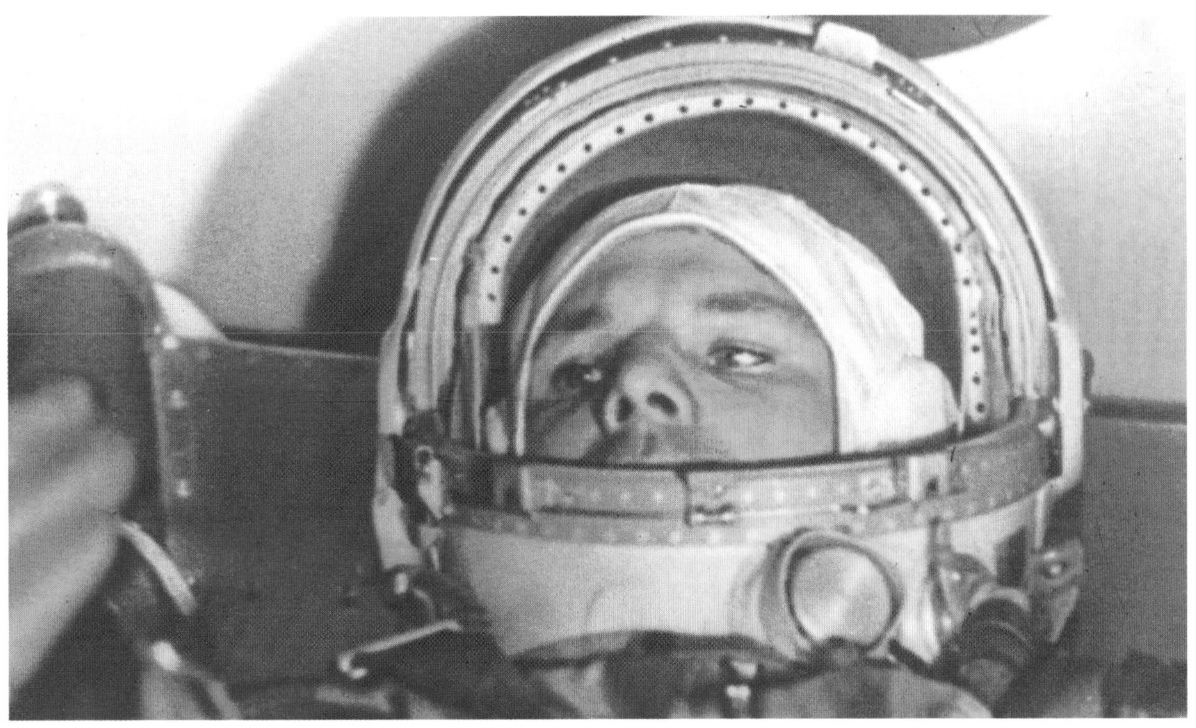

The first man in space, Soviet cosmonaut Yuri Gagarin.

1961
FEMALE PILL LAUNCHED

Gregory Pincus was an American endocrinologist who, in 1944, founded the Worcester Foundation for Experimental Biology. This became an important centre for the study of steroid hormones and mammalian reproduction. In 1951 he began to look at the anti-fertility properties of steroids. This led on to using synthesized hormones to inhibit ovulation and thus prevent pregnancy in laboratory animals. He combined the female hormones of oestrogen and progesterone and found that this inhibited the production of eggs and made the mucus produced by the cervix hostile to sperm. From this research he was able to perfect an oral contraceptive for women, which was launched in 1961.

1961
YURI GAGARIN ORBITS THE EARTH

On 12 April 1961, the Soviet cosmonaut Yuri Gagarin (1934–68) became the first man in space as he was launched into orbit in the *Vostok 1* spaceship. Gagarin, an air-force jet pilot, was chosen with the first group of Soviet cosmonauts in March 1960. His ship reached a maximum altitude of 327 km (203 miles) and circled the Earth once before landing near the Volga River. After the flight, Gagarin became training director of the womens' cosmonaut programme and returned to space for the *Soyuz* programme. He was killed in a MiG trainer jet crash in 1968. A crater on the far side of the Moon is named after him.

6 JUNE 1961
Carl Gustav Jung Dies

The Swiss psychiatrist Carl Gustav Jung dies at the age of 85. Together with Sigmund Freud, he is considered the founder of modern psychoanalysis, although he disagreed with Freud's emphasis on sexuality.

1961
BAY OF PIGS INVASION

In April 1961, a short-lived but potentially dangerous and ill-considered invasion took place in Cuba. Some 1,500 anti-Castro Cuban exiles had been formed into a fighting unit by the CIA and trained to overthrow the communist leadership. Following a landing in the Bay of Pigs, 145 km (90 miles) south-west of the capital Havana, the incursion only lasted four days. The project had been authorized by Eisenhower and was carried out during John F. Kennedy's presidency. Cuba had continually been a thorn in America's side and Castro was violently anti-American. Later, in 1962, Soviet missiles were installed on the island and Krushchev, by agreeing to remove them, narrowly averted war.

18 SEPTEMBER 1961
UN Leader Killed in Air Crash

Secretary-general of the United Nations, Dag Hammarskjöld, is killed when the plane carrying him to Ndola to meet with exiled Katanga leader Moise Tshombe plunges to earth without warning; there is speculation of sabotage.

1961
THE BERLIN WALL

The construction of the Berlin Wall was started in August 1961. It separated families and trapped people who had crossed to the other side of Berlin. For 12 years people had been escaping from East Berlin to West Berlin, and by 1961 their numbers were reaching thousands every week. Most of the people who escaped were skilled workers, doctors or engineers. The Wall was an attempt to stop the drain of people from East to West. It was very

Soldiers returning from the short-lived Bay of Pigs invasion.

effective, but it did not stop people trying to escape. The Wall also increased tension between the superpowers. The US president Kennedy visited West Berlin to show his support for its citizens.

1961
NUREYEV DEFECTS TO THE WEST

Rudolf Nureyev was a Russian ballet dancer with extraordinary technique and a compelling stage presence, who magnetized audiences with his passion. He trained in Leningrad and was then accepted as a soloist at the Kirov Ballet Company. He was billed as their principal dancer on its European tour in 1961, but he was apolitical, non-conformist and professionally ambitious. In Paris, he gave a superb performance of *Sleeping Beauty*, and then at

Armed guards patrolling the Berlin Wall, the barrier which divided Germany into East and West.

the airport refused to depart with the rest of the Company, seeking asylum in France. He danced with several companies until, in 1962, he became 'permanent guest artist' at the Royal Ballet with Margot Fonteyn as his partner.

After touring with the Kirov Ballet Company, the world-famous dancer Nuryev defected from Russia and sought political asylum in France.

1961
THE WRETCHED OF THE EARTH

Criticism of colonialism and the brutality of missionaries dates back to the time of Bartolome de Las Casas (1474–1566), a Spanish Dominican missionary who defended the rights of indigenous peoples in Latin America. Frantz Fanon's (1925–61) book about colonialism in Algeria, *The Wretched of the Earth*, published in 1961, was one source of the modern Liberation Theology movement. Liberation Theology saw Christ as the friend of the poor, who lived amongst them and died for them. It stressed biblical opposition to the pursuit of wealth and biblical teachings on justice. Archbishop Oscar Romero, who was assassinated by the El Salvador government for speaking out on behalf of the poor, was their leading martyr.

1962
THOMAS KUHN

Thomas Kuhn (1922–96), Professor of Philosophy at Massachusetts Institute of Technology, was responsible for a new understanding of how scientific models of the world develop. His major work was *The Structure of Scientific Revolutions* (1962), in which he rejected the view of empiricists that mankind was slowly evolving towards truth, and instead argued that man was simply creating coherent models that map reality, and that these collapse and are replaced whenever experiments reveal insoluble contradictions in the model. He called each of these accepted sets of theories paradigms. He concluded, like Karl Popper, that scientific theories cannot be true, but should be valued in accordance with their usefulness.

Model showing a DNA molecule; Watson and Crick received the Nobel Prize for their work on genetics.

1962
WATSON AND CRICK RECEIVE THE NOBEL PRIZE

Deoxyribonucleic acid (DNA) is the complex giant molecule that contains, in a chemically coded form, all the information required to build, control and maintain a living organism. In 1949 British molecular biologist Francis Crick and US biologist James Watson together began to research the molecular structure of DNA, trying to crack the code of nucleic acids within that molecule that enable characteristics to be passed down through generations. During the 1950s they realized that the molecule was two strands wrapped around each other in a spiral, or helix, each strand carrying a sequence of bases which carry the code of life. They were awarded the Nobel Prize for Medicine in 1962.

1962
EYEBALL TO EYEBALL

On 17 October 1962, John F. Kennedy, the president of the USA, was shown photographs of Soviet missile bases in Cuba. This meant that Soviet missiles could be launched at most US cities and there would be no defence against these attacks. After a week of intense

> 5 AUGUST 1962
> **Marilyn Found Dead**
>
> The body of film star Marilyn Monroe is found in her Hollywood bungalow, an empty bottle of sleeping pills by her side. Monroe had appeared in more than 20 movies and had established herself as the sex symbol of her generation.

Andy Warhol's famous Coca Cola bottle painting.

discussions, Kennedy decided to blockade Cuba and stop any more Soviet ships going there. For a week US forces were on full alert and many people around the world expected that nuclear war would break out. In fact Nikita Khrushchev, the Soviet prime minister, realised that he had made a mistake and sent two messages to Kennedy – one was threatening, the other conciliatory. Kennedy replied to the conciliatory message and the crisis was settled peacefully. The Soviet bases in Cuba were destroyed and the USA agreed not to interfere in Cuban affairs.

1962
ANDY WARHOL

Andy Warhol (1928–87) was the founder of Pop art. In 1960, he produced the first of his paintings depicting enlarged comic-strip images, and he pioneered the development of the process whereby an enlarged photographic image is transferred to a silk-screen which is then placed on a canvas and inked from the rear. This technique enabled Warhol to produce the series of slightly varied, mass-media images that he began in 1962. Incorporating such items as Campbell's Soup tins, Coca-Cola bottles and the faces of celebrities, most notably Marilyn Monroe and Chairman Mao, these works have been taken as comments on the banality, harshness and ambiguity of American culture. In these works, the same image is repeated across the entire surface of the canvas, and the aura of mass production is intensified by Warhol's technique rather than the serial repetition.

Hollywood sex symbol Marilyn Monroe, who was found dead in her home in August 1962.

Vietnam was in political upheaval, with people rioting against the government.

1963
THE RUSSIAN DROUGHT

In 1963, a disastrous drought in the USSR caused a decline of about 25 per cent in the country's wheat production. The government consequently needed large wheat stocks immediately. It purchased huge stocks from Canada and Australia, to the point where those countries' stocks were reduced almost to nothing. Then, in October 1963, the president of the USA, John Kennedy, authorized the first sales of surplus wheat to the USSR. An order for one million imperial tons of wheat, worth nearly $80 million, was placed by Russia with the Continental Grain Co., representing the largest individual sale in the history of the world wheat trade. By March 1964, the Soviet Union had contracted for the supply of more than 10 million tons of western wheat, and had become by far the world's largest importer.

1963
PROTESTS IN SAIGON

Quang Doc, a Buddhist monk, committed ritual suicide by burning himself alive in Saigon on 13 June 1963. Extremist Buddhists rocked the capital with rioting and protests against the maltreatment they received at the hands of President Diem's regime. The Vietnamese government was losing a war against the Vietcong; the government's position was not helped by its indifference and outright

JFK is shot in Dallas while driving through the streets with his wife Jackie.

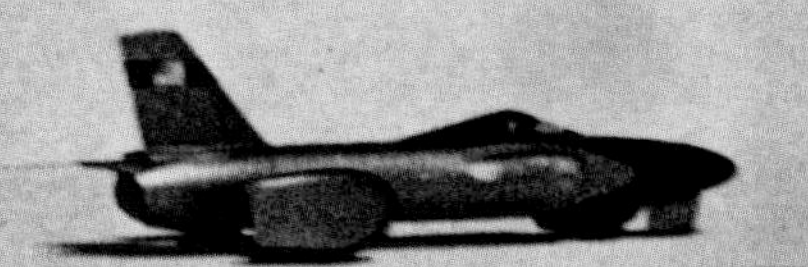

Spirit of America being slowed down by a parachute after breaking the world land speed record.

violence towards its own people. In August the army arrested 100 monks and 600 students who had been protesting. By September they were arresting civilian leaders at will. The US seriously considered a radical reappraisal of their role in the country and threatened a reduction in military and economic aid to Diem.

1963
JFK SHOT IN DALLAS, TEXAS

On 22 November 1963 John F. Kennedy was assassinated while on a state visit to Dallas, Texas. He was shot several times by rifle fire while being driven in an open-top car through the streets, with his wife Jackie sitting beside him. A gunman, Lee Harvey Oswald, was arrested shortly after and was named as the assassin. Oswald himself was shot and killed at point-blank range by Jack Ruby two days later, while under heavy police escort on a jail transfer. Oswald was an ex-marine who had gone to live in the USSR in 1959 and had returned when he could not become a Soviet citizen. Jack Ruby was a Dallas nightclub owner, associated with both the criminal underworld and the police. A number of conspiracy theories have been woven around the Kennedy assassination, which was investigated by a special commission headed by Chief Justice Earl Warren. The commission determined that Oswald operated as a lone assassin. It is, however, often speculated that Oswald was a 'patsy', someone set up to take the blame for the shooting. A later congressional report re-examined the evidence and determined that Kennedy 'was probably assassinated as a result of a conspiracy' though it did not venture into what that conspiracy was.

13 OCTOBER 1963

For My Next Trick...

Craig Breedlove breaks the land speed record in his specially designed car Spirit of America. He achieves 846.94 kph (526.28 mph), but has to swim for his life when the car dives into a pond. Clambering to safety, Breedlove jokes 'for my next trick, I'll set myself afire!'

1964
MARTIN LUTHER KING JR WINS NOBEL PEACE PRIZE

Martin Luther King Jr (1929–68) was a man of profound morality with a powerful belief in the rights of every person, of every race, religion and class, to have peace. He devoted his life to the fight for full citizenship rights of the poor, disadvantaged and racially oppressed in the United States. Inspired by the life of Mahatma Gandhi, he travelled widely, lecturing and writing on his dream for peace and equality. He organized a massive march on Washington in 1963 where, in his ingenious 'I Have a Dream' speech, he 'subpoenaed the conscience of the nation before the judgement seat of morality'. In January 1964, *Time* magazine chose King as Man of the Year, the first black American so honoured. Later that year he became the youngest recipient of the Nobel Peace Prize.

US Civil Rights leader Martin Luther King, Jr.

8 FEBRUARY 1964

Beatlemania Sweeps the US

The pop quartet from Liverpool, the Beatles, arrive at Kennedy Airport in New York to be greeted by thousands of screaming fans. The group are to appear on the Ed Sullivan Show the following evening and their success stateside seems assured.

1964
TONKIN GULF INCIDENT

After the Tonkin Gulf Incident in August 1964, in which the US navy claimed that two of its ships were attacked by North Vietnamese patrol boats, US Congress passed a resolution to take unlimited action to resolve the crisis in South-east Asia. An attack on a US base at Pleiku in February 1965 was used as the justification for starting air attacks on the North; these were to be a daily feature of the war until 1968. The US began sending in combat troops to Vietnam in April 1965, increasing steadily until March 1968. The political crisis simmering in Saigon was eased with the emergence of Nguyen Cao Ky as prime minister (1965–67), in the establishment of a new constitution in 1966, and with the election of Nguyen Van Thieu as president in 1967.

Refugees from Vietnam being helped by US marines.

1964
US CIVIL RIGHTS ACT

In response to spiralling violence against black and white civil rights activists, and following the murder of a number of American children and the bombing of dozens of black churches throughout the South, the US government passed several new laws, the most important of which were enacted in 1964 and 1965. The Civil Rights Act, passed in 1964, undermined the remaining structure of the Jim Crow laws (which had set up a racial caste system in the South) and provided federal protection for those fighting for civil rights. The Voting Rights Act (1965) provided for federal action to put an end to actions by local governments and individuals that interfered with the right of African-Americans to register and vote. Both these laws were upheld in challenges before the US Supreme Court.

1964
NELSON MANDELA IMPRISONED

African nationalist leader Nelson Mandela was a successful lawyer in Johannesburg before joining the banned African National Congress (ANC) in 1944. For the next 20 years he led a campaign of defiance against the South African government and its racist policies, and in 1961 he organized a three-day national strike in protest. Despite giving a memorable four-hour defence speech at his trial in 1964, he was sentenced to life imprisonment for political offences. He continued to be a powerful symbol of unity for the anti-apartheid movement and an international campaign for his release was launched, led by his wife, Winnie, who was herself continually subjected to restrictions on her own personal freedom.

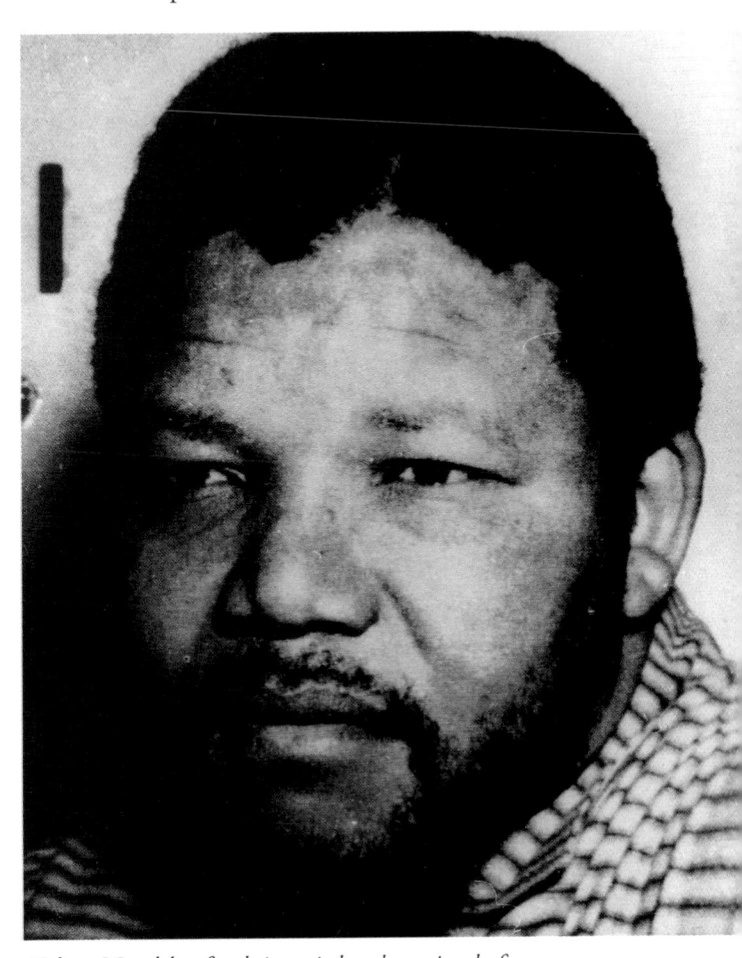

Nelson Mandela after being tried and convicted of political offences.

1964
JEAN-PAUL SARTRE DECLINES THE NOBEL PRIZE FOR LITERATURE

Existentialism swept through Europe in the wake of the Second World War, and Jean-Paul Sartre was its intellectual leader. Previously, he taught philosophy until he was drafted at the start of the war. Captured by the Germans, he managed to escape and became a leader in the resistance movement. After the war he devoted himself to writing, expounding in particular the existentialist philosophy. Sartre maintained that life had no purpose or meaning, beyond the goals that each person set for himself.
In 1964, he refused the Nobel Prize for Literature, saying that it was unfair to readers to add the weight of such extraneous influences to the power of the writer's words.

Jean-Paul Sartre, who refused the Nobel Prize for Literature.

30 JANUARY 1965

The Voice of a Nation Dies

World leaders join the British public in mourning the death of Sir Winston Churchill as he is laid to rest in a village churchyard in Oxfordshire. Churchill had been an active Member of Parliament for over 60 years and had led the country through the despair of both World Wars.

1965
BEATLES AWARDED MBES

The Beatles, a pioneering pop quartet from Liverpool, changed the world of music. They started off in black leather, conforming to American rock'n'roll standards. Then they changed into matching suits and turtlenecks and sang devastating pop harmonies that created hysteria. Headlines were full of 'Beatlemania', as their own songs took over the charts. They kept a sarcastic edge, and a witty irreverence despite the uproar. In 1963 at the Royal Command Variety Show John Lennon joked: 'The people in the cheap seats can clap, the rest of you rattle your jewellery.' Two years later they were outside Buckingham Palace posing with their MBEs, the youngest peacetime recipients of the honour.

1965
ASTRONAUTS IN SPACE

Colonel Alexander Leoner of the Soviet Union was the first man to leave his spacecraft and walk in space. Tethered only by a thin cord attached to his craft, the cosmonaut

Liverpool supergroup The Beatles showing off their MBEs.

emerged in a bright orange spacesuit and somersaulted against the heavens. Leoner remained outside for about 10 minutes and travelled 483 km (300 miles) in that short time, 4,828 km (3,000 miles) above a small, blue Earth. A few months later, an American, Major Edmund White, climbed out of *Gemini* while it was over the United States. He took photographs and was able to manoeuvre by using a compressed-oxygen gun to propel himself along. He spent about 14 minutes outside, and had to be persuaded to return to his craft.

1965
THE INDO-PAKISTAN (BANGLADESH) WAR

As a result of border violations, many Pakistanis crossed into Indian territory on 14 August 1965. The Indians rushed troops to seal the Haji Pir pass, leading to a large tank battle on 1 September. Under air cover, the Indians counter-attacked and crossed the border in the Lahore sector of western Pakistan, making thrusts towards Sialkot and the Sind. The ensuing tank battles were the biggest seen since the Second World War. On 22 September, after seven weeks of fighting, over 20,000 were killed or wounded, nearly 600 tanks destroyed and over 100 aircraft shot down. Under the terms of the Tashkent Agreement (1966), the two sides agreed to settle their disputes by peaceful means.

Alexander Leoner became the first man to walk in space.

1965
THE CULTURAL REVOLUTION

In 1965, Chairman Mao announced the beginning of the Cultural Revolution. This was in fact an attempt by Mao to regain his dominant position in the party. He set up soldiers called 'Red Guards', who put up posters throughout the country praising the 'thoughts of Chairman Mao', which were published in a 'Red Book'. They attacked teachers, intellectuals, scientists and civil servants, who were often humiliated by being tied up and forced to recite from Mao's book. All forms of traditional Chinese culture were ridiculed, as were all foreign influences. Within two years the country was in complete chaos and even Mao was forced to order the Red Guards to stop their attacks in 1967.

Mao Zedong, instigator of the Cultural Revolution in China, which was enforced through the military.

Mary Quant is widely credited with having invented the mini-skirt.

1966
MARY QUANT AWARDED THE OBE

Did she or didn't she invent the 'Mini'? Whatever the truth of the matter, it is generally agreed that Quant (b. 1934) popularized the look, along with the 'kooky' styles we now associate with the Swinging Sixties: black stockings, hot pants, tall boots, tight polo-necks, sleeveless shifts and pinafore dresses. Quant, who began making clothes in her bedsit, went on to open one of Britain's first concept boutiques, Bazaar, in 1955. Here, customers could buy 'a bouillabaisse of clothes and accessories' under one roof. Other shops followed, as well as a mail-order service, an American line, cosmetics, toys, hats, scarves, mugs and even bed-linen. In the interim, Quant designed for Alligator rainwear, Kangol and Dupont and continued to exploit and develop London street looks: woolly tights (1958), sleeveless shifts (1959), coloured nail varnish (1966) and vinyl hot pants (1970). In 1966, she was awarded the OBE.

1966
FLOODS IN FLORENCE

A combination of heavy rains and centuries of human neglect was the cause of the River Arno's overflowing its banks and flooding Florence, Italy, on 4 November 1966; 149 people drowned and over 100,000 citizens were trapped in their homes. Thousands of priceless art treasures were destroyed and thousands more damaged. The 64-kph (40-mph) flood tore through the city, the water rising in some places to 6 m (20 ft), submerging sculptures, paintings, mosaics and manuscripts in the city's libraries. The salvage operations revealed that the municipal treasury was depleted and that, despite flood plans since the 1600s, the city had done little more than replace the riverbanks with high walls.

1967
APOLLO SPACECRAFT BURNS

Virgil 'Gus' Grissom, Edmund White and Roger Chaffee entered *Apollo 1* on 27 January 1967 for a routine countdown test. The command module was filled with pure oxygen, as

> 28 MAY 1967
>
> **Sailing Solo Round the World**
>
> Sir Francis Chichester arrives back at Portsmouth after sailing alone round the world in a trip that covered 57,000 km (35,625 miles). Chichester, in his mid-sixties and suffering from cancer, is later knighted with the same sword used to knight Sir Francis Drake.

The aftermath of the floods in Florence – widespread destruction of property and loss of life.

was usual, and the test proceeded slowly. By 6.30 p.m., the simulated countdown had reached 10. Suddenly Grissom shouted, 'Fire in the spacecraft'. Seconds later, Chaffee called out, 'We've got a bad fire', and flames lashed from the capsule. Technicians tried to reach them, but the heat and smoke drove them back. The hatch, their only escape route, took over a minute to open, but the astronauts were unconscious in seconds from smoke inhalation. After their tragic deaths, the *Apollo* space programme was delayed for 18 months to produce a safer and more reliable craft.

1967
TORREY CANYON DISASTER

The massive tanker *Torrey Canyon* ran aground on a reef between the Scilly Isles and Land's End in Cornwall. Rocks ripped the bottom from the boat, and thousands of gallons of oil immediately began to pour from the jagged hole, causing a slick which covered some 675 sq km (260 sq ft) of sea water. On 28 and 29 March 1967, Royal Air Force bombers dropped explosives, aviation fuel and napalm to sink the wreck and burn away any remaining fuel. But it was too late for the beaches, which were polluted with a sludgy black mess. Birds' feathers clogged up with the sticky oil, making floating or feeding impossible. The beaches were cleaned up by the summer, but 25,000 sea birds had been killed.

The Argentinian revolutionary leader Che Guevara.

1967
THE SIX-DAY WAR

The Six-Day War grew out of the general Arab-Israeli struggle that had been ongoing for some years; Egypt had blockaded the Gulf of Aqaba, a vital transportation route to Israeli shipping – a move that Israel regarded as an act of aggression. Hostilities began on 5 June 1967 with a massive pre-emptive strike by Israel that crippled the Arabs' air capacity. Israeli forces then quickly moved to occupy the Gaza Strip and pushed into the Sinai. At the same time Israelis fought Jordanians in Old Jerusalem and advanced into Syria. By 10 June, when the fighting was halted, Israel controlled the entire Sinai Peninsula and all Jordanian territory west of the River Jordan, as well as the strategic Golan Heights of Syria. The Suez Canal was almost impassable until 1975.

10 SEPTEMBER 1967

Gibraltar Stays British

The citizens of Gibraltar reject claims of sovereignty made by General Franco of Spain and vote almost unanimously to remain a British colony. 12,182 of the population voted; of these only 44 were in favour of the change.

1967
CHE GUEVARA EXECUTED

The Argentinian communist revolutionary leader, Che Guevara, was born in 1928. He graduated in medicine at the university of Buenos Aires in 1953, but left Argentina soon after because of his opposition to Perón's government. He then joined Fidel Castro's revolutionary movement in Mexico in 1955

and played a significant role in the Cuban revolution in 1956–59. Following this he held government posts under Castro. An activist of revolution elsewhere, he became a hero of left-wing youth in the 1960s. After leaving Cuba in 1965 to become a guerrilla leader in South America, he was captured by government troops while trying to stage a revolt and was executed in 1967.

1967
FIRST HEART TRANSPLANT

Norman Shumway achieved the first successful heart transplant in a dog in 1958 and spent the next decade refining the technique and improving immune suppression in animal models. However, it was South African surgeon Christiaan Barnard who performed the first

General Franco of Spain, who hoped to gain sovereignty of Gibraltar.

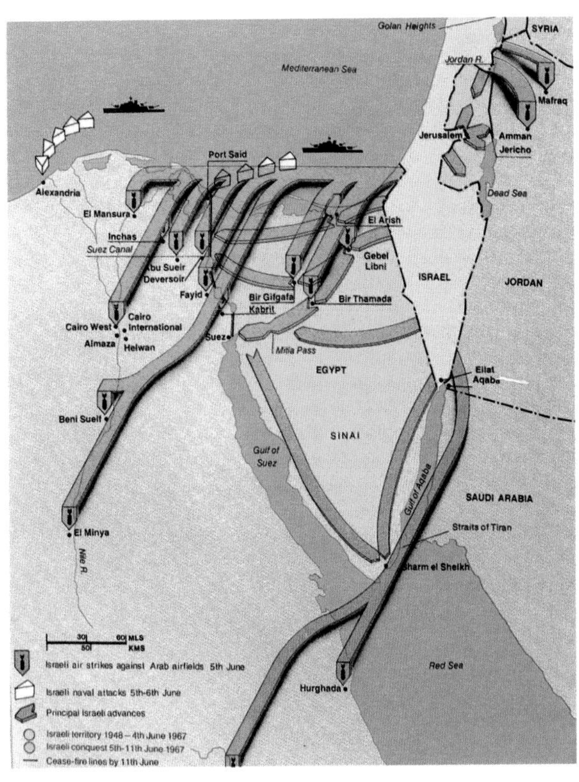

Map showing movements during the Arab-Israeli Six-Day War.

human heart transplant, on 3 December 1967 in Cape Town. The patient, 54-year-old Louis Washkansky, lived for 18 days. His success was followed by numerous attempts at other medical centres, with 101 heart transplants undertaken around the world within 12 months. Despite problems with immune rejection and poor survival rates, Shumway and Barnard continued developing their methods until 50 per cent of patients lived for at least five years after surgery.

Yuri Gagarin, the first man in space, who was killed in a fighter jet accident in 1968.

27 MARCH 1968

Gagarin Dies in the Air

The first man in space, Russian cosmonaut Yuri Gagarin, is killed in a MiG-15 jet training accident near Moscow. Gagarin, whose pioneering space journey will ensure his place in history for ever, was only 34 years old.

1968
THE TET OFFENSIVE

United States resolve was seriously shaken in February 1968 by the Tet Offensive, in which the communist Viet Cong guerrillas initiated major battles in Hue, Saigon and other towns. A crisis was reached in March 1968 when the US commander General Westmoreland asked for another 200,000 troops to go to Vietnam in addition to the 550,000 already there. By this time, there were also Koreans and Australians in Vietnam plus the 400,000 South Vietnamese under arms. Faced with a serious monetary crisis at precisely the same time, President Johnson decided against sending any more troops to Vietnam, and announced a limitation of bombing raids on the North. Before the end of 1968 the bombing had been halted completely and peace talks had opened in Paris.

1968
MARTIN LUTHER KING ASSASSINATED

At the height of his career, Martin Luther King called for a 'reconstruction of the entire society, a revolution of value', which gained him widespread support around the world, but also set up a network of conspirators who considered him to be a threat to Americanism. Early in 1968, King began to plan a multi-racial march on Washington to demand an end to all forms of discrimination and the funding of a $12-bn Economic Bill of Rights. While organizing the campaign, he flew to Memphis, Tennessee, to offer support to striking sanitation workers. On 4 April 1968, King was assassinated. The violent death of this moral and socially conscious man of peace sent shock waves around the country, and resulted in rioting in black ghettos. James Earl Ray was convicted of King's murder, but theorists believe that his death was planned by more than one man. In 1983, King's birthday was designated a national holiday.

1968
INVASION OF CZECHOSLOVAKIA BY RUSSIA

♲ The Prague Spring of 1968 turned into a Russian Winter as hundreds of thousands of Soviet troops brutally crushed the revolt in Czechoslovakia. Desperate Czechs attempted to stem the tide of tanks and troops with their bare hands as Alexander Dubcek, the reformist leader, was taken away in an armoured personnel carrier. Dubcek had hoped that the threat of invasion would not be carried out, but his beliefs were rapidly dispelled as the Russian tanks rolled across the border. As the invasion seemed imminent, prominent individuals switched sides and the Communist Party newspaper suddenly denounced the very reforms it had supported in previous weeks. According to the Soviet press agency, TASS, the Czechs welcomed the Russians with open arms, but pictures and reports from the country told a very different story. A one-hour strike was called on the 23rd to protest against the invasion. On the following day Dubcek began a series of discussions with the Soviet leadership. Even when the tanks disappeared in September the curfews and censorship stayed in place. More protests occurred in October when it was revealed that the Warsaw Pact troops would remain in the country for the foreseeable future. Desperate disobedience continued into November, with students occupying Prague University in protest against government repression.

The assassination of Martin Luther King caused widespread outrage and mourning.

The pioneering plane, ***Concorde****, the most famous supersonic aircraft.*

1969
CONCORDE'S FIRST FLIGHTS

The *Concorde* is the best-known supersonic transport (SST), the result of a joint initiative undertaken by the governments of Great Britain and France in 1962 to build a civil transport aeroplane that could fly at twice the speed of sound. The prototype made her first flight from Toulouse on 2 March 1969, and after considerable further development a lengthened and refined model entered service with British Airways and Air France on 21 January 1976. The *Concorde* had the longest and most thorough testing procedure of any commercial aeroplane. The *Concorde*, which flies at 2,333 kph (1,450 mph), did not achieve its goal of flying at twice the speed of sound until 4 November 1970.

1969
FIRST MAN ON THE MOON

Millions of television viewers from all around the world watched as Neil Armstrong, commander of *Apollo 11*, climbed down the ladder of *Eagle*, the lunar module. As he placed his foot on the surface of the Moon, his voice crackled through the static: 'That's one small step for a man, and one giant leap for mankind.' Armstrong was joined by Edwin 'Buzz' Aldrin, and the two men in the Moon's low gravity, leaving their footprints in the dust. The surface was like 'a fine powder ... it has a soft beauty of its own'. A few hours earlier, the world had heard: 'Houston. Tranquillity Base. The Eagle has landed,' and now there were men on the Moon.

Neil Armstrong, who successfully landed in the lunar module with fellow astronauts Buzz Aldrin and Michael Collins, and took the first steps on the moon.

1969
WOODSTOCK POP FESTIVAL

Monterey may have been the first, but Woodstock was the biggest. Nearly half a million people gathered in the fields of a farm in upstate New York for a celebration of peace, love and music. Thunderstorms crackled overhead, and the torrential rain turned the ground into a mudslick, but still the bands played on. A little-known folk singer, Richie Havens, made history when he opened the festival; Sweetwater, who were meant to be first on, had got stuck in one of the 16-km (10-mile) tailbacks that radiated out from the venue. Sly and The Family Stone, and English rockers The Who were the stars of Saturday. By the Sunday, inadequate sanitation and lack of food and drink were beginning to take their toll. Helicopters airlifted supplies to the uncomfortable audience. Joe Cocker wowed the crowd with his uncoordinated dancing, and Crosby, Stills, Nash and Young played their second-ever gig in front of that vast crowd. At the end of the evening, Jimi Hendrix played a charged set, which finished up with a twisted, searing 'Star Spangled Banner'. Max Yasgur, owner of the farm, was impressed that 'Half a million kids can get together for three days and have fun and music, nothing but fun and music.'

from the Woodstock Festival, the largest pop music its time.

13 MAY 1969

Riots in Malaysia

196 people are killed and a further 439 injured when rioting breaks out between Malays and Chinese in the Malaysian capital of Kuala Lumpur. Emergency rule is established and remains in place until December of the same year.

1969
EDWARD KENNEDY INVOLVED IN CHAPPAQUIDDICK INQUEST

Following an accident in which his friend Mary Jo Kopechne died, presidential candidate Edward Kennedy appeared in court on 20 July 1969. The car carrying the senator and Kopechne crashed on Chappaquiddick island, but eight hours lapsed before Kennedy reported the incident. He pleaded guilty to the charge of failing to report an accident and announced at the end of the month that he would not be standing for president in 1972. The exact details of the case may never be known, but why Kennedy took so long to tell the police about the incident is still one of the most perplexing issues surrounding the case.

MULTIPLEX
LADY HERRON

Chapter 8

1970–1979

The first Earth Day took place on 22 April 1970 to discuss environmental issues.

1970
EARTH DAY

On the first Earth Day, 22 April 1970, millions of Americans joined in teach-ins, demonstrations and rallies in major cities across the country, to show support for the protection of the environment, and awareness for the dangers caused by pollution and other environmental issues. The Earth Day received an amount of corporate opposition, but ended as a great success. The long-term consequences of this event were substantial, leading to important legislation, including the establishment of the Environmental Protection Agency, a 25 per cent reduction in air pollution and the rehabilitation of half of the polluted rivers of the US. The Earth Days, which are held every year, remain major events.

1970
JANIS JOPLIN DIES

Musician Janis Joplin grew up in Texas listening to Bessie Smith and Leadbelly, and started out singing country music and the blues. In San Francisco she developed a style of her own, a raunchy wail of a voice that ached with vulnerability and power. She got herself a hell-raising image too, glittering in bangles and satins, going on drinking sprees, and cursing out anyone who crossed her. She was a sensation at the Monterey Pop Festival and her album *I Got Dem Ol' Kozmic Blues Again* was full of hollers and moans. On the day she died from a heroin overdose, she was working on her new album. *Pearl* was released posthumously.

Janis Joplin, who died of a heroin overdose.

17 APRIL 1970

Apollo 13 Back to Earth

Jim Lovell, John Swigert and Fred Haise, the three astronauts manning the Apollo 13 space craft, land back on earth safe and well after a harrowing trip. The planned Moon landing had to be aborted after an explosion in the service module.

An exultant Pelé celebrating one of his many goals in the World Cup.

1970
PELÉ'S WORLD CUP

Brazil played Italy in the 1970 World Cup Final in Mexico's intense heat and altitude. Their 4–1 win put the Jules Rimet trophy in their custody for a record third time and enabled them to keep it permanently. Brazil's confidence in their attacking skills did cause them to be vulnerable in defence at times, and the Italians were well equipped to exploit this. After Pelé had risen to a Rivelino cross to head Brazil in front after 18 minutes, careless play by midfielder Clodoaldo in trying an impudent back-heel in his own half gave Boninsegna the chance to equalize. When Gerson put the Brazilians 2–1 ahead with a shot from outside the box in the 66th minute, Brazil's play was switched into carnival mode. Five minutes later, a Gerson free-kick was touched on by Pelé to enable Jairzinho to maintain his record of scoring in every game in Mexico. But the best Brazil goal was saved for last. The move leading up to it began with a Gerson dribble past five players. As the attack developed through Rivelino, Jairzinho and Pelé, Brazil's right-back and captain, Carlos Alberto, pushed forward to join in the fun. Pelé waited for him to arrive and played the ball into his path to allow the skipper to thunder the ball into the net.

1970
JIMI HENDRIX DIES

Jimi Hendrix was born in Seattle, but started roaming after playing in local bands and doing a stint in the army. In London in 1966 he formed the Jimi Hendrix Experience, and set about taking the music world by storm. His electric-guitar playing was legendary, a kind of innovative buzz of controlled feedback and melodic riffs. He was also a dazzling showman, slinking on stage in velvet and then smashing or burning his guitar. His first album *Are You Experienced?* was a psychedelic blaze of chords with Dylan-inspired lyrics. His later recordings anticipated dub and ambient music. He died of an overdose on 18 September 1970.

Jimi Hendrix, symbol of the 1960s rock revolution, who died from an overdose in 1970.

The Ugandan political leader Idi Amin.

1971
IDI AMIN SEIZES CONTROL OF UGANDA

Ugandan soldier and politician Idi Amin was born in 1925. He joined the British (later to become Ugandan) army and rose through the ranks, becoming a colonel in 1964. A friend of the prime minister, Milton Obote, he was made commander-in-chief of the army and air force, but when relations between them worsened, Amin staged a coup in 1971, dissolving the Parliament and establishing a military dictatorship, taking legislative and executive powers into his own hands. Amin then proceeded to expel all Ugandan Asians and many Israelis in 1972, seized foreign-owned businesses and estates and ordered the execution of thousands of his opponents, making his bloodthirsty regime notorious worldwide.

1972
SALT

In 1969 the superpowers began Strategic Arms Limitation Talks. These were aimed at limiting the numbers of the very biggest nuclear weapons. The first treaty, known as SALT 1, was signed in 1972. Its most important clause was a five-year moratorium on the building of strategic weapons. This agreement did not lessen the risk of nuclear war, the superpowers had more than enough weapons already, and it did not affect intermediate or tactical weapons, but it was the first agreement of its kind. SALT 2 was agreed in 1979. This was a much more important treaty as it limited the number of strategic weapons that the two superpowers could build. Each would have no more than 2,500. However, the treaty was never ratified by the US Congress, because of the Soviet invasion of Afghanistan in December 1979.

The pocket calculator, invented by Sir Clive Marles Sinclair.

13 JUNE 1971

The Pentagon Papers

After a Supreme Court ruling that the New York Times should be allowed to print them, the first extracts from the Pentagon Papers are published in the newspaper. The report studies the origins and policies of the United States regarding the Vietnam War.

1972
THE POCKET CALCULATOR

The British inventor Sir Clive Marles Sinclair (b. 1940) was a pioneer in the fields of microelectronics and industrial design, producing such items as a 340-g (12-oz) hand-held personal computer and a pocket-sized television set. Largely self-taught, Sinclair formed the Sinclair Radionics company in 1972 and produced some of the first multi-function electronic calculators and digital watches. His first pocket calculator was only 1 cm (½ in) thick and 12 cm (5 in) long. The most innovative and complex calculator of its time, it possessed a 7,000-transistor integrated circuit and was the first to be powered by a wafer-thin battery. After the company failed in 1979, Sinclair founded Sinclair Research Ltd, which produced the phenomenally successful ZX 80 computer.

1972
10,000 PEOPLE KILLED IN MANAGUA

A series of earthquakes, measuring 6.25 on the Richter Scale, hit Managua, Nicaragua, on 21 December 1972. Managua was levelled and turned into an inferno that killed 7,000 people and made 200,000 homeless. Seventy-five per cent of its buildings were destroyed and another 15–20 per cent were left uninhabitable. The population of 325,000 was reduced to 118,000. Incredibly, there was almost no damage a mere few kilometres from Managua and the catastrophe was caused because the city was built on a fault line. Had it been just 40 km (25 miles) away the tragedy would not have occurred. The lesson was not learnt, though, and the city was rebuilt on the same fault and suffered more earthquakes.

Lava flow from the Helgafell volcano threatens the harbour on the west coast of Iceland.

2 FEBRUARY 1972

British Embassy Burned

The British Embassy in Dublin is set alight by protestors in the Republic's capital; the demonstrators are angered at the killing of 13 people in Londonderry by British paratroopers three days previously.

1973
VOLCANIC ERUPTION IN ICELAND

On 23 January 1973 a mile-long fissure in the side of the long-dormant Helgafell volcano began to erupt. A rain of ash and cinder buried Vestmannaeyjar, a town in southern Iceland on Heima island, forcing the evacuation of most of the 4,500 inhabitants. A more serious disaster was avoided by residents who managed to divert some of the lava by bulldozing it out of the way and by using hoses to chill the lava. The eruption did not subside until June, when most of the evacuees returned and removed the thick deposits of ash that had covered the town's buildings. Vestmannaeyjar subsequently made a complete recovery from this disaster.

1973
THE YOM KIPPUR WAR

On 6 October 1973, Egypt and Syria, frustrated by Israel's refusal to give up Arab territory, joined to launch a surprise attack on Israeli occupation forces. The Syrians, aided by troops from Jordan and Iraq, initially made some gains in the north, but by 11 October they had been turned back, and the Israelis advanced into Syria. In the south, the Egyptians

One result of the Arab-Israeli war was a dramatic increase in the price of oil. The following year, however, Britain discovered oil in the North Sea.

crossed the Suez Canal and penetrated about 10 km (6.2 miles) into the Israeli-occupied Sinai before they were stalled. On 16 October the Israelis counter-attacked and invaded Egypt itself. A cease-fire took effect on the Syrian front on 22 October and in Egypt two days later. Although militarily won by Israel, Egypt, by the initial performance of its army, managed to turn the war into a psychological victory.

The Egyptians crossed the Suez Canal and penetrated into Israeli-occupied territory before being routed.

1973
ARAB–ISRAELI WAR TRIGGERS OIL EMBARGO

✽ While Israelis celebrated Yom Kippur in 1973, the Egyptians stormed across the Suez Canal and surged into the Sinai desert. The Arab States, responding to the US financial and political support of the Israelis, increased oil prices by 70 per cent and announced a rolling cut in oil production of five per cent per month. Western Europe would suffer, too, from the price rise and the production cut, leading to petrol shortages and rationing. Hundreds of petrol stations closed as refined petroleum became ever more scarce. In the UK, the government imposed a road speed limit of 80 kph (50 mph). Idi Amin announced the 'Save Britain' campaign as Arab oil producers doubled the price. By January 1974, the war was over and Britain had discovered oil in the North Sea.

1973
STUDENT RIOTS IN ATHENS

The government of George Papadopoulos was overthrown on 28 November 1973 by the Greek militia. The rhetoric and approach were very similar to those used in 1967 when the colonels, who staged a coup, accused the government of weakness for believing that they would retain power only until the situation had been stabilized. The coup ended a week of violence in which 10 people died. Tanks were used against the students of Athens Polytechnic where 5,000 were protesting against the lack of political and academic freedom. The martial law that had been declared by Papadopoulos had triggered the coup, with the Greek troops taking up strategic positions around the capital in the early hours of the morning.

E. F. Schumacher encouraged the use of Intermediate Technologies that could help developing countries.

The flag of the European Union, with the Union Jack of Great Britain.

1973
SCHUMACHER'S *SMALL IS BEAUTIFUL*

E. F. Schumacher's *Small is Beautiful: A Study of Economics as if People Mattered* was published in 1973. In it he challenged the vast institutions that were emerging in both capitalist and communist countries and called for small communities, decentralization and technology on a human scale. Excessive size was, he believed, the cause of unemployment, poor working conditions, inequality and a decline in freedom. In particular he was keen to help poor countries develop without suffering the problems of what he termed 'giantism', and to this end he helped develop 'Intermediate Technologies', machines that could be owned and used on a village scale – an approach that has now been widely adopted.

Studies into genetics have opened up new opportunities for genetically modified foods and new chemicals and drugs.

1973
POST-INDUSTRIALISM AND THE REDEFINITION OF WORK

Sociologist Daniel Bell (b. 1919) argues that the original Protestant work ethic underlying capitalism will collapse as a result of the massive productive capacity of modern technology. This is argued in his books, *The End of Ideology* (1960), *Towards a Post Industrial Society* (1973), *The Coming of Post Industrial Society* (1973) and *The Cultural Contradictions of Capitalism* (1976). Modern capitalism requires consumers in pursuit of leisure and so is moving us towards a world where work is no longer seen as a virtue. Professor Charles Handy points in a similar direction, predicting the end of the full-time nine-to-five job and forecasting instead that people will increasingly work part-time on a freelance basis.

1973
GENETIC MANIPULATION

After it was discovered how DNAs and their genes work, scientists set about trying to alter the genes of species to achieve new characteristics. Gene splicing, the insertion of bits of new DNA into an existing DNA strand, was invented in 1973 by American scientists Stanley Cohen and Herbert Boyer. This enabled scientists to produce transgenic species. Transgenic, or genetically engineered, species could thus possess desired characteristics which made them economically more viable through resistance to disease and pests, higher yields and so on; or they could be used to produce valuable chemicals, drugs or hormones for medical use.

21 FEBRUARY 1973

Libyan Aircraft Shot Down

A Libyan aircraft carrying 113 civilians, is shot down over the Sinai Desert by Israeli fighter jets. The airliner had allegedly strayed off course. Only five of the passengers survived the crash.

1973
BRITAIN JOINS THE EEC

The EEC proved very successful economically. Trade between the members increased and in 1961 Britain applied to join. Britain had not taken part in the earlier developments towards economic unity because of its links with the Commonwealth, but it soon became clear that membership of the EEC was very advantageous. However, in both 1963 and 1967, Britain's applications for membership were vetoed by France. The French president, Charles de Gaulle, believed that Britain was too closely linked to the USA to be a real member of the EEC. Britain eventually joined in 1973, along with Denmark and Ireland. In the 1980s Spain, Portugal and Greece were admitted and in the 1990s Sweden, Austria and Finland.

1973
FAMINE IN ETHIOPIA

Africa depends upon farm products for the survival of the 12 billion people inhabiting its 12 countries. The lack of rainfall is a natural phenomenon and consequently drought and famine hold the upper hand over the populace. In Ethiopia the start of the more recent famines was in November 1973; during this one year, an estimated 100,000 died as a result of famine and attendant malnutrition. The western world failed to respond with aid because of the economic crisis caused by OPEC's oil-price increase. Little meaningful help arrived until the famine peaked in 1984–86 when millions of Ethiopians were threatened with starvation and hundreds died of it each day.

Victims of the drought in Ethiopia.

The flag of the state of Israel, of which David Ben-Gurion was one of the founders.

1973

LAUNCH OF THE CAT SCAN

Godfrey Hounsfield, a British electrical engineer, headed the team that pioneered the development of computerized axial tomography (CAT) in 1973. His team was working on the project at the same time as American physicist Allan Cormack, though neither team knew this. They shared the Nobel Prize for Medicine for the CAT scan device in 1979. The CAT scan enables detailed X-ray pictures of 'slices' of the human body to be produced and displayed as cross-sections on a viewing screen. Using views taken from varying angles, a three-dimensional picture of any organ or tissue irregularities in the body can be analyzed and used as an aid in diagnosis without the need for surgery.

1973

BEN-GURION DIES

David Ben-Gurion was born in Poland in 1886. Attracted to the Zionist Socialist movement he emigrated to Palestine (1906) where he worked as a farm labourer and formed the first Jewish trade union in 1915. From 1921 to 1933 he was general secretary of the General Foundation of Jewish Labour and in 1930 he became leader of the Mapai party. As defence minister he presided over the Israeli army's development into one of the Middle East's strongest. A founder of the state of Israel in 1948, he became the country's first prime minister 1948–53 and again 1955–63. On retiring from politics he remained a symbol of the Israeli state until his death in 1973.

11 SEPTEMBER 1973

Chilean President Killed

President Salvador Gossens Allende of Chile is killed in an uprising that overthrew his Marxist government; the coup marks the culmination of years of opposition to his socialist regime.

The Opera House, one of the most dramatic pieces of modern architecture in the world.

1973
SPANISH PREMIER ASSASSINATED

In December 1973, Spanish premier Admiral Luis Carrero Blanco was travelling to Mass in his car when a bomb blasted it 20 m (65 ft) into the air. The car was hurled over the church and landed on the second-floor balcony of a nearby building. Blanco was pulled out alive from the wreckage but died shortly after. The bomb was planted by the terrorist organization Basque Homeland and Liberty (known as ETA). Blanco was General Franco's hand-picked successor as head of government and effectively the man in power owing to Franco's ailing health. Franco relinquished the premiership to Prince Juan Carlos in 1973, but remained head of state until his death in 1975.

15 APRIL 1974

Patti Hearst Joins in Raid

Patti Hearst, daughter of millionaire William Randolph Hearst, re-emerges as an armed accomplice in a bank raid organized by the Symbionese Liberation Army, the gang that kidnapped her.

1973
THE SYDNEY OPERA HOUSE

Jorn Utzon's Sydney Opera House was the product of a competition won in 1956, nearly 20 years before the building was actually completed. Despite Utzon (b. 1918) resigning as architect before completion, it remains one of the world's most dramatic, beautiful buildings. His design was distinguished by the roof, a series of interlocking shells which stand on a podium surrounded by Sydney Harbour. Each of these segments was generated from a single sphere, an approach which Utzon described as 'additive architecture'. The shells were made from cast-in-situ and prefabricated concrete. The ribs of the fan vaulting, also concrete, were clad in ceramic tiles, which were

*The **New York Post** headlines the Nixon Watergate Scandal that culminated in his resignation.*

positioned to emphasize the roof curves and shimmer with reflected light. The main concert hall seats 2,900, with a separate opera house accommodating another 1,547. Instead of being lowered from fly towers, the scenery is raised from beneath the main stage, which means that the usual bulk is avoided.

1974
NIXON RESIGNS AFTER WATERGATE

Richard Nixon was re-elected as president in 1972 in a landslide victory over George McGovern. He resigned amidst controversy in 1974 over the Watergate affair. Watergate, a US political scandal, was named after the building in Washington, DC, which had housed the Democrats' campaign in the 1972 presidential elections. Five men, hired by the Republican Committee to Re-elect the President (CREEP), were caught after breaking into Watergate with electronic surveillance equipment. For two years, investigations were run by the media and a Senate committee and it was revealed that the White House was implicated in the break-in, and that there was a 'slush fund' used to finance unethical activities. In August 1974, President Nixon was forced by the Supreme Court to surrender to Congress tape-recordings of conversations he had held with administration officials, and these indicated his involvement in a cover-up. Nixon resigned rather than face impeachment charges on three counts: for obstruction of the administration of justice in the investigation of Watergate; attempting to use the IRS (Internal Revenue Service), FBI and CIA as weapons against political opponents; and failure to produce 'papers and things' as ordered to the Judiciary Committee. The only US president to have left office by resignation, he was granted a pardon later in 1974 by President Ford.

Patti Hearst in front of the Symbionese Liberation Army insignia, the group who kidnapped her.

The first Volkswagen, known as the 'people's car'.

1974
VOLKSWAGEN GOLF

Giugiaro (b. 1938) is considered to be the world's most influential motorcar designer. Having studied at the Turin Academy of Fine Arts, he joined the Fiat styling centre at the age of 17. In 1959, he became head of the styling department at Carrozzeria Bertone, where he worked on the BMW 3200CS (1961), Alfa Romeo Giulia GT (1963) and Fiat 850 Spider (1965). In 1967, Giugiaro formed Italdesign with Aldo Mantovani and Luciano Bosio, to offer pre-production services beyond straightforward design to motorcar industries. Services included styling, feasibility studies and the construction of models and prototypes. Among designs created under the Italdesign umbrella were the Volkswagen Golf (1974) and Fiat Panda (1980). The Golf offered the 'two-box' solution: with sharp-edged contours and a vigorous break between the engine compartment and the passenger area – a design solution which was much copied. The Golf replaced the Beetle in 1974.

1974
CYCLONE IN AUSTRALIA

On Christmas Day, 1974, cyclone Tracey struck Darwin, north Australia, causing the immediate deaths of 44 people and injuries to many more. Ninety per cent of Darwin's buildings were destroyed, leaving 25,000 out of the city's population of 32,000 without shelter. Relief was made all the more difficult by Darwin's remote location and the fact that it was accessible by only one major road. Civilian and military aircraft were drafted in and shuttled in food and supplies. Prime Minister Whitlam cut short a European tour because of the disaster, flying back to be with his people. He made a firm pledge that the city would be rebuilt.

A cyclone in northern Australia at Christmas 1974 destroyed 90 per cent of the buildings in Darwin.

1975
THE FALL OF SAIGON

Contacts between Hanoi and Washington during 1972 led eventually to the signing of the Paris Treaty in January 1973. US forces finally left South Vietnam in March 1973, and for two years the South Vietnamese government of Nguyen Van Thieu sought to continue the US policy of pacification. But the Viet Cong provisional revolutionary government of South Vietnam was making substantial political gains in the countryside and in late 1974 North Vietnam breached the cease-fire with a final offensive against the South. By March 1975 South Vietnamese morale had collapsed and in April the communist forces took Saigon with only a limited amount of fighting. The war was over and Vietnam was reunited as the Socialist Republic of Vietnam in July 1976.

11 JULY 1975

Ancient Army Discovered

Archeologists working near the ancient city of Xian in China, uncover a huge collection of 6,000 'terracotta' warriors, built to guard the tomb of the first emperor of the Ch'in dynasty. The army is complete with weapons, horses and chariots.

1975
MINERALS

❁ In order to use minerals for industrial production, rocks containing the mineral, in the form of ore, must be extracted and processed. Metallic minerals are sometimes combined to form alloys, for example steel. The extraction and processing of minerals is expensive, energy intensive and requires advanced technology. Many developing companies have rich mineral deposits but lack the capacity to exploit them. Help is often provided in the form of finance and technical expertise from a multi-national corporation. The EU imports 70 per cent of the minerals it needs, including more than 95 per cent of its copper, chromium and manganese. In 1975, to secure its supply, the EU (European Community) signed an agreement, the Lomé Convention, with 45 developing countries to guarantee prices and amounts of important minerals.

In April 1975, communist forces were able to seize Saigon with only limited resistance.

The Apple I computer was the first to be sold complete with all the necessary attachments.

1976
THE APPLE I COMPUTER

The electronics engineer Stephen Wozniak, (b. 1950), together with Steve Jobs (b. 1955), built a revolutionary microcomputer which was to form the basis of Apple Computer Company's success and helped create the enormous personal computer industry of the 1980s. Wozniak and Jobs formed Apple in 1976, after building a prototype computer, 'Apple I', which was user-friendly, intended for single users, and the first personal computer to be sold complete with all the necessary elements, for use 'off the shelf'. One important aspect of 'Apple I' was the mouse: the hand-held controlling device which replicated hand movements to select services from the computer screen. The computer's styling was influenced by that of Mercedes Benz cars; the result of this was soft lines but stark detailing. Apple's innovations paved the way for desk-top publishing (DTP).

1976
PICTURES OF MARS

The *Viking* spacecraft was launched to find out if there was life on Mars. Previous pictures of the planet's surface had been taken from a distance and had given a generalized impression of the cold, red planet. *Viking* landed on the Plains of Gold in July 1976, and within minutes its camera was sending out clear pictures of the surface of Mars. It looked flat, scattered with small, sharp rocks and a few large boulders. The ground was red, iron-rich clay and the sky a strange pink, probably from the tiny particles of red dust suspended in the air. Over 52,000 photographs were sent back to earth and the planet was observed in greater detail than had ever been possible before.

*The **Pathfinder** rover vehicle that supplied the first pictures from the surface of Mars.*

1976
GENETIC DETERMINISM

In *The Selfish Gene* (1976), Professor Richard Dawkins (b. 1941) argued that the process underlying life and evolution is the survival and replication of the fittest gene. Derived directly from Darwin's theory, Dawkins suggested that plants and animals were merely the machines that genes used to survive. Although accused of reductionism by his opponents, he argued that any basic unit that self-replicated – whether a gene, a process or an idea – was capable of evolution through natural selection. This meant that not only would individual animals evolve, but so would artefacts, cultures and religions, communities and ecosystems. He also argued that 'God' was merely an idea that used a whole range of effective techniques to survive; a potential weakness of this argument is that it could be applied to any idea, including his own.

> 9 SEPTEMBER 1976
> **Death of Mao**
>
> Chairman Mao, Communist leader and head of the People's Republic of China, dies at the age of 82. He won his party leadership through the 'Cultural revolution' which was characterized by oppression and disruption.

Professor Richard Dawkins derived his theories directly from Darwin's theories of evolution.

1977
BOKASSA CROWNED

Jean-Bedel Bokassa was commander-in-chief of the Central African Republic from 1963 until, in December 1965, he led the military coup that gave him the presidency. On 4 December 1976 he proclaimed the Central African Empire and one year later crowned himself emperor for life. In all, £30 million was spent on his coronation, with £2 million spent on the crown alone, paid for by his patron, the president of the French Republic. His regime was characterized by state violence and cruelty. Overthrown in 1979, he was in exile until 1986. Upon his return, he was sentenced to death but this was commuted to life imprisonment in 1988.

1977
DEATH OF STEVE BIKO

Stephen Biko (1946–77) was an influential leader of the Black Consciousness Movement in South Africa who became a martyr to the anti-apartheid cause. In 1968, as a medical student, Biko founded the South African Students' Organization (SASO), which actively campaigned against racial discrimination. In 1975 and again in 1976 he was arrested and held for more than 100 days without being charged or put on trial. In August 1977, Biko was arrested for a third time at Port Elizabeth, where he died in custody after being taken by truck while unconscious to Pretoria, 1,190 km (740 miles) away. Although the police claimed that he died as the result of a hunger strike, the post-mortem examination disclosed that his death was caused by blows to the head. The police were absolved of blame, leading to public outcry around the world.

Rare photo of the Black Consciousness Movement leader Steve Biko, who died in mysterious circumstances while in jail.

1978
FIRST TEST-TUBE BABY

In-vitro fertilization (fertilization in glass) is the process allowing eggs and sperm to unite in a laboratory to form embryos. The embryos produced are then implanted into the womb of an otherwise infertile woman. The work was pioneered by an English obstetrician and gynaecologist, Patrick Steptoe, who, with his colleague Robert Edwards, was the first to accomplish the successful implantation of an egg fertilized outside the human body into the uterus. The first 'test-tube' baby was Louise Brown, who was born by Caesarean section in 1978. Since then the field has been extended to the birth of a baby from a frozen embryo and from a frozen egg.

16 MARCH 1978

Amoco Cadiz Disaster

The Amoco Cadiz supertanker hits bad weather on her way to Rotterdam from the Persian Gulf and breaks apart on rocks, releasing her cargo of crude oil into the water; 22,000 seabirds die despite attempts to clear the mess.

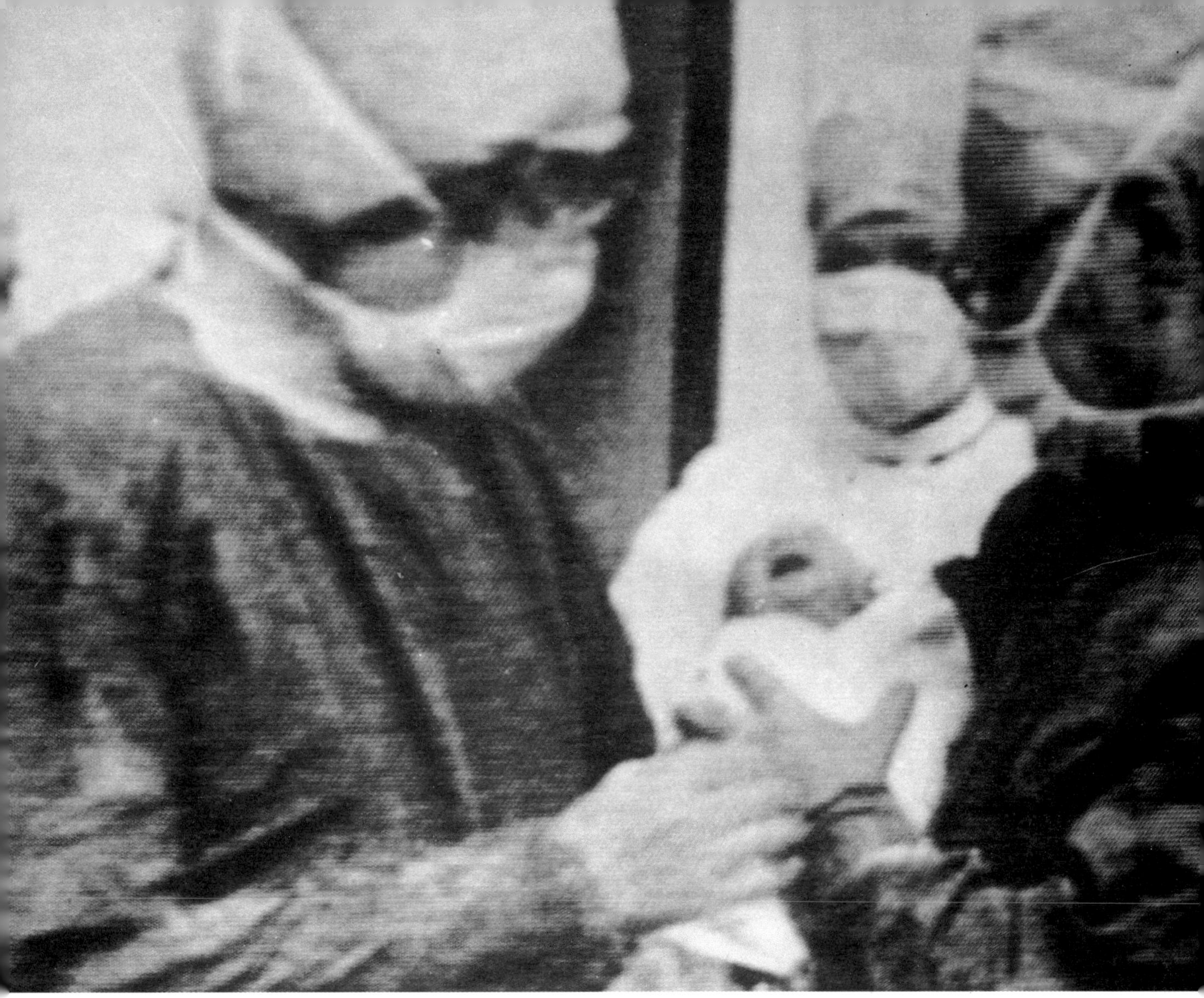

Television image of the birth of Louise Brown, the first test-tube baby.

1978
JACQUES DERRIDA AND DECONSTRUCTIVISM

Jacques Derrida was born in Algeria in 1930. His way of thinking developed as a response to that of Heidegger, although he was also influenced by Nietzsche and Ferdinand de Saussure. He felt that metaphysical philosophy was without meaning, that it had reached the end of its history and that the only true philosophy concerned the nature of being. His greatest work was *Writing and Difference* (1978). The question he asked was: 'what can we say about Being without resorting to any metaphysical assumptions?'. He tried to answer this by deconstructing philosophical statements on this matter and showing their limitations, contradictions and false assumptions.

1978
MASS SUICIDE IN JONESTOWN

The self-styled Reverend Jim Jones (1933–78) originally preached his ideas to San Francisco's black community. He established his group, known as the People's Temple of the Disciples of Christ, in 1974. Jonestown, the commune of the sect, was built north-west of Georgetown, Guyana. Following the shooting of Leo Ryan, a US congressman, and three newsmen performing an unofficial investigation into the group, Jones gave a final sermon, then instructed his followers to imbibe cyanide mixed into a soft drink. In all, 789 people died, according to the official Washington/CIA report, during the mass suicide of 17 and 18 November 1978. Jones himself died of a gunshot wound to the head.

1978
SONY 'WALKMAN'

The 'Walkman', introduced by the Sony Corporation in 1978, represented a significant change in the Japanese industry's approach to styling. Until this point, companies had paid little attention to styling, which they believed added minimal value to a product. The 'Walkman' was the brain child of Sony chairman Akio Morita. Aimed at teenagers, the personal stereo – the ultimate personal accessory – used existing technology (the transistor radio), but repackaged it into a 'must-have' item, with a belt latch, colourful buttons and a pocket-sized format. The original 'Walkman's were metal, but by the mid-1980s, colourful plastic became the standard. The 'Walkman' became an essential fashion accessory of the 1980s.

Sony released their 'Walkman' in 1978, aimed at the teenage market; today it is one of youth's essential symbols.

The flag of the European Union, which led to establishment of the European Monetary System.

1979
VIETNAMESE INVADE CAMBODIA

A vicious series of border clashes between Vietnam and Cambodia erupted into full-scale war when the Vietnamese deposed the Cambodian dictator, Pol Pot. The new Vietnamese-backed administration was quick to distance itself from the excesses of Pol Pot. Within days of the administration's taking control thousands of skeletons had been uncovered as mute testimony of the 'killing fields' of Cambodia and the 'Year Zero' policy of the old regime. Systematically, the Khmer Rouge had slaughtered all 'intellectuals' and opponents of their rule. Whole villages had been wiped out and the country was in a state of terror. Despite attempts to bring Pol Pot to justice, he managed to retain a degree of control in certain parts of the country for many years.

1979
MARGARET THATCHER BECOMES BRITAIN'S FIRST FEMALE PRIME MINISTER

Margaret Thatcher had trained as a barrister before joining politics. In 1970 she became education minister under Edward Heath. She was the unexpected victor in the 1975 Conservative leadership election when she defeated Heath. Building up support for the party, she won the election in 1979 and

Margaret Thatcher celebrates becoming Britain's first female prime minister.

became Britain's first female prime minister. During her first term she sent British troops out to recapture the Falkland Islands from Argentina. Following victory in the Falklands her popularity soared and she was re-elected. Her second term was marked by the miners' strike (1984–85), which ended in the miners' defeat and with power shifted away from the unions. She narrowly avoided an IRA bomb in October 1984 which exploded at the Conservative conference. Victory again in 1987 made her the first prime minister in 160 years to be elected for a third term but she became increasingly isolated by her autocratic stance. In 1989 she introduced the unpopular community charge or 'poll tax', which caused violent protest marches on Britain's streets. In 1990 splits in the Cabinet over Europe and consensus government led to a leadership challenge. Thatcher resolutely stood in the first round before resigning and giving her support to John Major, who replaced her as prime minister and Conservative party leader.

1979
EMS AND EMU

The European Monetary System (EMS) aimed to aid financial co-operation and to establish monetary stability within the European Union (EU). It came into force in 1979 as a means of correcting the fluctuations in exchange rates that followed the 1974 oil crisis. The central component of the EMS was the exchange rate mechanism (ERM), a voluntary system of partly fixed exchange rates, based on the European currency unit (ECU, the standard monetary unit, the level of which was set according to a basket of currencies of member states). Participating currencies under the ERM were allowed to fluctuate in relation to each other and to the ECU within a fixed band only. The ERM was a stepping stone to European monetary union (EMU), which began on 1 January 1999. Proponents of EMU claimed that a fixed exchange rate would act as an anchor against inflation. Opponents feared loss of national autonomy over monetary and exchange-rate policy.

31 MARCH 1979
Three Mile Island Disaster

A potentially explosive bubble of hydrogen gas develops inside a crippled reactor at the nuclear plant on Three Mile Island, Pennsylvania; a mass evacuation campaign is put into effect, although the crisis is kept under control and only small amounts of radioactivity are released.

1979
JAMES LOVELOCK AND THE GAIA HYPOTHESIS

The Gaia hypothesis was first outlined by biochemist James Lovelock in his major work, *Gaia* (1979). The hypothesis suggested that the planet Earth, its soil, oceans, atmosphere and biosphere all constitute a self-regulating system that could be thought of as living. He has often been accused by scientists of arguing that the Earth is conscious. Although this is a view that is held by many of his supporters, it actually forms no part of Lovelock's theory. His studies of atmospheric chemistry, which led him to discover the hole in the ozone layer and the wide distribution of pesticides, also provided much evidence for the theory. His work was largely responsible for the greater awareness of the effect man-made products and actions have had on the planet.

1979
EARL MOUNTBATTEN MURDERED

Louis, 1st Earl Mountbatten of Burma, was born in Windsor in 1900. The great-grandson of Queen Victoria, he served at sea in the First World War and during the Second World War was chief of combined operations in 1942 and commander-in-chief in South-east Asia in 1943. As the last viceroy of India (1947) and first governor-general of India until 1948, he oversaw the country's transition to independence. Later, he returned to service at sea and was 4th sea lord (1952–55) and appointed 1st sea lord (1955–59). He was murdered by an IRA bomb aboard his yacht while sailing near his holiday home in County Sligo in the Republic of Ireland.

5 MARCH 1979
Volcanoes in Space

The US spacecraft Voyager 1 sends back pictures from its exploratory mission to Jupiter; these confirm that the planet has rings like Saturn and also show an erupting volcano on one of the planet's moons.

The funeral of Lord Mountbatten, killed by an IRA bomb in the Republic of Ireland.

1979
AYATOLLAH KHOMEINI RETURNS TO IRAN

The Iranian Shi'ite Muslim leader Ruhollah Khomeini was born in 1900. He held the title Ayatollah, which means 'sign of Allah', when he became the chief teacher of Islamic philosophy and law. He was exiled from Iran (1964) for opposition to the pro-western regime of the Shah. Ayatollah Khomeini continued to campaign against the Shah from his exile in France, demanding a return to the principles of Islam. The pressure on the Shah became so great that he left the country in 1979 and the Ayatollah made a triumphant return and became virtual head of state. Iran underwent an 'Islamic Revolution' involving a return to strict observance of Muslim principles. Relations with the US worsened inexorably when a group of Iranian students took 63 Americans hostage in Tehran, demanding the Shah's return to face trial. The Shah's death in 1980 did little to alleviate the crisis, the hostages finally being released in 1981.

*The **Voyager 1** spacecraft discovered rings around the planet Jupiter.*

Ayatollah Ruhollah, who inspired great adulation in Iran, returns home after his exile in France.

1979
THE RUSSIAN INVASION OF AFGHANISTAN

On 25 December 1979, Soviet forces invaded Afghanistan and quickly won control of Kabul. But the government, dependent on Soviet military forces, was unpopular, and the rebellion intensified. During the next few years about three million war refugees fled to Pakistan and 1.5 million fled to Iran. The anti-government guerrilla forces included dozens of factions. They operated from bases around Peshawar, Pakistan and Iran. Weapons and money from the United States, Saudi Arabia, Iran and China sustained them. During the 1980s Soviet forces increasingly bore the brunt of the fighting. By 1986 about 118,000 Soviet troops and 50,000 Afghan government troops were facing roughly 130,000 guerrillas. Estimates of combat fatalities range between 700,000 and 1.3 million people. The Soviets completed their withdrawal in 1989.

Chapter 9

1980–1989

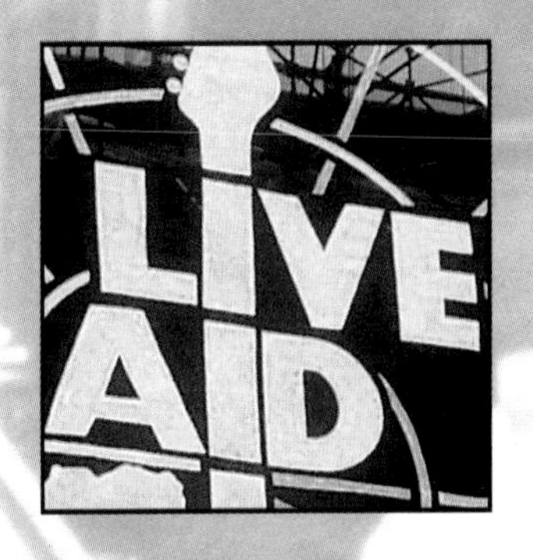

1980s
ROBOTS

Not only has the computer changed people's personal and business lives, it has also changed manufacturing. In many factories, robots can perform simple tasks faster and more accurately than people. When computers are used to design, make and assemble product parts, this is called Computer Integrated Manufacturing (CIM). Computers are able to control robots, which can be adapted to do new tasks very quickly, simply by changing the computer program, whereas people need to be retrained for new tasks. The use of robots, first employed in factories in the 1980s, enabled smaller and more efficient works possible: robots take up less space and are flexible. A robot can make a small number of one product and then switch to making a different one. Factories can thus produce the wider range of low-cost products that customers now want.

Iraqi president Saddam Hussein, who ordered his troops to invade Iran in 1980.

Ronald Reagan, former movie star, became president of the United States in 1980.

1980
RONALD REAGAN BECOMES PRESIDENT

Ronald Reagan was born in Illinois in 1911 and became a Hollywood actor in 1937. He appeared in over 50 films including *Bedtime for Bonzo* in 1951 and *The Killers* in 1964. As president of the Screen Actors Guild 1947–52 he became a conservative, was critical of bureaucracy that stifled free enterprise and he named names before the House Un-American Activities Committee. In 1962, He joined the Republican party and his term as governor of California (1966–74) was marked by battles with students. He lost the Republican presidential nominations in 1968 and 1976 to Nixon and Ford respectively. He won it in 1980 and became 40th US president, beating Jimmy Carter.

1980
IRAQ INVADES IRAN

In 1980, Iraqi president Saddam Hussein invaded Iran, hoping to reverse the 1975 border settlement and perhaps to gain control of the rich, oil-producing Iranian province of Khuzestan. Although Iraqi forces won early successes, Iran rallied, held the invaders, formed new armies and eventually took the offensive. Iran mounted offensives all along the border between the two countries, but particularly in the south, where Iran tried to capture Al Basrah, Iraq's main port. Iraq stubbornly resisted; it held back Iranian troops with superior firepower and gas warfare, while the Iraqi air force attacked Iranian cities and oil installations, as well as tankers approaching or leaving Iranian ports in the nearby Persian Gulf. An agreement for a cease-fire was eventually reached in August 1988 with the help of the United Nations.

1980
THE RISE OF MICROSOFT

William Henry Gates III was born in 1955. In 1975, when he was just 19 years old, Gates dropped out of Harvard and joined his schoolfriend Paul G. Allen to establish the company Microsoft. They began by adapting the computer language BASIC, which was used on large computers, for use on the earliest commercially available microcomputers. In 1980 Microsoft began its domination of the global computer industry when Gates licensed an operating system called MS DOS to IBM for use in the personal computer (PC) that it was planning to develop. IBM's PC came on the market in 1981 and by the mid-1980s MS DOS had become the major operating system for American PCs.

Bill Gates, the founder of the Microsoft Corporation; today Gates is one of the richest men in the world.

> 19 MAY 1980
> ## US Volcano Erupts
> A series of earthquakes causes the volcano Mount St Helens, in the state of Washington, to erupt; although warning signs had caused evacuation of the surrounding area, 38 people are still killed as a result of the eruption.

1980
THE BIRTH OF SOLIDARITY

After three months of strikes and demonstrations, Polish workers, led by dockers and the strike leader Lech Walesa, wrung concessions from the hard-line Polish government. The agreement, signed on 30 August 1980, allowed independent trade unions the right to strike, the release of political prisoners and the easing of government censorship. The defeat of the Polish government sent tremors throughout the Eastern Bloc. Arguably, the defeat of the communist government in Poland was the first step in the collapse of the Russian domination of Eastern Europe. Lech Walesa would become the leader of his country and General Jagielski would face criminal charges before the end of the decade. Although the Polish press condemned the strikers, they represented a democratizing movement that would sweep the communist government from power.

5 JULY 1980
Borg Wins Again

Swedish tennis star Bjorn Borg takes the Wimbledon Men's Singles Title for a record fifth consecutive time. The champion beats hot-headed American John McEnroe in five sets.

1980
THE RESURGENCE OF ISLAM

The Islamic revival that has shaken Iran, Afghanistan, Algeria and most of the Muslim world since 1980 has several aspects that are hard to disentangle. It is both a spiritual revival, although most of the mystic sects have been subjected to harsh oppression, and a militant response to the economic and intellectual dominance of the West. The Islamic

The Qur'an, the Holy Book of the Islamic faith, which has undergone a revival since the 1980s.

The fairy tale wedding: Prince Charles marries Lady Diana Spencer.

Revolution in Iran, led by the Ayatollah Khomeini, marked the start of the movement, which inspired the Taliban movement in Afghanistan, the Hezbollah in Palestine and terrorist groups in many other nations. It is probably too early to tell whether the intellectuals, whose main concerns are cultural and spiritual, will gain the upper hand or whether the fundamentalists will instigate increasingly violent attacks on secular societies.

1980
JOHN LENNON MURDERED

When John Lennon was shot outside the Dakota building in New York in December 1980, he was one of the most famous men in the world. In the 1960s, as a member of The Beatles, he had made jangly pop an art. Post-Beatles, working with his wife Yoko Ono, he made music that was more experimental and challenging, the pop chords giving way to primal screams. Meanwhile his political statements and rallying for world peace had made him the voice of a generation. Mark Chapman, although a fan, had decided Lennon was the 'anti-Christ'. He had asked for Lennon's autograph, and later the same day he gunned the star down outside Lennon's home.

A generation mourned after John Lennon was gunned down outside his home.

1981
PRINCE CHARLES AND LADY DIANA MARRY

Charles Philip Arthur George is the eldest son of Queen Elizabeth II and Prince Philip, and heir to the British throne. He became Prince of Wales in 1958, was invested at Caernarvon in 1969 and served in the RAF and the Royal Navy (1971–76). In July 1981 he married Lady Diana Frances Spencer, the younger daughter of the 7th Earl Spencer, at St Paul's Cathedral; she was the first English bride of a royal heir since 1659. Their first child was Prince William Arthur Philip Louis who was born in 1982 and their second son, Prince Henry Charles Albert David, was born in 1984. The couple were separated in 1992, amid much publicity.

1981
FIRST FLIGHT OF THE US SPACE SHUTTLE

The Space Shuttle was the first reusable spacecraft. Until then, creative energy had been focused on winning the race to be first on the Moon. Monster rockets had to be developed rapidly. They could be used only once, but they would get you there first. After Neil Armstrong planted the American flag on lunar soil, scientists could turn their attention to smaller, more economical projects. The Space Shuttle would be a delivery vehicle, a flying laboratory to repair and recover faulty satellites. The Space Shuttle could remain in space for up to eight days on a normal run. With extra supplies, missions could be extended for up to 30 days. The Shuttle's first launch was on 12 April 1981.

The launch of the space shuttle ***Columbia****.*

30 MARCH 1981
Assassination Attempt on Reagan

US president Ronald Reagan is shot in the chest by John Hinckley as he leaves a hotel in Washington; the president is rushed to hospital where a bullet is removed from his lung. Three others were wounded in the shooting.

1981
VIETNAMESE BOAT PEOPLE

In the years from 1979, more than 1.4 million Vietnamese, including large numbers of ethnic Chinese, fled the country by sea, to escape the new communist regime in Vietnam. They risked death and piracy in order to escape, and as many as 50,000 of these 'boat people' may have perished in flight. Partly due to the mass media, who widely publicized their cause, nearly a million settled abroad. The exodus of refugees fled the country in small, unseaworthy craft and sailed to neighbouring Thailand, Malaysia, Singapore, Indonesia, the Philippines and Hong Kong. Their plight caused governments world-wide to increase the number of Vietnamese refugees admitted for immigration. In 1981, the US admitted a total of 133,000 refugees.

1981
BOBBY SANDS DIES

On 5 May 1981, Bobby Sands became the first of 10 Provisional IRA hunger strikers to die in the H block of Belfast's Maze Prison. Sands, 27, died after 65 days without food.

Sands had recently been elected to Parliament, in a by-election in the Northern Irish constituency of Fermanagh and South Tyrone, despite the fact that he was serving a 14-year sentence for possession of firearms. His hunger strike was in protest against the demands for the reintroduction of special category status for Republican prisoners. He was buried in the Milltown cemetery in Belfast on 7 May, in a Republican plot. Nine other prisoners on hunger strike died between May and July of 1981, drawing worldwide attention to the Northern Irish cause.

Ronald Reagan was shot in the chest in March 1981; the bullet lodged in his lung and was removed in an emergency operation.

1981
POPE JOHN PAUL II SHOT

† Born in Krakow, Poland, Karol Wojtyla took the name of John Paul II when he was elected pope in 1978. The previous pope, John Paul, had died after serving only 33 days. Wojtyla was the first non-Italian pope to be elected since 1522. He is famed for his worldwide trips, his preaching to huge audiences and his endorsement of traditional Catholic views. He was shot and wounded in St Peter's Square, allegedly by Mehmet Agca, a Turkish national, in May 1981. It was believed the assassination was attempted because of the pope's outspoken support of the Roman Catholic Church and the Solidarity trade union in Poland. Agca was acquitted for lack of evidence.

Pope John Paul II was shot and wounded in St Peter's Square, allegedly by a Turkish national, who was later released due to lack of evidence.

The TGV train, which went on to hold the world speed record for rail travel.

1981
FIRST CASES OF AIDS IN THE US

News reports from the US in December 1981 told of a worrying new sexually transmitted disease prevalent among a small population of homosexual men. Acquired immunodeficiency syndrome (AIDS) is the progressive destruction of the immune system by the human immunodeficiency virus (HIV). Research carried out between 1982 and 1984 proved that AIDS had spread beyond its originally supposed risk group and now included heterosexual men and women with multiple sex partners, haemophiliacs and habitual intravenous drug users. HIV is generally spread by exchange of infected blood or sexual fluids. The virus was thought to have originated in Africa. By 1991, 323,378 cases had been reported to the World Health Organization.

1981
TGV TRAIN SERVICE BEGINS IN FRANCE

France's TGV (*Train à Grande Vitesse*) began service from Paris to Lyon on 22 September 1981. Powered by electricity and capable of 380-kph (236-mph) speeds, it was Europe's first super-high-speed passenger line and it was extended to reach Marseilles by 1983. The fastest scheduled passenger train runs in the world are those of France's TGV Atlantique, which travel between Paris and various cities in western France, at 300 kph (186.4 mph). The TGV uses 'dedicated track' over much of its route and has permanently linked cars. It employs electric-powered locomotives, and its fuel consumption per passenger is about one-fifth of that used by aeroplanes. The TGV has been called the 'star train' of the 1980s.

14 SEPTEMBER 1982

Princess Grace Killed

The former movie star, Princess Grace of Monaco, is killed when her car careers off the edge of a mountain road. The princess, who gave up her film career on her marriage to Prince Rainier III of Monaco, was 52 years old.

1982
THE FALKLANDS WAR

Negotiations to settle the sovereignty dispute between Argentina and Great Britain over the Falkland Islands, began in the mid-1960s at the United Nations. The talks were still in

YOUR NEXT SEXUAL PARTNER COULD BE THAT VERY SPECIAL PERSON.

THE ONE THAT GIVES YOU AIDS.

Poster warning of the dangers of the AIDS virus.

progress in April 1982, when Argentine forces invaded and occupied the islands for 10 weeks in an attempt to settle the issue by force. The Argentines were defeated by a British task force and formally surrendered on 14 June. Despite being numerically superior, the Argentines were out-fought and out-commanded by the British. Casualties were comparatively light, despite the use of modern weaponry. Argentina continued to claim the islands; the British government refused to participate in further negotiations, but the two nations resumed diplomatic relations in 1990.

1983
MASSACRES IN ASSAM

On 20 February 1983, over 600 Muslims were massacred in one of the worst cases of sectarian violence since India and Pakistan became separate countries. Indira Gandhi sacked the state government of the Punjab in October for failing to deal with continued religious and political unrest. In the following year, the violence flared up again. Throughout May Hindus and Muslims clashed in the Bombay area, resulting in the deaths of another 100 people. In June, the Indian military launched Operation Blue Star to storm the Golden Temple of Amritsar that had been held by militants. Ninety soldiers and 712 extremists died. In October Indira Gandhi was murdered by her own Sikh guards.

British marines exercizing during the Falklands conflict.

In 1983 US troops invaded the island of Grenada to restore control after the premier Maurice Bishop had been murdered.

1983
FIRST VIDEO GAME SYSTEM

In 1958, an American scientist, William Higginbotham, invented the first video game. By 1971, a commercially produced model, known as 'Computer Space', was brought out by Nolan Bushnell, and 1983 saw the first home video game system, by Nintendo. Flight simulators were first developed in the 1980s, comprizing an artificial cockpit mounted on hydraulically operated legs. The concept of virtual reality was thus born and developments have continued apace. Stereoscopic helmets, data body pads and data gloves have been experimented with in conjunction with hydraulically operated platforms, in attempts to fool the human mind into believing what it sees and feels. Applications for virtual reality so far include: military and surgical training, architectural design and entertainments.

1983
US INVADES GRENADA

A coup in 1979 on the island of Grenada ousted the prime minister, Gairy; the new premier, Maurice Bishop, appealed for calm. By October the island had become independent of the UK and all appeared quiet. In 1983, another coup, backed by the army, murdered Bishop and seized power. The Americans troops swiftly responded by invading the island. They had been sent to protect the 1,000 or more Americans, including those attending the medical school in the capital, and to stop the building of a fighter base. Resistance was quickly dealt with, despite the involvement of over 600 Cubans. Bishop's body was found with other murdered islanders in November.

1 SEPTEMBER 1983

Korean Plane Attacked

A Korean airliner carrying 269 people is shot down by a Soviet military plane; everyone on board is killed in the crash. The Soviets claim that the Boeing 747 was on a spy mission, but the reason it had strayed into Russian air space is not established.

1984
E-MAIL AND INTERNET

The technical foundations for the internet and WWW (World Wide Web) were developed as a project, funded by the Advanced Research Project Agency (ARPA), to build an electrically run communications network able to withstand damage by nuclear warfare. Work began in 1984, and with extra funding from the United States' National Science Foundation, was able to link up American universities, via five super computing centres. By the early 1990s the service became cheap enough for domestic use. Sending and receiving e-mail (electronic mail), searching for information on the internet and advertising on web sites became a familiar feature of modern life by the end of the twentieth century.

1984
TORVILL AND DEAN

Perfection occurs rarely in sport. But on 14 February 1984, at the Sarajevo Winter Olympics, it did. That was the night Jayne Torvill and Christopher Dean – Britain's legendary ice-dancing pair – scored perfect marks for their performance, an interpretation of Ravel's *Bolero.* Nine judges all gave the British pair the maximum six mark for artistic impression. It was such a landmark performance and score – the first time nine perfect sixes had been awarded – that many believe no other ice-dance pair will ever again reach such incredible heights. Afterwards, Dean said that the two had not suffered from nerves on the night. He admitted that '... it couldn't get any better than that', but his main worry was that now they had achieved the perfect score, he had no idea what they would do next.

Ice dancers Jayne Torvill and Christopher Dean, who scored an unprecedented nine sixes at the 1984 Olympics.

1984
LIBYANS EXPELLED FROM THE UK

Following the murder of policewoman Yvonne Fletcher outside the Libyan Embassy in St James's Square in London, the Libyans were given seven days to leave the country. The

Terry Waite, who was instrumental in the release of four Libyan hostages in 1985.

policewoman was apparently shot from one of the rooms of the embassy, which led to a siege of the building. The officer was on duty during an anti-Gaddafi demonstration outside the embassy. Britain broke off diplomatic relations with Libya in protest at the fact that the embassy had been used as a base for terrorist activity in the capital. On 22 April 1984, 30 Libyan diplomats left the country. In June British prime minister Margaret Thatcher called on the West for 'relentless action' against terrorists.

1985
BRITISH HOSTAGES FREED

Under intense pressure and described as 'state sponsors of terrorism' by Ronald Reagan, the Libyan government finally agreed to release four British hostages in February 1985. The four had been held for nine months. Instrumental in the release was Terry Waite, the special representative of the archbishop of Canterbury. In the following year, Libya clashed with the Americans in the Gulf of Sirte. In 1986, Libyans were implicated in the planting of a bomb on a TWA airliner, which prompted the US to respond by bombing Libya in April. They had hoped to kill the Libyan president, Colonel Gadaffi.

1985
GORBACHEV

In 1985, Mikhail Gorbachev became the president of the Soviet Union and announced

The Soviet premier Mikhail Gorbachev, whose reforms finally led to the end of the Cold War.

The wreck of the 'unsinkable' ship, the ***Titanic****, was finally located in 1985.*

his policies of Perestroika and Glasnost. Perestroika involved the restructuring of the Soviet economy and Glasnost meant openness. This applied both internally and externally. Gorbachev was aware that the Soviet Union was bankrupt and that he had to find ways of saving money as quickly as possible, so he immediately restarted disarmament talks with the USA and became very well known and very popular in the West. He was able to develop a close friendship with the Western leaders, which enabled a number of treaties to be signed in the years from 1986 to 1991. In 1989 Gorbachev and President Bush of the USA were able to announce that the Cold War was over.

1985
JOINT FRENCH–US TEAM LOCATES WRECK OF *TITANIC*

Robert Ballard of Woods Hole Oceanographic Institution in Massachusetts and Jean-Louis Michel of the Institute for the Research and Exploration of the Sea in Paris headed a joint US–French expedition to locate the fated British ocean liner, *Titanic*, which had struck by an iceberg and sunk off the coast of Newfoundland in 1912. Ballard's *Argo* – a submersible sled with a camera – photographed the sunken vessel 4 km (2½ miles) under the ocean surface, 650 km (400 miles) south-east of Newfoundland, preserved almost intact 4,000 m (13,000 ft) beneath the ocean's surface. The search had taken 16 days. It was the first sight of the *Titanic* in nearly 75 years.

19 DECEMBER 1984

Hong Kong to Return to China

Britain signs an agreement with the People's Republic of China in Beijing, agreeing the terms of Hong Kong's return to China in 1997. The treaty establishes that sovereignty of the area will return to China, but that its capitalist status is to be retained for another half-century.

8 APRIL 1985

Murdoch Buys Hollywood

Media magnate Rupert Murdoch buys out the film company Twentieth Century Fox for more than £200 million. The company has been steadily making a loss in recent years, but Mr Murdoch hopes to turn its fortunes around.

1985
LIVE AID

The world became a 'global jukebox' on 13 July 1985, the day of the Live Aid concert. In 1984 musician Bob Geldof had been appalled by pictures of the famine in Africa, and decided to help. He persuaded 40 pop stars to come to a recording studio and the single 'Do They Know It's Christmas' was released. The proceeds raised £8 million for famine relief. Live Aid was the follow-up, a 16-hour concert which would take place in England and America simultaneously. It would be broadcast to every country in the world. Once again the stars gathered, appearing for free. They performed for just 17 minutes each, a traffic-light system warning them to get off stage for the next act. Status Quo kicked off with 'Rocking All Over The World', Paul McCartney played 'Hey Jude' to a massive audience at Wembley Arena, who sang the words for him when his microphone cut out. Phil Collins managed to appear at both venues, thanks to *Concorde*. But it was Queen who stole the show with Freddie Mercury's charismatic performance and their vibrant rock music. By the end of the evening an estimated 1.5 billion people had watched the event and $50 million had been raised to help the people in Ethiopia.

1985
COLOMBIAN VOLCANO ERUPTS

In September 1985 initial rumbles from the 4,940-m- (16,200-ft)-high Nevada del Ruiz volcano had worried residents of nearby Armero and Chinchina, but government officials played down any dangers, saying that it was only a mudslide down the flank of the mountain and that there was no hazard. This had drastic consequences when the volcano erupted on 13 November. Fireballs were flung from its peak, and millions of gallons of water careered down the mountain, creating mud and forming into a 45-m (150-ft) wave that flattened vegetation and set fire to trees. In all, 22,490 residents of the towns were crushed, drowned and buried beneath the molten mud or were burnt to death.

Icons of the pop world united in the charity event Live Aid, a massive concert to raise finds for the starving in Africa.

The signs warning of a possible eruption from the Colombian volcano were ignored, resulting in thousands of deaths.

1985
EARTHQUAKE IN MEXICO

Towns in three provinces of Mexico were devastated by the earthquake of September 1985. Measuring a huge 8.1 on the Richter Scale, the quake was felt in Houston, Texas, 1,200 km (745 miles) to the north, and Guatemala City, 1,000 km (620 miles) south. Forty per cent of homes in Ciudad Guzman and one-third of Mexico City was destroyed. The City's central hospital toppled, medical supplies within catching alight. There were 1,000 people in the building and hundreds died, trapped between collapsing floors, some surviving the blast but dying of smoke asphyxiation from the fire. Rescue workers were still digging and finding survivors seven days after the initial blast. The total death toll was 9,500.

1985
BECKER WINS WIMBLEDON

Becker's victory in the 1985 Wimbledon final over South African Kevin Curren – 6–3, 6–7 (4–7), 7–6 (7–3), 6–4 – meant that the record books had to be rewritten. At the age of 17 years and 227 days, he had become the tournament's youngest winner. In addition to this, Becker became the first unseeded winner and first West German champion. Becker's dominance was emphasized on match point, when he produced an explosive serve which caught the edge of Curren's racket before flying into the crowd. A disconsolate Curren said that Becker could be number one in the world one day. 'He is only 17 and has got a lot of time for improvement.' When Becker entered the post-match press conference, the reporters broke into spontaneous applause. When he was told that he had won £130,000, he replied 'That's a lot.'

Mexico City after the earthquake that ravaged it in 1985.

1985
ROBERT MAPPLETHORPE PHOTOGRAPHS *TULIP*

Mapplethorpe (1946–1989) began his career as an independent film maker and sculptor. He frequently used photographs in collages, and by the late 1970s had drawn considerable attention to his own photography: he is best-known for intense black-and-white compositions in which the subject appears as object, even icon. Mapplethorpe's gallery shows scandalized some viewers and critics with their juxtaposition of straight portraits and elegant still-lifes, such as *Tulip*, with overtly homoerotic, even sadomasochistic, male nudes. Mapplethorpe later became successful as a commercial fashion photographer and celebrity portraitist. Learning in 1986 that he had AIDS, he used a series of self-portraits to help focus attention on the disease.

Robert Mapplethorpe's ***Tulip****, a fine example of his intense study of flowers.*

22 JUNE 1986

The Hand of God

The controversial footballer Diego Maradona scores the winning goal in Argentina's World Cup semi-final clash with England by punching the ball into the net with his hand. The referees allow the goal to stand, causing public outrage. Maradona, tongue-in-cheek, describes the goal as scored by the 'Hand of God'.

1986
OIL PRICES PLUMMET

At the end of 1985 the Organization of Petroleum Exporting Countries (OPEC) announced that it was abandoning its official pricing structure based on restricting production. From now on, it would sell oil at whatever price it felt was right. In November 1985 oil prices were set at $27 a barrel, but by the end of January 1986 it had fallen to $15. Prices continued falling up to March, reaching a price under $10 a barrel. In August, the OPEC members announced that they would restore the old restrictions on production. As a consequence, the prices began to stabilize at $13–14 per barrel. By the end of the year, despite arguments between the OPEC members, the price had fixed at $18 based on a 7 per cent cut in production.

1986
US *CHALLENGER* EXPLODES AFTER TAKE-OFF

The 25th mission of the *Challenger* space shuttle had been postponed and delayed four times, before its crew of seven rode out to the launch pad on the morning of 28 January 1986. After a cold night at Cape Canaveral, the launch tower sparkled with icicles, but the countdown went ahead. A few seconds after launch, puffs of smoke emerged from the right-hand booster, but *Challenger* continued to climb normally. Fifty-eight seconds later, a small flame appeared, and the space shuttle was engulfed in a huge fireball. *Challenger* was torn apart by aerodynamic forces. The fragments, including the crew compartment, continued upwards for another few moments, and then splashed down into the Atlantic Ocean. All seven on board were killed.

Diego Maradona's infamous 'Hand of God' goal in the 1986 World Cup.

Checking the levels of radiation after Chernobyl, a nuclear disaster that had repercussions for many years afterwards.

1986
CHERNOBYL

♲ The results of the world's worst nuclear disaster were first detected in Sweden, then in Finland, Denmark and Norway, where huge increases in radioactivity had been measured. Satellite pictures revealed that the top of a Soviet nuclear reactor had blown off, and a fire followed. The aftermath of the disaster is well known: the radiation alerts in nearly every European country, children kept indoors, the slump in milk and meat sales because of fears of contamination. In Kiev, 100 km (62 miles) south of Chernobyl, citizens suffered burns and sickness. Experts differ in their estimates of the number of additional cancers that might be caused by the Chernobyl radiation, but the most conservative is 10,000 in Russia and 1,000 in the rest of Europe.

1986
SWISS CHEMICAL PLANT FIRE CAUSES ENVIRONMENTAL DISASTER

The River Rhine has long been a symbol of mythical purity, but in 1986 it became an emblem of pollution. After a fire at the Sandox chemical plant, firefighters washed about 30 tons of highly toxic, liquid pesticide into the river. The full scale of the disaster became apparent when fishermen began hauling hundreds of thousands of dead fish from the water. Some of the chemicals gradually diluted, but large amounts of non-soluble mercury drifted along almost as a solid body. Water that was once clear and flowing was silvered over with poison, its fish stocks were depleting and it was becoming undrinkable. A powerful German ecological lobby demanded tough anti-pollution laws to prevent such a disaster from ever occurring again.

Terry Waite (centre), who had helped with the release of hostages previously, was taken hostage himself in 1987.

6 MARCH 1987
Zeebrugge Ferry Disaster

The Herald of Free Enterprise car ferry capsizes shortly after leaving the Belgian port of Zeebrugge on its way to Dover; Dutch and Belgian rescue teams arrive on the scene swiftly, but it is too late for many passengers trapped in the ferry, or suffering exposure in the icy waters.

1987
TERRY WAITE KIDNAPPED

Terry Waite was born in Cheshire (1939) and educated in London and the US. He was appointed lay training adviser to the bishop of Bristol (1964–68) and the archbishop of Uganda, Rwanda and Burundi (1968–71), and consultant with the Roman Catholic Church (1972–79). From 1980 he worked as religious adviser on Anglican Communion affairs to the then archbishop of Canterbury, Dr Robert Runcie. Possessing great diplomatic skills, Waite undertook many overseas assignments until, on 20 January 1987, he was seized in Beirut, Lebanon, while seeking to negotiate the release of European hostages. Taken hostage himself, Terry Waite was captive from 1987 until his release on 18 November 1991.

1987
THE IRANGATE SCANDAL

Irangate was the 1987 US political scandal over the sale of arms to Iran via Israel. This broke the law prohibiting the sale of US weapons for resale to a country listed as a

Lieutenant-Colonel Oliver North is sworn-in before he gives evidence at the Irangate trial.

'terrorist nation', and the law requiring sales above $14 million to be reported to Congress. Lieutenant-Colonel Oliver North, a military aide to the National Security Council, and security adviser John Poindexter were both tried in 1987 on charges of obstructing congress and unlawfully destroying government documents; they were found guilty in 1989–90. The Congressional Joint Investigative Committee reported that the president bore 'ultimate responsibility' but found no firm evidence that Reagan had been aware of the deal.

1987
KLAUS BARBIE ARRESTED

♲ German Nazi Klaus Barbie was a member of the SS from 1936. He was known as the 'Butcher of Lyon', as SS commander in Lyon his crimes included rounding up Jewish children from an orphanage and torturing Resistance leader, Jean Moulin. He was involved in deporting Jews from the Netherlands (1940) and in tracking down Jews and the Resistance in France (1942–45). He escaped capture in 1945 and was employed by US intelligence services in Germany before moving to Bolivia with his family in 1951 and working as a businessman. Barbie was expelled from Bolivia (1983) and was arrested and convicted of crimes against humanity in France in 1987.

The anti-Semitic Klaus Barbie, who was convicted of crimes against humanity.

1987
BLACK MONDAY

In just one day £50 billion was wiped off the value of UK quoted companies. Panic gripped the stock market as it mirrored the Friday falls in Wall Street and Tokyo. Hong Kong closed their market for a week. Although this was the sharpest fall in stock market history (10 per cent), twice as bad as the worst day of the Great Crash of 1929, it did not rival the massive losses in America. The market had been expanding for five years with share values rising by almost 400 per cent. The root cause of the collapse has been much debated, but the probable reason was the huge US trade deficits and rising interest rates.

Black Monday in Britain: the stock market crashed, taking £50 billion with it.

1987
GALES IN THE BRITISH ISLES

On 16 October 1987 a television viewer rang the meteorological office and asked if a hurricane was due to hit the British Isles. The question was laughed off but within hours the southern parts of Britain were hit with gusts of winds reaching 177 kph (110 mph). By the morning at least 17 people were dead and there was an estimated £300 million of damage created. The London fire brigade received a record 6000 emergency calls in 24 hours. Thousands of homes had collapsed and roads and railways throughout the south were blocked by fallen trees. Kew Gardens lost one-third of its trees and Sevenoaks in Kent lost six of the oaks that make up its name.

1987
THE *SPY CATCHER* SCANDAL

Peter Wright's *Spy Catcher* set off ripples of unease in the Thatcher government of 1986. His memoirs discussed his years as an MI5 officer and included revelations about the illegal activities of MI5 in Britain. The government launched a campaign to stop newspapers from publishing any information received from Peter Wright. A high-court judge agreed, saying that Britain's security forces must be seen to be leakproof. Ironically, the book could be bought in any bookshop in America. In July 1987 an

13 OCTOBER 1988

Turin Shroud a Fake

After centuries of being regarded as a sacred relic by Catholics the world over, the Turin Shroud – a piece of cloth imprinted with the image of a crucified man, and believed to have been the shroud in which the dead Christ was buried – is proved to be a clever forgery. Carbon-dating puts the shroud at around 700 years old.

Hurricane Gilbert hits Jamaica after passing through Texas and Mexico.

action was brought against *The Times* for publishing an extract. Eventually the government's case was overturned and *Spy Catcher* became a bestseller.

1988
AUSTRALIA'S BICENTENARY

Captain James Cook discovered Australia in 1770, but it was not until 1787 that the British decided that it would be an ideal place for a penal colony. The following year 736 convicts were landed at Sydney Cove, New South Wales, under the control of Governor Arthur Phillip. As far as non-Aboriginal Australians are concerned, 26 January marks the birth of their nation. When the Bicentenary fell in 1988 the event was celebrated throughout the country with a huge range of civic and ceremonial activities. One of the youngest developed countries in the world and the only single-state continent had come of age. The events attracted thousands of visitors.

1988
HURRICANE GILBERT HITS JAMAICA

Hurricane Gilbert cut a 4,000-km (2,500-mile)-wide path of destruction as it crossed the Caribbean westwards from 12 to 19 September 1988. In all, it wreaked $10 billion worth of havoc and killed more than 350 people, causing winds of up to 322 km/h (200 mph). First hitting land in Texas and crossing through Mexico and the Dominican Republic, Gilbert had already caused damage and death but squarely in its path was Jamaica. It hit Kingston with winds of 233 kph (145 mph) and lifted the roofs from 80 per cent of homes, making 500,000 homeless. Twenty-five people died on Jamaica; the banana and poultry crops of the entire island were wiped out and all communications were lost for several days.

Unprecedented gales swept through Britain in October 1987, causing millions of pounds worth of damage.

The Berlin Wall, a symbol of separation and conflict for so long in Europe, is finally torn down in 1989.

1988
ARMENIAN EARTHQUAKE

An earthquake measuring 6.9 on the Richter Scale struck Soviet Armenia on 7 December 1988. The worst quake in 80 years, it destroyed two-thirds of Leninakan, Armenia's second largest city, and eliminated 20 villages and towns. Officially 28,854 were killed, 12,000 were injured and 400,000 were made homeless, although unofficial reports put the casualties at 55,000. Much of the extensive loss of life was due to faulty construction of the houses. Built cheaply and carelessly in the Brezhnev era, they simply folded and crumbled inwards on their inhabitants. Gorbachev was in New York on a diplomatic mission at the time but rushed home when the news reached him.

1989
THE WALL COMES DOWN

Since 1945 the Soviet Union had kept military forces in the countries of eastern Europe. Those countries had been cut off from the West by the Iron Curtain that Stalin had built in 1945–46. The most famous example of the Iron Curtain was the Berlin Wall, which had been built on Khrushchev's orders in 1961. These actions had been very expensive. In 1989 Mikhail Gorbachev, the Soviet president, began to withdraw forces from eastern Europe in an effort to save money. The West German government paid the expenses of the forces, which left East Germany. As Soviet troops withdrew, country after country left the Warsaw Pact and threw off Communism. Finally, in November 1989, crowds in Berlin began to dismantle the Berlin Wall. By the end of the year pieces were being sold as souvenirs.

1989
SATANIC VERSES

Salmān Rushdie was born in India into a Muslim family; he later lived in Pakistan before moving to the UK. His novels include *Midnight's Children* (1981), which won him the Booker Prize, and *Shame* (1983), which was a satire and revisionist history of Pakistan. In 1988 he wrote *The Satanic Verses* (the title refers to deleted verses from the *Qu'ran*), which offended many Muslims with its alleged blasphemy. The book was banned in India in 1988 and in 1989 Iran's Ayatollah Khomeini issued a death threat. Demonstrations followed, in which

> 3 DECEMBER 1989
>
> **End of the Cold War**
>
> The summit between US president George Bush and Soviet leader Mikhail Gorbachev, held on ships in the port of Valletta in Malta, ends with a declaration that the Cold War is over and a new era of co-operation is to begin.

Police were forced to guard Salman Rushdie after death threats were issued on the release of his ***Satanic Verses****.*

copies of the book were burnt along with effigies of the author. Rushdie was forced to go into hiding under police protection.

1989
TIANANMEN SQUARE MASSACRE

In June 1989, the Tiananmen Square massacre in Beijing brought a tragic end to six weeks of pro-democracy demonstrations by Chinese students and workers. The demonstrations began as a display of mourning for the death of former communist party leader Hu Yaobang and gathered momentum during a visit to China by Mikhail Gorbachev in mid-May. By that time, more than one million people a day were in Tiananmen Square demanding that government leaders end corruption and instigate political reform. Martial law was declared on 20 May, and the People's Liberation Army was summoned to clear the capital. On the night of 3–4 June, PLA units cleared Tiananmen Square and killed almost 1,000 civilians in the immediate area. Thousands of students and others were arrested and executed.

Armed tanks were brought in to control the riots involving Chinese students and workers in Tiananmen Square.

Marlboro
BOSS
POWERED by
HONDA

Chapter 10

1990–1999

1990
NELSON MANDELA FREED

From 1964 to 1982 Nelson Mandela was imprisoned at Robben Island Prison, off Cape Town. He was then kept at the maximum security Pollsmoor Prison until 1988, at which time he was hospitalized with tuberculosis. Mandela inspired continued support among South Africa's black population and his imprisonment became a major issue in countries worldwide that disapproved of apartheid. Many countries banned the import of South African goods. The government, led by President F. W. de Klerk, released Mandela (aged 71) from prison on 11 February 1990 after the ban on the ANC had been lifted. He entered into negotiations with the government about a multiracial future for South Africa.

Nelson Mandela celebrates his freedom after 22 years of imprisonment.

Kuwaiti soldiers cheer and wave at the end of the Gulf War.

1990
THE GULF WAR

The Gulf crisis began in August 1990, when Iraq, led by President Saddam Hussein, invaded and annexed Kuwait. Between August and November the United Nations Security Council passed a series of resolutions that culminated in the demand that Iraq withdraw unconditionally from Kuwait by 15 January 1991. By that time, some 500,000 allied ground, air and naval forces – chiefly from the United States, Saudi Arabia, Great Britain, Egypt, Syria and France – were arrayed against an Iraqi army estimated at that time to number 540,000. The land offensive, Desert Storm, was launched and within 100 hours the city of Kuwait had been liberated, and tens of thousands of Iraqi troops had deserted, surrendered or been captured or killed.

1990
LECH WALESA WINS ELECTIONS IN POLAND

Polish trade union leader Lech Walesa founded the independent trade union, Solidarity, in 1980. A series of strikes organized by Walesa drew wide public support and substantial concessions from the Polish government until Solidarity was outlawed in 1981 and Walesa arrested, following the imposition of martial law by General Jaruzelski. He was released in 1982 and awarded the Nobel Peace Prize (1983). After leading more strikes during 1988 he negotiated an agreement with Jaruzelski (1989) in which Solidarity once more became legal and a new 'socialist democracy' was founded. The coalition government, elected in September 1989, was dominated by Solidarity and Walesa went on to be elected president by a landslide in 1990.

Lech Walesa set Poland on the path to democracy after his support of workers on strike overturned the government policies about trade unions.

1 APRIL 1990

Riots at Strangeways

Riots break out in Strangeways Prison in Manchester in protest against the appalling conditions in which the prisoners are held. Inmates took prison wardens by surprise during morning prayers and soon overran the building, some even climbing to the roof to make their protest.

1990
GERMAN REUNIFICATION

On 2 October 1990, the reunification of Germany took place. East Germany, a centrally planned economy, was reunified with West Germany, one of the world's most highly developed and successful economies. In 1988 output per wage earner and wages in East Germany were about half of those in West Germany. East German factories consumed almost twice as much energy as West German factories to produce goods of the same value. State control in East Germany had perpetuated inefficiency: people's continuing employment did not depend on their skill or willingness to upgrade. In the free market arena of reunified Germany, many from the east found it difficult to obtain work. Within a year, Germany's unemployment rate had soared to three million.

1990
OIL PRICES

From the 1960s the United States and most other non-communist countries were increasingly dependent on oil from the Persian Gulf region. In 1973–74, the Organisation of Petroleum Exporting Countries (OPEC), many of them Arab states, acting in concert, abruptly quadrupled the price of oil. Some countries are particularly vulnerable to any fall in the oil price; in Saudi Arabia, for example, oil and refined petroleum account for about 90 per cent of exports. A further doubling of the oil price in 1979 drove up inflation in several developed countries. Oil is vital to both producer and consumer countries and often engenders conflict. In 1990 Iraq invaded oil-rich Kuwait causing oil prices to leap. An American-led alliance drove the Iraqi forces out but only after they had set fire to most of Kuwait's oil wells.

The invasion of Kuwait by Saddam Hussein sparked the Gulf War between the UN and Iraq.

1990
THE GUINNESS SCANDAL

Hints of a scandal involving several major business personalities hit the headlines as early as 1987. During the Guinness bid to buy Distillers, individuals had invested in Guinness to inflate the value of the shares. Ernest Saunders, the Guinness chairman, was sacked, charged with perverting the course of justice, ordered to repay £5 million to Guinness and later jailed. Gerald Ronson, head of the Heron International Group, was charged with stealing £6 million from Guinness, and merchant banker Roger Selig of Morgan Grenfell charged with the theft of £2.95 million. The ripples of stock market manipulation and illegal share dealings led to a major Department of Trade and Industry investigation aimed at clamping down on insider dealing.

1990
TRANS-ANTARCTICA EXPEDITION BY DOGSLED

In 1990, Will Steger and Jean-Louis Etienne completed the first dogsled trip across 6,115 km (3,820 miles) of Antarctica. Steger, an American explorer, had previously reached the North Pole accompanied by five American and Canadian explorers in 1986, assisted only by dogs, and they were the first to reach the pole without mechanical assistance since Robert E. Peary planted a flag there in 1909. The Antarctica expedition set out to achieve the same milestone in the South. Explorations of the Antarctic have continued since that time, with satellites showing new and undiscovered areas of the globe still untouched by humans. The continent is of particular interest to environmental scientists because its thick covering of ice – on average 2,000 m (6,500 ft) deep – holds the history of the Earth's atmosphere.

1 DECEMBER 1990

Two Nations Meet Under the Sea

English and French workers celebrate deep underground as the tunnel linking the two countries finally meets in the middle. This is the service tunnel section of the Channel Tunnel; hopes are that the rail service should be established by 1991.

The Channel Tunnel was finally opened in 1994 after years of planning and construction and at a cost of more than £10 billion.

1991
THE BREAK-UP OF YUGOSLAVIA

The wars in Yugoslavia began in summer 1991, after Slovenia and Croatia declared their independence. In July of that year, the Yugoslav People's Army (JNA), which consisted mainly of Serbs, intervened in Slovenia with the intention of removing the Slovenian government and disarming its defence forces; Slovenian troops repelled the Yugoslav forces after 10 days. The war in Bosnia began in the spring of 1992, when the new government declared independence from Yugoslavia. Serbian nationalists within Bosnia violently occupied more than 60 per cent of Bosnian territory; thousands of Muslims and Croats were murdered or expelled from their homes. The tribunal for massacring civilians during the war indicted more than 50 Bosnians, the majority of whom were Serbs. They included Bosnian Serb leader Radovan Karadziç and military commander Ratko Mladiç.

Robert Peary (left) was the first to reach the South Pole in 1909.

Publicity campaign, warning of the dangers of the AIDS virus and promoting public awareness and acceptance of the disease.

1991
ROBERT MAXWELL DIES

Jan Ludvik Hoch was born in Slatina-Selo in Czechoslovakia in 1923. He managed to escape the Holocaust and fled to France and then to Britain where he changed his name to Ian Robert Maxwell. After the war he obtained German academic and scientific papers and published them all over the world. He founded the Pergamon Press in 1951 and by the 1960s he was a major force in publishing. He also served as a Labour MP until 1970. In 1981 he bought the British Printing Corporation, selling it in 1987. He then purchased the Mirror Group, using it as a foundation to create Maxwell Communications. He secretly siphoned off $1.2 billion to support his shaky empire. Faced with exposure, he died after falling off his yacht in 1991.

1991
AIDS CLAIMS FREDDIE MERCURY

Superstar Freddie Mercury died of an AIDS-related illness on 24 November 1991. The flamboyant star had been the lead singer of Queen for nearly 20 years. The band's music – basic hard rock glammed over with lush production values – and their outrageous stage shows won them huge popularity worldwide. The single 'Bohemian Rhapsody' became their best-known song, an operatic pop anthem with falsetto backing, and layer upon layer of vocals. The single stayed in the charts for nine weeks. Just a short time before his death Freddie Mercury re-released the single and donated all the proceeds to an AIDS charity. The band refused to continue without their front-man: 'Without Freddie there is no Queen.'

1991
KURDISH REFUGEES FLEE

President Bush's call for the Iraqi people to overthrow Saddam Hussein was embraced by rebel factions, and the Kurds responded with an uprising in the north that was brutally suppressed by Saddam's remaining forces. The suppression created an enormous refugee problem, as hundreds of thousands of Kurds fled their homes. International mass media widely publicized the plight of the Kurds, who crowded into the frozen mountains above the Turkish border to escape Saddam's plans for mass genocide. As the death toll among the Kurds mounted, US military forces built camps for them in northern Iraq. The administration of these camps was later assumed by the United Nations. Coalition forces began policing a 'no fly' zone for Iraqi aircraft in the south in August 1992.

1992
DENMARK VOTES AGAINST THE MAASTRICHT TREATY

The European Economic Community (EEC) was founded in 1957–58 to oversee the economic integration of the nations of western Europe. The EEC joined with

> 19 APRIL 1991
> **Kurdish Refugees**
>
> Thousands of US, British and French troops prepare to advance into the north of Iraq with plans to establish camps for the floods of Kurdish refugees fleeing from the fighting; an invisible barrier along the 36th Parallel defines the zone in which the UN will attack Iraqi aircraft.

European fuel communities forming the European Community or EC (1967). Success of the trade policies sponsored by the EC made its members more receptive to greater economic and political union, which yielded the Treaty on European Union (Maastricht treaty) in 1991. In a 1992 referendum on EC policies the Danish people soundly rejected the treaty. Denmark had joined the EC in 1973, triggering referendums and debates elsewhere in the Community. The Danish government then proposed modifications to the treaty and a second referendum (1993) approved it.

President George Bush made calls to the Iraqi people to overthrow their leader Saddam Hussein.

The Euro, the new single currency that is being phased in throughout Europe as the new millennium dawns.

1992
A SINGLE MARKET

The EEC became the European Community in the 1970s and then became known as the European Union in the 1990s. This was a sign that the Community was changing significantly. In particular a much higher level of integration was taking place. Taxes and laws were being brought into line. In 1992 the Single Market was set up; all goods and people could now travel freely throughout the member countries. Work permits were not required. Terms for a single currency were agreed in 1997, and came into effect in 1999. Co-operation between police and armed forces increased and the Community, in addition, began to be seen as a political force. It attempted to intervene in the Balkans and made common representations on worldwide issues.

1992
RIO AND AFTER

One of the signal accomplishments of the UN Conference on Environment and Development in Rio de Janeiro in 1992 (the Earth Summit) was the official linking of environment and development issues. Yet, while the world's population grew by about 450 million in the subsequent five years, biological wealth and diversity diminished; and an estimated 1.3 billion people were too poor to meet their basic needs for food and shelter. The broad goals of the Summit were laid down in Agenda 21, which recognized that 'an environmental policy that focuses mainly on the conservation and protection of resources without consideration of the livelihoods of those who depend on the resources is unlikely to succeed'. By 1996, 117 governments had formed commissions to develop national sustainable development strategies.

1992
RACE RIOTS IN LOS ANGELES

In response to the acquittal of four white policemen charged with beating Rodney King, a black motorist, Los Angeles exploded into racial violence in 1992. The Los Angeles riot was the largest and most dangerous since the turn of the century: more than 60 people were killed and 2,383 injured by the time local and

23 JULY 1992
First Woman Rabbi

Naamah Kelman is ordained in Jerusalem as a rabbi of Reform Judaism; this is the first time a woman has been ordained in the Jewish religion.

federal law enforcement personnel were able to restore order. The riots cost the city over $800 million in damages, but the issue of greatest concern was the volatility of the black response, which included unprovoked attacks on white civilians, clashes between black rioters and non-black merchants and widespread looting and arson outside the ghetto area. Two of the four white policemen were later convicted in the Supreme Court.

Riots broke out in Los Angeles after four white policeman were freed from the charge of beating a black man to death.

1992
PALESTINIANS DEPORTED FROM ISRAEL

War and dissent had torn the Holy Land apart for centuries. The Palestinians, stateless and in their eyes living in an occupied land, had suffered deportations on several occasions before 1992. In 1948, directly after the war and the founding of the state of Israel, 780,000 Palestinians were forced out to make room for Jewish immigrants from Europe and from the Arab world. The plans for Palestinian self-rule on the Gaza Strip and the West Bank meant that more Palestinians would be displaced and deported to these areas. The new zones, economically weak and reliant on Israel, became new hotbeds of dissent and fundamentalism.

The holy capital of Jerusalem, where the first woman rabbi was ordained in 1992.

1993
WORLD TRADE CENTER BOMBED

On 26 February 1993, a 550-kg (1,210-lb) bomb was packed in a van and detonated inside the garage of the World Trade Center. It ripped a 60-m (197-ft) crater in the basement of the world's second tallest building. The explosion killed six and injured over 1,000. At the time it was believed to be the most destructive terrorist attack in the history of the USA. The mastermind behind the bomb was Sheikh Omar Abdel-Rahman, a fundamentalist Muslim leader. In the days following the explosion US investigators discovered that this attack was just the first of a series that had been planned by an Islamic group.

The aftermath of the IRA bomb that exploded in the City of London, injuring 44 people.

12 MARCH 1993

Bombings in Bombay

A series of car bomb explosions tear through the streets of Bombay, killing as many as 300 people, injuring hundreds more and leaving behind a wave of destruction; conflict between Hindus and Muslims had killed hundreds in the city just two months previously.

1993
ISRAELI–PALESTINIAN PEACE ACCORD

With funds drying up and support diminishing, the Palestinians realized that the opportunity of a peaceful settlement was their only option. Luckily, a Labour government had come to power in Israel and it was committed to the implementation of Palestinian autonomy within a year. A series of secret meetings were held in Norway between January and September and on the 13th a historic agreement was signed. Both the Palestinians and the Israelis agreed to recognize each other and over a five-year period the Gaza Strip and the West Bank would be given over to the Palestinians. Self-rule has been a delicate issue and zealots from both sides continue to do their best to derail the agreement.

1993
BILL CLINTON BECOMES US PRESIDENT

Bill Clinton served as governor of Arkansas in 1979–81 and 1983–93 and established a liberal and progressive reputation. He won the 1992 presidential campaign focusing on domestic issues and the ailing economy. In 1993 he was sworn in as the 42nd US president and the first Democrat in the White

Bill Clinton is sworn-in as president of the United States.

House for 13 years. As president he brought in a variety of anti-crime measures and helped pull America out of recession. In foreign affairs he backed the Israeli-PLO peace accord in Washington in 1993 and withdrew US peacekeeping forces from Somalia in 1994. Although his party suffered a huge defeat in the November 1994 mid-term elections, he was himself re-elected as president in 1996. 1998 saw on trial for impeachment, but he retained his popularity with the public.

The Hubble telescope has enabled humankind to learn about the universe beyond our planet.

1993
HUBBLE TELESCOPE REPAIRED

The 1993 launch of the space shuttle *Endeavour*, to repair the Hubble telescope, combined high technology with down-to-earth practicality. On its 11-day mission, the craft reached 579 km (360 miles) above the earth. Its crew managed the tricky manoeuvre of snaring the $3-bn telescope to replace eight electrical fuses and install two pairs of gyroscopes. They were outside the shuttle for a gruelling eight hours, wrestling with jammed doors on the telescope. Eventually the only way they could get them to close was by tying them together with an improvized luggage strap! They also fitted the telescope with corrective optics, so that it could see to the edge of the Universe, possibly unravelling the secrets of the world's beginning.

Molecule showing the structure of DNA, the genetic make-up of human beings.

1993
JURASSIC PARK GROSSES $500 MILLION

The monster movie is not dead. In 1993 Steven Spielberg's dinosaurs stalked across the screen with ripping teeth and gripping claws, and into box-office records. *Jurassic Park* grossed $500 million worldwide. Special effects had moved on oceans since the days of *Jaws*, where the shark looked distinctly suspect in close-up. These giant reptiles were hi-tech marvels, huge, menacing and frighteningly realistic. The film was based on a novel by Michael Crichton, in which a billionaire tycoon biologically engineers dinosaurs from fossilized DNA and decides to open a living museum. The film's gigantic profits made the production budget seem like a snip at $60 million.

1993
WACO SIEGE

David Koresh formed the Branch Davidian sect in 1959. The sect was a splinter group, formed out of another group which itself had broken away from the Seventh Day Adventist Church. The charismatic leader took his followers to Waco, Texas, and formed a commune. Koresh became more dictatorial as time went on, instructing that he was a messiah and that all the women in the group were his God-given wives. Authorities were alerted over the stockpiling of weapons there and a siege was born in 1993. The fiery demise of the compound claimed the lives of Koresh and 74 of his followers, with four federal agents killed in the preceding shoot-out.

1993
CHRISTIE'S GRAND SLAM

It was not until the early 1990s, that – already in his '30s – Linford Christie produced his best form and was recognized as the supreme runner on both sides of the Atlantic.

24 NOVEMBER 1993

Teenagers Guilty of Murder

Two 14-year-old boys are convicted of the murder of two-year-old James Bulger, who was stoned to death by the side of a railway line in Liverpool; the boys are the youngest murderers in recent history.

A victorious Linford Christie flying his country's flag after taking the 100 m gold medal.

By 1993, Christie had won athletics' sought-after grand slam, taking first place in the Commonwealth Games, European Championships, Olympics and World Championships. The Commonwealth title was the first one he gained, winning in the 1990 games. The same year, he won the European title, the first of six he would win. The biggest title of all, the Olympic title, came next. Aged 32, Christie was in the best form of his life. He had lost only once all season. In the final, Christie produced one of the performances of his life. After 60 m, he was clear of the field and pulled away to claim Britain's second 100-m gold medal in 12 years. Christie was the oldest man by four years to win the Olympic gold medal. In Stuttgart in 1993, he completed the set, taking the gold and setting his fastest-ever time.

1994

PLANE CRASH KILLS RWANDAN PRESIDENT

Certainly the worst instance of genocide in Africa's history occurred in Rwanda from April to August 1994. On 6 April a plane carrying President Habyarimana of Rwanda and neighbouring Burundi's President Ntaryarima was shot down near Kigali airport by Hutu extremists. A planned massacre of the Tutsi minority ensued, with killer squads of Hutu slaughtering indiscriminately. They had already murdered over 2,000 before the death of the President; now they were unchecked. On the 7th, Prime Minister Uwilingiyimana was murdered. The UN arrived in May and attempted to establish safe areas. The Tutsi Rwandan Patriotic Front was particularly active by now, taking control of the country by August. In all, one million were killed and millions became refugees.

Nelson Mandela after his inauguration as president of South Africa.

1994
NELSON MANDELA BECOMES PRESIDENT OF SOUTH AFRICA

A year after his release from prison, Mandela was chosen as deputy president of the ANC (the president Oliver Tambo being ill) and he replaced Tambo as president in July 1991. His wife, Winnie, however, had not escaped controversy. In 1989 she was involved in the abduction of four youths, one of whom, Stompie Seipei, was later murdered. Winnie Mandela was convicted of kidnapping and assault and in 1991 was given a six-year jail sentence with the right to appeal. In April 1992 she and Nelson separated after 33 years of marriage. In the same year she resigned from her ANC leadership posts. In September 1992, Mandela and President de Klerk agreed to speed up the creation of an interim government under which reforms could take place; they agreed, in 1993, to the formation of a government of national unity after free, non-racial elections. Mandela and de Klerk were awarded the Nobel Peace Prize in 1993, for their efforts to end apartheid, and in April 1994 Mandela was elected president and introduced many new initiatives to improve standards for the black population. Winnie Mandela was given the post of deputy arts and science minister in Mandela's 1994 government but was expelled in 1995. She and Nelson were divorced in 1996.

1994
OPENING OF THE CHANNEL TUNNEL

After more than six years of construction and at a cost of more than £10 billion ($15 billion), the English Channel Tunnel was officially opened on 6 May 1994, by Queen Elizabeth II of Britain and President François Mitterrand of France. The Channel Tunnel, or 'Chunnel' as it is sometimes called, consists of two single-track tunnels with a service tunnel running between them. The tunnels run for 50 km (31 miles) at an average depth of 40 m (131 ft) beneath the Channel seabed from terminals in Folkestone, England, and Calais, France. With 38 km (24 miles) of the system running under the sea, the tunnel is the world's longest underwater tunnel. The Channel Tunnel connects the railway networks of British Rail (BR), French Railways (SNCF) and Belgium Railways (SNCB). The railways' new Eurostar trains carry passengers and freight directly between Britain and continental Europe.

1994
AUSTRALIAN FOREST FIRES

In most years drought affects some part of Australia. The country also suffers from localized flooding and tropical cyclones. South-eastern Australia (which includes Tasmania) has the highest occurrence of bush-fires in the world. The only other areas in the world that can rival the danger levels are California and parts of the Mediterranean. During 1994 bush-fires swept through New South Wales. The dangers from the fires caused the evacuation of the outskirts of Sydney. This was well-timed, as the fires blazed their way into the suburbs, destroying hundreds of homes. All the southern states are subject to hot, dry winds that can make fires commonplace.

1 MAY 1994

Ayrton Senna Killed

Brazilian Formula 1 racing champion Ayrton Senna is killed when his car spins out of control and crashes into a wall during the San Marino Grand Prix; his death comes just a day after Austrian racer Roland Ratzenberg is killed on the same track during a qualifying race.

Ayrton Senna, who was killed on the track at the 1994 San Marino Grand Prix.

1995
JAPANESE EARTHQUAKES

On 17 January 1995 the most violent earthquake to have struck Japan since 1948 hit Kobe, Osaka and Kyoto in Japan's industrial heartland. The 20-second seismic wave reached 7.2 on the Richter scale, ripped through motorways and railway tracks, and hurled concrete from rooftops. More than 600 after-shocks followed the first tremor. Scores of fires caused by fractured gas pipes raged out of control and, with roads blocked, helicopters were used to douse the flames. At least 1,800 people were killed by the initial blast with the death toll finally reaching around 6,000. In Kobe 100,000 people spent the night in shelters and about 650,000 homes were without power.

A Russian soldier in the ruined capital city of Grozny, during the Chechnyan war.

1995
RUSSIANS WAGE WAR IN CHECHNYA

Secessionists emerged in 1991, taking advantage of the USSR's decline in power. Dzhozkhar Dudayev was elected Chechin president in October, declaring independence the following month. He was a nationalist and extremely anti-Russian. In 1992, Chechnya divided into two republics and by 1993 the economy was in such a bad state that he dissolved the parliament. In 1994 armed pro-Russian rebels attempted to depose him, but they failed. On 11 December the Russians invaded and attempted to seize the capital, Grozny. By March 1995 over 40,000 Russians managed to take Grozny. Casualties were high on both sides. Chechin rebels resisted for some time before a degree of order was restored.

1995
DESTRUCTION AND PARTITION OF SARAJEVO

Heavy shelling of Sarajevo resumed in April 1995. The Serbian stranglehold over the town could not be broken by the Bosnians. In May the UN Commander General Rupert Smith issued an ultimatum to the Bosnian Serbs and the Bosnian government to withdraw their heavy weapons from Sarajevo.

2 FEBRUARY 1995
Floods in the Netherlands

In an large-scale emergency operation across the Netherlands, nearly 250,000 people are evacuated from their homes as a result of widespread flooding, which experts fear could destroy the dikes and create extensive damage.

Bombing raids followed, with the Serbs taking 300 UN soldiers hostage. They were released by June and a multi-national UN force was flown in to protect the safe areas. Given that Sarajevo had a mix of ethnic backgrounds, there was no alternative but to partition the town, along with most of the rest of the region.

1995
ETHNIC CLEANSING IN BOSNIA

Throughout the 1990s the town of Srebrenica was at the centre of conflict between the predominantly Muslim population and the Serbs. The United Nations declared the town as one of the safe areas for Muslims, but despite this the Bosnian Serbs laid siege to the town and took control of it in July 1995. Following the siege, the Serbs murdered thousands of Muslims, expelling the rest. When Bosnia and Herzegovina were partitioned in 1995, Srebrenica was included in Serb-held territory. For most of the post-Yugoslavian period, a great deal of the violence was centred on the aim of creating ethnic purity in areas that had once had a mixture of cultures. Ethnic cleansing displaced more than a third of the population of Bosnia and Herzegovina. In July 1995 at the International War Crimes Tribunal for the Former Yugoslavia at The Hague, Radovan Karadziç was indicted for war crimes. He was the leader of the so-called Republika Srpska (Serb Republic) in Bosnia. His military commander, Ratko Mladiç was also charged with genocide and crimes against humanity.

The effect of the war in Sarajevo – an old man leaves the soup kitchen with his rations.

Torrential rain caused floods throughout France, Germany, Holland and Belgium.

The victory speech at the Quebec referendum after a close-run campaign ended in a 'no' vote for separation from Canada.

1995
QUEBEC SAYS *NON* TO SEPARATION FROM CANADA

The separatist group Parti Quebécois (QC) agitated for a referendum to push forward a separation of the province from the rest of Canada. When it came in October 1995, they were narrowly beaten. They lost by just 54,000 votes, with 50.6 per cent of the Quebec electorate voting to remain part of Canada and 49.4 per cent voting for sovereignty. The situation was further complicated by the claims of the native Canadian Indians that 10 nations plus the Inuit (Eskimo) lay claim to 1.5 million sq km (580,000 sq miles) of Quebec. It was clear that the claims of the French-speaking separatists were but one of the major considerations regarding the future of the province.

1996
THE INTERNET ASSISTS IN APPREHENDING A CRIMINAL

After much criticism of the Internet for its poor content, it hit headlines in May 1996 when, for the first time, the FBI captured one of the '10 most wanted fugitives' using the Internet. A netsurfer in Guatemala saw Leslie Rogge's picture on the FBI homepage and reported seeing him to American officials. In response, Guatemalan national police and US diplomatic security launched an extensive search which ended on 18 May when Rogge surrendered at the US Embassy in Guatemala City. Rogge was a convicted bank robber who had escaped custody by bribing a guard in

The Internet page which contains pictures of fugitives in the hope that the public will aid apprehension.

American football star O. J. Simpson's trial for murder was followed by millions via the media.

1985. He was charged with bank robbery, interstate transport of stolen property and wire fraud.

1996
O. J. SIMPSON ACQUITTED

♲ In 1996, American football star Orenthal James (O. J.) Simpson (born 1947) was, in an internationally televised trial, acquitted of the first-degree murders of his ex-wife, Nicole Brown Simpson, and her friend Ronald Goldman. O. J. and Nicole Simpson, who had two children, were divorced in 1992. After midnight on 13 June 1994, the two victims were found stabbed to death outside Nicole Simpson's condominium in the Brentwood section of Los Angeles. O. J. Simpson, who lived 3 km (2 miles) away, had left late on the previous evening for a long-planned trip to Chicago. On 17 June O. J. was charged with the murders and, after a televised police chase, he appeared before the Los Angeles Municipal Court where he entered a plea of not guilty. He was held without bail in the Los Angeles Prison until trial. The trial was presided over by Judge Lance Ito, and 12 jurors found him innocent of all charges – causing reactions of jubilation and disbelief around the world. The media interest in the trial was unprecedented.

MARCH 1996

Ban on British Beef

The European Commission places a ban on exports of British beef and its by-products, after it is revealed that a small proportion of animals have been infected with a fatal illness called bovine spongiform encephalopathy (BSE).

1997
PATHFINDER ON MARS

A robot explorer from the *Pathfinder* mission touched down on the surface of Mars in the early hours of 5 July 1997, and sent back pictures of a planet which is 500 million km (312 million miles) from Earth. The photographs were proof that the *Pathfinder* was on stable ground after hurtling down on to the dusty plains of *Ares vallis*. It was the first time a rover had been put on the Martian surface, and that a craft had landed on a planet without orbiting it. The robot, *Sojourner*, moves at just under 1 cm (half an inch) per second, identifying soil and rock samples. The *Pathfinder* stayed in place, sending back pictures and information on Martian weather and its atmosphere.

1997
BRITISH RETURN HONG KONG TO CHINA

Britain first used Hong Kong as a naval base in the nineteenth century. It was ceded to Britain forever in 1842 after the end of the Opium Wars. The New Territories were leased to Britain in 1898 on a 99-year lease. Talks regarding the return of Hong Kong and the other territories began in 1982. The Sino-British Joint Declaration of 1984 was signed in Beijing and bound Britain to return the territories in 1997. Under this agreement Hong Kong would become known as the Hong Kong Special Administrative Region of China and be allowed to retain many of its own social, legal

The Prince of Wales and the Governor of Hong Kong watch the celebrations as it is handed back to China.

*The **Pathfinder** vehicle that sent back the first pictures from the surface of Mars.*

15 OCTOBER 1997

Breaking the Sound Barrier

Squadron leader Andy Green breaks the sound barrier on land in Richard Noble's Thrust 2 car. The record was made at Black Rock, and saw the car reach a top speed of 1,227.952 kph (763.035 mph).

and economic systems for another 50 years after the handover. The Tiananmen Square massacre in 1989 threatened to derail the negotiations and by the early 1990s emigration from Hong Kong had reached an average of 60,000 per year, the majority of the emigrants leaving for Canada and other Commonwealth countries. In July 1993 China established a Hong Kong government in waiting, but Hong Kong government elections in March 1995 showed that the majority of the people were against pro-mainland candidates. The convincing victories in both the local elections and those for the Hong Kong Legislative Council caused China to think again. Now that the handover has been completed, the region has suffered periodic economic and political uncertainties, culminating in the halving of the share values of companies traded on the Hong Kong stock exchange.

1997
DIANA, PRINCESS OF WALES, KILLED IN PARIS

The youngest daughter of the 7th Earl Spencer married Prince Charles in 1981. They had two sons, William and Harry, but the couple separated in 1992. They were divorced in 1996. Although linked with other suitors, Diana appeared to be more interested in supporting causes as diverse as the arts, children's charities, AIDS and the campaign to eradicate the use of land mines. Since her marriage to Charles she had been the target of the media who had relentlessly pursued her since the engagement was announced. In the last few months of her life she was linked to Dodi Al Fayed, the son of the owner of Harrods. Rumours of an engagement spread, renewing media interest. She died in controversial and, as yet, unresolved, circumstances in an underpass in Paris in August 1997. The world was shaken by her death and her funeral received unprecedented coverage.

Diana, Princess of Wales, just a few months before she was tragically killed in a car accident.

10 APRIL 1998

Peace in Northern Ireland

The culmination of the peace talks in Northern Ireland is the Good Friday Agreement, which finally gives hope for an end to the country's Troubles. Prime ministers Tony Blair and Mo Mowlam agree terms that are 'satisfactory' to all parties.

1997
FOREST FIRES IN ASIA

Burning to clear land for farming and plantations is common practice in Indonesia and the region, but coupled with a severe drought the situation got desperately out of hand in 1997. The hundreds of forest fires swathed the whole region in a yellow smoke, bringing visibility down to 90 m (100 yds). Numerous deaths were reported and more than 50,000 people fell ill in the region as a result of the smoke. At least five other countries were affected by the fires in Indonesia: Malaysia, Singapore, Brunei, the Philippines and Thailand. Thousands of firemen were deployed to contain the fires, but to little effect. Tourism, the electronics industry and agriculture were all affected by the disaster.

1997
THE SPICE GIRLS

'Girl Power' stormed the charts in 1997. It was the manifesto of an all-girl band, the Spice Girls. They had four consecutive Number One singles, three of which went straight in at the top. The songs were pretty and sassy, clean commercial pop, but the band became a phenomenon in an industry which had been dominated by the 'boy bands'. The five girls were called Mel B, Mel C, Geri, Victoria and Emma but the press quickly dubbed them: 'Scary Spice', 'Sporty Spice',

The forest fires in Indonesia covered cities in a blanket of smoke for hundreds of miles around.

The Spice Girls, an all-female band, which became the pop sensation of the 1990s.

'Ginger Spice', 'Posh Spice' and Baby Spice'. Even campaigning politicians were asked who their favourite Spice Girl was. The band signed several lucrative deals with crisps and drinks manufacturers, assuring their financial future. Geri left the group amidst controversy in 1998, but the other four continued without her, causing a sensation on both sides of the Atlantic.

1998
CRISIS IN THE GLOBAL ECONOMY

❁ In the late 1990s, an economic crisis occurred in South-east Asia and spread across the world. In July and August 1998 alone, four trillion dollars were wiped off the value of shares worldwide. Commodity prices, including oil and grain prices, collapsed to their lowest level in real terms since the 1930s. The Asian 'miracle' came to grief as a result of massive speculation against fixed currencies. Singapore, for example, had pegged its dollar to the US since the early 1970s and had succeeded in attracting huge flows of inward investment. China's devaluation of its currency in 1994 was a last straw. Just as the other Asian economies were moving into a boom, their fixed link to the dollar was making exports uncompetitive. Inflation rose. One by one the countries were gradually forced off the dollar peg, currencies plunged and stockmarkets crashed. Leading economists suggested exchange controls as the least damaging way out of the crisis.

Glossary

AIHSMA
Practice of campaigning for civil and human rights by non-violent means, as demonstrated by Mahatma Gandhi.

ALLIES, THE
Term commonly used to describe the Entente countries – Britain, France and Russia – during the First World War.

ANTI-SEMITISM
Practice of persecution or prejudice against Jews, based in the belief of the inferiority of the race.

APARTHEID
Afrikaans word used to describe the segregation of races in South Africa, based on a belief in white superiority.

AXIS POWERS
Collective name for the alliance of Nazi Germany, Japan and fascist Italy, from 1936 until then end of the Second World War.

BLOCKADE
In military terms, the cordoning off of certain areas, particularly sea ports, to prevent trading with enemy nations.

BOERS
Dutch, Flemish and Huguenot settlers in South Africa, who revolted against settlements of British colonists at the turn of the century.

BOLSHEVIKS
Followers of a political ideology rooted in the establishment of a workers' socialist state, leading to the Russian Revolution in 1917.

BOOKER PRIZE
Prize awarded annually since 1969 for a work of fiction by a British or Commonwealth writer; established by the Booker McConnell company.

BOOTLEGGING
Practice of making or trading in illegal alcohol during the period of Prohibition in the United States.

CAPITALISM
Economic system based on private ownership of property and exchange, with an emphasis on the material and the freedom of individual profit-making.

CARBON-DATING
Method of dating organic archeological finds by measuring the content of radioactive carbon within the artefact.

CIVIL RIGHTS MOVEMENT
Campaign in the United States during the 1960s in which people fought for equal rights for black Americans; the best-known leaders of the movement include Martin Luther King and Malcolm X.

COALITION GOVERNMENT
Temporary alliance between political parties, when two or more govern a country together, generally in times of national crisis, such as the World Wars.

COEXISTENCE
Policy by which different factions, races or cultures agree on mutually acceptable terms to enable peaceful existence with one another.

COLD WAR, THE
Ideological and political tensions, dating from the end of the Second World War (1945) to the 1990s, between the Soviet Union and the United States; characterized by nuclear threats, arms races, espionage and destabilizing governments.

COLLECTIVISM
Political system whereby ownership of means of production belongs to the people or state rather than the individual.

COLONIALISM
Practice of acquiring new territories or colonies, through conquest or agreement, and maintaining control of them under the empire's government.

COMMONWEALTH, THE
Association made up of states that have at one time been ruled by Britain and which recognize the British monarch as head of the Commonwealth.

COMMUNISM
Classless economic system of public ownership, where producing goods a nd food is a communal activity for the general good; made popular in the nineteenth century by theorists such as Karl Marx and continued in many countries throughout the twentieth century.

CONGRESS
The United States' federal legislature, made up two bodies: the Senate and the House of Representitives.

CONSTITUTIONALISM
Belief maintaining that states be defined by a body of fundamental laws on government and the judiciary, concerning individual freedom.

DEPRESSION, THE
Economic crisis of the early 1930s, characterized by mass unemployment and recession, most notably in the United States.

DEVOLUTION
Process whereby certain powers are passed, or devolved, from central government to regional governments; devolution occurred in Scotland and Wales in 1997.

DUMA
Russian parliament or assembly established in 1905, creating a constitutional monarchy; overthrown in 1917.

EXISTENTIALISM
Philosophical movement pioneered by John-Paul Sartre which emphasizes personal experience and belief, and responsibility of the individual.

FASCISM
Authoritarian political movements, particularly powerful in the 1930s–40s, where democracy and liberalism were abandoned in favour of nationalistic ideology; fascist regimes often fell under the leadership of a dictator.

FUNDAMENTALISTS
Those who believe in strict adherence to and hold a belief in all the teachings of the holy books (the Bible in Christianity, the Qur'an for Muslims).

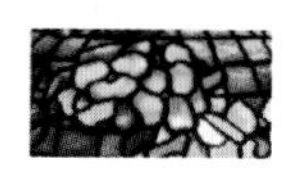

GENOCIDE
Intentional persecution and murder of a group of people, whether based on nationality or religion.

GLASNOST
Policy instigated under the leadership of Mikhail Gorbachev in the USSR, encouraging openness and public accountability.

GUERRILLAS
Groups of armed militants that combat traditional – and usually larger – forces; guerrilla warfare is usually politically motivated.

HOLOCAUST, THE
Name generally used to describe the widespread persecution and execution of Jews by the Nazis during the Second World War; more than six million are believed to have died in concentration camps during the Holocaust.

KHMER ROUGE
Military organization under the control of Pol Pot in Cambodia, enforcing his rule by means of fear, violence and execution for those who dissented.

MANIFESTO
Public declaration by a group, movement or party, particularly political, of intent and policies

MARTIAL LAW
National state in which civil law has been overthrown by military factions, ruling the country and enforcing laws by military means.

MARXISM
Political practice founded in the nineteenth century by Karl Marx, among others, and perpetuated by leaders in the twentieth, serving against capitalism, particularly imperialism, and emphasizing communism.

NAPALM
Ingredient made from petrol to make it extremely incendiary, used in firebombs, a particularly common weapon used during the Vietnam War.

NATIONALISM
Ideological movement to build national identities, reviving interests in native languages, histories and traditions; extreme nationalism is viewed as fascism.

NATIONALIZATION
Process by which privately owned industries or businesses are placed under the control of the state or government.

NAZISM
German fascist regime of the National Socialist Party, led by Adolf Hitler, who desired an empire for what he called his 'Aryan' race.

NOBEL PRIZE
Annual awards given for outstanding contributions in certain fields of human endeavour, including science, literature, medicine and peace.

PACIFISM
Belief that war cannot be justified and is immoral; those who refused to fight on such grounds were termed 'conscientious objectors'.

PERESTROIKA
Policy introduced by Soviet leader Mikhail Gorbachev in which the country's economy is restructured.

PRIVATIZATION
Process by which state or government owned institutions are sold off to private companies or individuals.

PROHIBITION
Reform movement that began officially in 1920 in the United States, which made it illegal to produce, sell or consume alcohol.

PSYCHOANALYSIS
Practice by which mental and emotional illness is treated by discussion and analysis of a patients conscious and subconscious (i.e. dreams) thoughts.

RECESSION
Temporary period of economic decline, characterized by decrease in public expenditure and national prosperity.

RED ARMY
Special army created in Russia in the 1920s by Leon Trotsky and enhanced later by Joseph Stalin; its emphasis lay on the offensive and on mechanization.

REFERENDUM
Vote made by the general electorate on a decision of public importance; or a vote taken by members of a political union, party or group to determine an opinion on an issue.

REICHSTAG
German Parliament or sovereign assembly, between the years 1919 and 1933, before Hitler's Nazi Party seized control.

RICHTER SCALE
Seismological scale ranging from 0 to 8, used as a method for espressing the intensity of earthquakes.

SENATE
Political body representing the upper chamber of the US legislature; also applicable to Australia and Canada.

SINGLE MARKET
Policy which allows free trade and travel throughout member countries, born from the European Union.

SOLIDARITY
Independent trade union founded in Poland in 1980 by strike leader Lech Walesa after a series of strikes.

SOVIET
Countries dominated by communist Russia after 1922, i.e. Estonia, Ukraine, Uzbekistan were termed Soviets within the Union of Soviet Socialist Republics (USSR).

SS
Military body within the Nazi party during the 1930s and 40s which comprised special security forces including Hitler's personal bodyguard.

SUFFRAGISM
Belief in the extension of suffrage, generally to women and the working classes, traditionally denied the right to vote.

SUMMIT
Meeting of heads of state in order to agree practical solutions and or methods of solving global or political issues.

THIRD REICH
Political body in Germany under the control of the dictatorship of Adolf Hitler between 1933 and 1945.

TROUBLES, THE
Term used to describe the political unrest in Northern Ireland since the 1970s, characterized by acts of violence and terrorism.

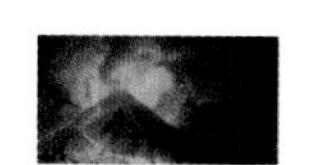

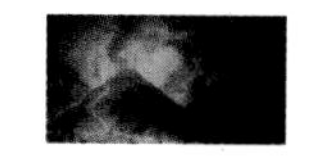

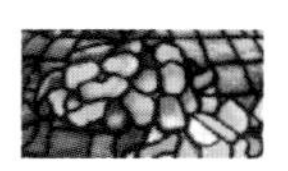
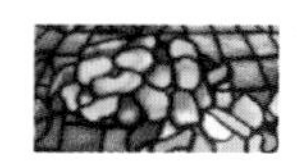

Bibliography

Boorstin, D. J., *The Discoverers*, London, 1991

Brogan, Hugh, *The Pelican History of the United States of America*, London, 1986

Brogan, Patrick, *World Conflicts*, London, 1985

Calvocoressi, Peter, *World Politics Since 1945*, New York, 1991

Chacoliades, Militiades, *International Economics*, New York and London, 1990

Clutterbuck, Richard, *International Crisis and Conflict*, London and Basingstoke, 1993

Dawson, Lorne L. (ed.), *Cults in Context: Readings in the Study of New Religious Movements*, Toronto, 1996

Eliade, Mircea, *A History of Religious Ideas*, Chicago, 1984

Gilbert, Martin, *Second World War*, London, 1989

Grove, Noel, *National Geographic Atlas of World History*, Washington, DC, 1997

Hall, Michael, *Leaving Home*, London, 1997

Hanbury-Tenison, R. (ed.), *The Oxford Book of Exploration*, Oxford, 1993

Hillier, Bevis, *The Style of the Century*, London, 1983

Hobsbawn, E. J., *The Age of Extremes*, 1919–1991, London, 1994

Kenyon, N. D. and C. Nightingale, *Audiovisual Telecommunications*, London, 1992

Loudon, Irvine, *Western Medicine*, Oxford, 1997

Macfarlane, L. J., *The Theory and Practice of Human Rights*, London, 1985

Messadie, Gerald, *Great Modern Inventions*, Edinburgh, 1991

Messenger, Charles, *The Century of Warfare: Worldwide Conflict from 1900 to the Present Day*, London, 1985

Solomon, Robert C. and Kathleen M. Higgins, *A Short History of Philosophy*, Oxford, 1996

Taylor, A. J. P., *From the Boer War to the Cold War*, London, 1995

Tomlinson, Jim, *Public Policy and the Economy Since 1900*, New York, 1990

Woolf, Stewart (ed.), *Nationalism in Europe*, London, 1996.

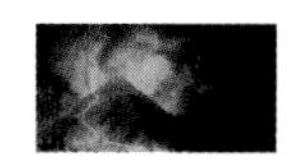

Picture Credits

Allsport: pp. Otto Greule 95(b), Gary Mortimore 237, Ben Radford 217(l)

Allsport/Hulton Getty: pp. 41(b), 60, 65(b), 82, 138, 140

Anglepoise Ltd. of Redditch: pp. 89

The Architectural Association: pp. 106(t)

Christies: pp. 16, 42(r), 71, 122, 161 (t), 204, 216

Clicks Digital Image Management: pp. 150(b)

Empics: pp. Seven Simon 179(t)

FBI Home Page: pp. 242(b)

Foundry Arts: pp. 16(b), 103,133,183(b)

Image Select: pp. 20, 64, 88(l), 108(l), 118, 158, 190(t), 199(b)

Image Select/Chris Fairclough: pp. 34(r), 45(l), 61, 108(r), 144, 233(b)

Image Select/Ann Ronan: pp. 29(r), 130, 143

Interface Digital Library Ltd. : pp. 196(l)

International Buisness Machines Corporation: pp. 126(t)

Joseph E. Seagram & Sons Inc: pp. 145

L.A.T. Photographic: pp. 239

London Transport Museum: pp. 87(b)

Mary Evans: pp. 10, 11, 12(b), 13, 15(all), 18(b), 21 (b), 22, 24(r), 25, 26, 27, 29(l), 31, 37(all), 38(b), 41, 42(l), 43, 45(r), 47, 48, 50(all), 51, 52(t), 58(t), 59(t), 63, 66, 68(all), 72, 78, 84(t), 87(t), 93, 95(t), 97, 109, 111, 113(all), 114, 119, 126(b), 136, 166, 171, 193(t), 213, 229(b)

Pictorial Press: pp. 44(t), 147(r), 161(b)

Quadrant: pp. 67(b), 73(b) Autocar: pp. 163, Anthony R. Dulton: pp. 208

Sanders, N. J.: pp. 36

Still Pictures: pp. 116, 247

Topham: pp. 30, 34(l), 35, 39, 41(t), 46(all), 48, 49, 54, 66, 67(t), 69, 70(t), 73(t), 74(t), 75, 76(r), 84(b), 85, 88, 94,98, 101(B), 107,110(l),120,121,123(b), 127, 131 (all), 132, 135, 137(all),,141 (all), 142(b), 146, 151, 154(r), 155, 156(all), 160, 162(t), 168(t), 169, 174(t), 179(b),180(r), 181, 183, 184(r), 186, 187, 188, 190(r), 191, 192(l), 193, 194, 195, 196(t), 198, 203, 209, 210, 212, 211, 218, 222, 223, 226(t), 230, 232, 235(t), 236, 238

Topham/Associated Press: pp. 17, 18(t), 19, 21 (t), 38(t), 40, 54(b), 59(b), 62, 65(t), 70(b), 74(l), 79(t), 86, 90(t), 90, 91, 99, 100, 106(b), 1 10(r), 112, 115(all), 117, 119(r), 124, 134(t), 139(b), 147(l), 149, 150(t), 154(l), 157, 162(b), 165(l), 167(b), 168(b), 170, 171(r), 172, 173, 174(b), 178, 182, 185(l), 186(t), 189(all), 192(r), 197, 199(t), 202(all), 205(t), 206, 207(all), 215(all), 217(t), 219(all), 221(all), 223(b), 226(b), 228, 235(b), 240, 241(t), 242(t), 243, 244(all)

Topham/Press Association: pp. 12(t), 14, 28, 53, 58(b), 63(r), 92, 96, 101(t), 120(b), 134(b), 142(t), 148, 159(all), 164, 165(r), 167(t), 175, 180(l), 205(b), 214, 220, 227, 229(t), 231(l), 233(t), 234, 245, 246

Travel Photo International: pp. 77

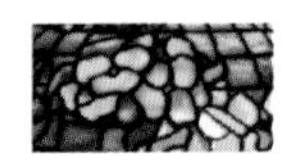

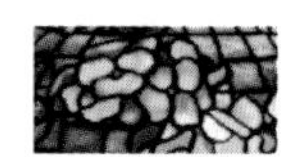

Index

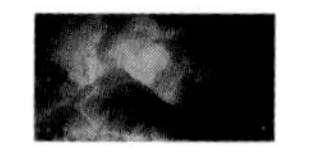

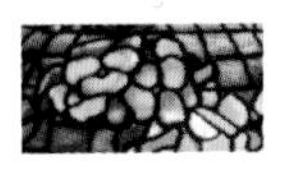

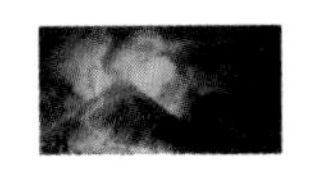

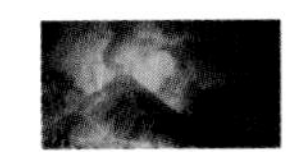

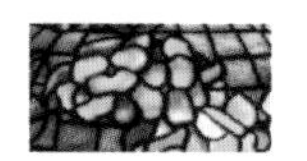

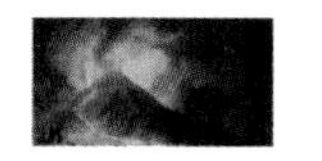

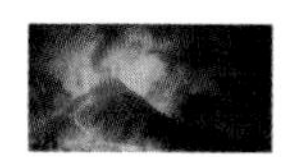

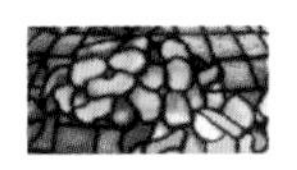

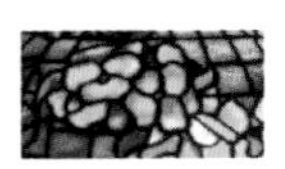

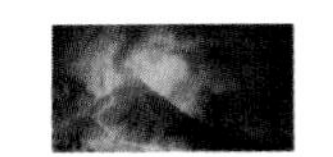

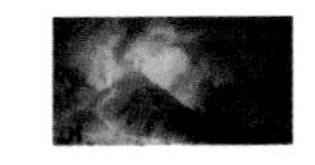

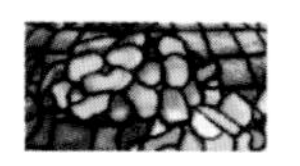

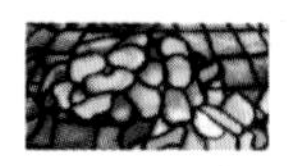

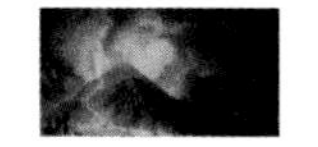

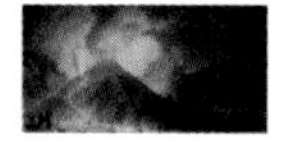